Global Pop *From* a Catholic Perspective

"The population of the world in 1950 was 2.5 billion. In the year 2000 it will be about 6 billion. How the Catholic Church has reacted to this amazing phenomenon is the subject of this important book. Its author, faithfully reflecting official Catholic teaching, is creative, constructive and compelling in his conclusions. This book is indispensable reading for everyone concerned with the exploding population of the global village."

Robert F. Drinan, S.J.
Professor, Georgetown University Law Center

"The Catholic moral tradition has a lot to bring to the mainstream global conversation on population and ecocidal consumerism. Hamstrung by its taboos in reproductive ethics (contraception, sterilization, abortion) it has not been an effective voice. John Schwarz, in this excellent book, respects the tradition by a critique that is at once gentle and powerful."

Daniel C. Maguire
Author with Larry Rasmussen of
Ethics For A Small Planet, Suny Press, 1998

"John C. Schwarz tells us in the introduction that he has written a respectful inside critique of the Catholic perspective on global population for the non-expert in theology and demography. He has succeeded admirably in achieving his purpose.

"Schwarz's approach is truly Catholic in the best sense of being universal and all-inclusive while avoiding one-sided reductionism. He sees the global population problem and solutions to it connected with economic and ecological perspectives. Too often Americans have tended to see the population problem without any necessary connection to economic development. In addition, Schwarz is very familiar with developments in contemporary Catholic moral theology and as a skilled pedagogue presents his reasoning in a clear and convincing manner as he develops his Catholic perspective on global population."

Charles E. Curran
Elizabeth Scurlock Professor of Human Values
Southern Methodist University

*"In his **Global Population from a Catholic Perspective** John Schwarz has supplied an all-embracing resume of the world's demographic situation. With the number of the globe's inhabitants rising from one billion in 1800 to an estimated eight billion in 2050, Schwarz challenges the papal reluctance to acknowledge the inhuman situation in which at least one billion human beings now exist. He suggests that alleviating such degradation demands global family planning on a catholic or universal scale."*

Francis X. Murphy, C.SS.R.
Professor emeritus Academiae Alfonsianae Roma

Global Population from a

Catholic

Perspective

John C. Schwarz

XXIII

TWENTY-THIRD PUBLICATIONS

Mystic, CT 06355

To the children
of my family,
of your family,
of every family everywhere—
but especially to
children born in great poverty
our young sisters and brothers…
wherever…

Twenty-Third Publications
185 Willow Street
P.O. Box 180
Mystic, CT 06355
(860) 536-2611
(800) 321-0411

ISBN: 0-89622-932-7

Library of Congress Catalog Card Number 98-60484

Printed in the United States of America

A.M.D.G.

Contents

Part II
Reflections on a Pastoral Theology of Global Population

Acknowledgments

I am most particularly and personally indebted to my wife, Catherine, for her sustained support throughout a prolonged time, which made the book possible. Also to Dr. C. Alison McIntosh, Director of the Population Fellows Program, University of Michigan School of Public Health, for invaluable consultation; to Neil Kluepfel and Dan Connors of Twenty-Third Publications for exceptionally helpful suggestions and guidance.

I am sincerely grateful to the following for permission to use published materials: the editor of *Theological Studies* (Georgetown University, Washington, DC) for extensive material from a 1974 issue on population; to the Park Ridge Center for the Study of Health, Faith, and Ethics (Chicago, Illinois) for extensive use of their "Religious Perspectives on Population, Consumption and Environment—A Report of an Interfaith and Interdisciplinary Forum"; to the Worldwatch Institute (Washington, DC) for a complete editorial from their magazine; to The University of Michigan Press (Ann Arbor, Michigan) for textual and chart material from *Population-Environment Dynamics: Ideas and Observations,* Gayle D. Ness, William D. Drake, Steven R. Brechin, eds., copyright by the University of Michigan 1993; to The Liturgical Press (Collegeville, Minnesota) for material from *Jesus, The Compassion of God,* by Monika Hellwig; to The Food First Institute (Oakland, California) for textual and chart material from *Taking Population Seriously,* by Frances Moore Lappé and Rachel Schurman; to *Commonweal* magazine (New York) for extensive material, 1994, by an author under a pseudonym; to Betsy Hartmann (Population and Development Program, Hampshire College) for material from her *Reproductive Rights and Wrongs;* to Orbis Books for material from Joseph Gremillion's *Gospel of Peace and Justice;* to *The National Catholic Reporter* (Kansas City, Missouri) for a complete editorial; to Joel E. Cohen (Laboratory of Populations, Rockefeller University) for material from his article in *The Sciences.*

I also thank Sister Nancy Sylvester, I.H.M., for critiquing early segments of the manuscript. I must conclude not only in customary form but in utter truth that final results remain the author's sole responsibility.

The population of the world at mid-century was 2.5 billion; some time in 1987 it passed 5 billion. The increase in the past 40 years has equalled the total increase over the millions of years from when the human species emerged until 1950.

—NATHAN KEYFITZ[1]

Our Perplexing Population: Disputes and the Catholic Voice

NOT OFTEN THESE DAYS DOES THE NEWS PROVOKE A SMILE rather than a frown. But one is amused when a Louisville, Kentucky, newspaper states that "the total number of births in the 1950s was larger than ever seen in the U.S.—due mostly to the number of women having babies." Although that seems beyond dispute, little else in the realm of human reproduction and global population is so fortunate. Controversy and dispute are rampant.

Population data that some consider obvious in their significance are nonetheless sharply disputed by others. For example, consider these demographic statistics: within the next generation the populations of Pakistan, Bangladesh, and Nigeria will, combined, jump from 318 million to a projected 714 million—more than double.[2] These beleaguered nations already rank sixty-seventh, sixty-eighth, and seventieth among ninety-three nations on the *International Human Suffering Index* (Denmark is first, best; U.S.A., fifth; Japan, seventh).[3] Ever-increasing distress for these nations seems evident. Yet some serious observers, often economists, assert that economic and technological advances will in due time balance the negative factors connected to such growth of human numbers.

Surveying the multiple controversies, Marguerite Holloway writes, "At times it seems there are as many opinions concerning what—if anything—to do about population growth as there are people on the planet. Bitter schisms often divide groups arguing for women's rights, family planning and health, environmental protection, reduced consumption of natural resources, economic development and population control."[4] The list goes on.

Quoted above, Nathan Keyfitz spotlights the basic startling data of accelerating global population. Greatly to his credit Keyfitz is notably respectful of divergent interpretations of population data. Nevertheless he states that "the preponderance of data and common sense insist that decisive and effective action be taken to address the population dilemma."[5]

Among the many dimensions of population phenomena, a remarkably accelerated rate stands out. In my opening lines from Keyfitz at the head of this Introduction, note "in the past 40 years...." In the overview of Pakistan, Bangladesh, and Nigeria, note "within the next generation...." While by no means the same in all regions (some population rates are declining) the historical aggregate picture shows a very sharp swing upward in absolute numbers.

The Catholic Role—Official and Otherwise

The Catholic Church, at its most official institutional and doctrinal level, participates in the controversy, with its own interpretation of global population concerns.[6] That interpretation (to be detailed later in these pages) is characterized by a reserved skepticism coupled with, paradoxically, numerous clear acknowledgments of the reality of population increase as a problem. By reason of its diplomatic status in the world political arena (not enjoyed by other religious bodies), along with its potent historic moral force, the Vatican exerts distinct influence on population issues both in the United Nations and in nations where the Catholic populace remains numerically significant (e.g., Philippines; see Chapter Two, discussing the U.N.).

The Church in recent years has increasingly acknowledged that growing populations in some regions give cause for concern (see especially Chapters Two and Five)—and hence for remedial action. But in the area of remedial methods—notably artificial contraception, sterilization, and abortion—the Church has an unbending stand and words of caution and prohibition that reverberate widely in world forums of discussion, if they are not dismissed out of hand.

The stand of the Church in the latter half of the twentieth century emerged most publicly, of course, in *Humanae Vitae* (*On Human Life,* 1968), the formal pronouncement of Pope Paul VI, reinforcing the Church's historic prohibition of artificial birth control. That stand has been vigorously maintained by Pope John Paul II in writings, disciplinary actions against dissent, and speeches in nations visited worldwide. Indeed John Paul II has raised the prohibition to a central point of doctrinal emphasis. All this is obvious to anyone paying attention, as obvious as that "the total number of births in the 1950s was ...due mostly to the number of women having babies."

So why a book, this *new* Catholic "interpretation"? If *the* Catholic "interpretation" is already established, globally and formally pronounced in capital letters, what remains to be said? A fair question.

I offer evidence that another approach—perhaps several other approaches—can be drawn legitimately from Catholic, Christian, Judeo-Christian, and broadly moral-ethical sources. The official Catholic stance is not exempt from reassessment. That stance is in fact contested by *many* of the Church's own most reputable scholars. The "official stance" deserves the honor of a respectful, conscientious hearing by Catholics throughout the world. One would be surprised if by this time it had not received such a hearing by adult, informed Catholics.

Yet more remains to be said and to be heard. Many rich resources must be consulted, relevant to global population concerns:

- Scripture, especially the example and teaching of Jesus,
- many leading Catholic and non-Catholic scholars,
- Catholic laity,

• medical professionals,

• demographers and population specialists,

• service and caring personnel in Third World nations,

• "ordinary" citizens living in the actual circumstances of population-related distress—especially women and children.

All deserve to be heard. The Vatican voice must be heard, yes—as well as *many other* voices who share the human scene, responsible for it in varying ways. These too deserve a role in the formation of our moral and theological perspectives.

But having described so huge a task one can only start, can only try, can only say something, not everything. At least one can do that much, hoping others will discuss, reflect, and add.

For Whom?

I have written this book as an introduction for non-experts. My intended readership is educated laity, not professional theologians, ecclesiastics, or professionals in the various areas of population studies. I propose that university courses in ethics and religious studies, and courses in Christian and Catholic social philosophy and theology, would find it useful.

Although not directed to professional theologians I suspect some of them may find this exploration provocative, since very little theological reflection on the topic exists. My deliberately extensive source references may suggest the breadth of relevant material available—awaiting further analysis and integration. On many of these vastly complex issues I can only touch briefly.

I hope, moreover, to be heard across confessional lines, by concerned fellow Christians and non-Christians. Many in the demographic fields are also troubled by the official Catholic positions. Perhaps they will find more hopeful perspectives in these pages, perspectives still informed by the ethical and spiritual values of historic Catholicism—by no means abdicated herein.

Positions Emphasized

This book will discuss and emphasize the following positions, while acknowledging and respecting opposing views. All "sides" have a contribution to make in such momentous issues.

1. Although the Catholic doctrines most explicitly applied to

population concerns—prohibitions directed to artificial means of contraception, plus sterilization and abortion—were not formulated in reference to global population issues primarily, these issues now constitute an urgent and sufficient motive to reassess the official Catholic positions. Major transitions in world history have often affected religious perspectives and theology.

2. Population or demographic issues are themselves in dispute; a growing consensus, however, acknowledges a serious problem even if the exact dimensions remain uncertain. Population statistics are, after all, merely one mode of representing vast circumstances of human suffering, indignity, and injustice—"overpopulated" or not. As such these call out to Christian concern and gospel values, to the conscience of all persons of human sensitivity. To human need and deprivation the Church has often responded well—and sometimes not so well. It can never justifiably cease to reassess its response.

3. "Population problems" are far more than merely phenomena of numbers and fertility. They are at least equally problems of resource use and abuse in *both* Third World and First World societies, of social justice and injustice, of economic and political exploitation, of basic health care, of human dignity and family dignity, and of the vastly disregarded role of women and children.

4. Catholic *positive* contributions have been extensive and diverse— and perhaps largely overlooked. Meanwhile, the Church's *negative*, adversarial prohibitions have dominated in the news media and popular consciousness. But by its medical, social, educational, and spiritual services the Church has contributed incalculably to human well-being— a strong factor in demographic realities. Domestic and international social justice has increasingly occupied a major role in Catholic theological and pastoral emphases.

5. The official Catholic position concerning artificial means of birth control should not be presented to the world at large as *absolute moral doctrine beyond dispute or exception* when in fact the issue remains seriously and responsibly contested within the Church itself.

6. Concerning contraception, sterilization, and abortion, the official

Catholic prohibition—absolute and exceptionless—is seriously inconsistent with other equally important areas of Catholic moral and social teaching (e.g., war, capital punishment) where exceptions are affirmed—or differences in decisions of conscience respected.

7. The indicated Catholic positions on contraception, sterilization, and abortion conflict with the Vatican's own repeated acknowledgments of today's population challenge. Moral prohibitions rooted in private, individual ethics are no longer an adequate response to massive public, national, and international phenomena of population.

8. Catholic moral doctrine is not immutable. It has changed in the past and can do so again.

9. Personal reproductive decisions by the women and men directly affected—even the most obscure peasant or *favela* resident—must be understood as decisions that profoundly and wholly engage conscience, culture, faith, love of family, economic situation or status, health and medical resources, instincts of sheer survival, protection against gross exploitation, as well as response to the grace of God immediately present to such distressed persons. Thus, no single formula, no "one size fits all" morality or spirituality can possibly encompass or prescribe for such complexity.

10. Global ecological or environmental issues must concern theology, religion, and the Church. Indeed since humankind itself exists as part of the created natural order, while also transcending it, the realities of ecology constitute the very foundation and context within which demographic phenomena occur. How human beings treat, exploit, manage, damage, and consume their natural environment is profoundly a religious and humanistic concern. Human fertility and human numbers are major elements within that scheme, within those patterns.

Since much of this is controversial, one additional emphasis needs underscoring: how we approach dissent and dispute in religious and theological issues. Christian history far too often displays rank antagonism, even outright severity—all in the name of God—toward those with whom we disagree. The editors of *Commonweal*, a respected Catholic journal, offer this good counsel:

Controversy need not be a symptom of institutional weakness, decay, or even disunity; it is often a sign of intellectual vitality and passionate attachment. Much depends on how the parties involved in any dispute conduct themselves. Are they willing to listen to one another? Or do they condemn first and ask questions later? Do they presume the best about each other's motives? Or the worst? Even rarer, are they open to the possibility of learning something, even from their critics?[7]

Recommending that to others, I apply it to myself as well.

Plan of the Book

This book has two parts. Part I provides a basic summary of the global population issue; additionally, numerous aspects of the global situation appear throughout the text. However, readers interested in that problem itself will need to look elsewhere for a full treatment. My goal is to examine specifically the role of the Catholic Church in that problem, its attitudes and policies toward it, and how its doctrine does, could, and should relate to the problem, in the author's view. Therefore, I look at the Catholic record—what the Church has done and not done, said and not said, positive (especially Chapter Three) and negative (especially Chapter Four).

Part II connects this study with the contemporary revisioning of moral theology and extends the critique into more particular areas, including abortion. The crucial impact and significance of Christ's compassion will be explored. Consistency within Catholic moral and social thought will be applied to the official stance on population, along with assessments of Catholic relationships with science and ecology—both of which clearly carry large implications for population issues. Chapter Nine reports on a modest but significant interfaith, international conference on population issues—exemplifying admirable cooperation, analysis, and recommendation. The final chapter completes the connection with contemporary moral theology and the moral choices that will influence the future of humankind.

Along the way I explore and recommend approaches and attitudes toward the population challenge that Catholics generally, and the Church officially, could adopt, and from which the Church could learn.

Four appendices are included: (1) a concise (editorial) analysis of "the socioeconomic inequity" that sustains high population rates; (2) a brief statistical sketch of "whole nations in poverty," one major component of population problems; (3) an editorial urging attention to the chronic indebtedness of impoverished nations, supportive of high fertility rates; (4) an ardent statement, written for this book, from a priest discussing Catholic social and moral teaching in his Third World experience.

A "Critique from the Inside"

I propose and conceive of this book as a respectful "critique from the inside." This means, first, that I write as a lifelong Roman Catholic, most assuredly intending to remain such. I write with sympathy and affection for my Church, with respect for its rich tradition, with profound appreciation for all it has meant in my life. I'm a product of Catholic education, with twenty-six years of membership in the esteemed Society of Jesus (the Jesuits), ordained to the priesthood (1955), and now married (in the Church) as many years. My wife, Catherine, and I together represent some forty-six years in Roman Catholic religious communities.

In my Jesuit years principal assignments included teaching theology at the University of Detroit (my own alma mater), serving as personal assistant to the chief executive ("provincial") of our Detroit Province, and serving as pastor for seven years in a major Detroit parish (Gesu) in the turbulent 1960s—a time of massive change in city, country, and Church as well. In no spirit of boast I recall the truly remarkable cardinal archbishop of Detroit John F. Dearden, with whom my contacts were numerous, graciously speaking (1969) of my parish work in a letter I cherish and retain. The cardinal referred to "dedicated service...soundness of judgment, your candor and sincerity [which] enabled you to make a contribution I valued highly. And for this I am profoundly grateful." I have never quoted this before in public, and do so here only to establish a background, to define the professional and personal "inside" from which I write.

Upon resigning from the Jesuit Order I added a master's degree in social work (University of Michigan) to my licentiate in theology and master's in philosophy (Loyola University, Chicago). After thirteen years on the staff of the Washtenaw County Community Mental Health Services I was, with my wife's generous and essential support, able to enter upon, in effect, a third religious career-phase of adult education in parishes, Catholic and Protestant. I have commonly dealt with social issues and Catholic socio-religious perspectives applying to peace, the economy, and environmental issues (as well as issues of personal spirituality and religious practice). The Diocese of Lansing selected me for its "Respect Life Award" (1989), acknowledging my work in peace and justice education.

The book is further an "inside critique" in the sense that its lines of argumentation and documentation draw heavily on Catholic sources. This is deliberate, seeking to demonstrate that change and development are warranted by our own tradition, our own values—that such change is an essential component of the Judeo-Christian experience. Today just such change is needed in the official Catholic positions vis-à-vis global population concerns. That "case" for change is best and most responsibly argued "from the inside."

There is, moreover, a solid, if often overlooked tradition of valid dissent within Catholicism, documented frequently in these pages (see "Dissent," in Chapter Two). A moment's reflection reveals that growth, change, and adaptation are inseparable from a broad-based process that, at the start, is usually called dissent.

So if I undertake an appraisal of my church in the painful issues of global population I surely do not engage in the "Catholic bashing" regrettably familiar today. The Roman Catholic tradition, with all its human flaws and undeniable deficiencies, has been and remains a source and context of wisdom for countless millions, of inestimable guidance for life—and beyond.

The reader, then, must judge if the foregoing validates the claim of a "critique from the inside." "Inside" does not mean official, or somehow authorized. I speak in my own name only. It is sufficient for me if "inside" means authentic—and to that extent credible.

Two Encounters

Two simple encounters brought this issue to a point of personal emphasis. The first occurred when teaching at Memorial Christian Church, Ann Arbor, concerning the American bishops' 1986 pastoral letter on the economy. A local physician active in social causes stated in the question period that, "No matter how well your church speaks of social justice it's all nullified in global matters by the stand on birth control." I disagreed, and said so. But I kept his pointed comment in mind.

A second encounter: reading R. J. Blackwell's *Galileo, Bellarmine & the Bible*.[8] The author, a philosopher at St. Louis University, states, "Despite massive changes since the age of Galileo the Catholic conception of the nature of religious faith and the logic of centralized authority related to it seem to remain untouched. Could there be a second Galileo affair? What has been learned from the first?" These are startling questions. Could such a monumental fiasco, or something in that general category, happen again? Is it already happening? Is ecclesial authority today less defensive, more flexible, more open? Blackwell wondered, and I wonder. My Chapter Seven will offer evidence of real progress. But is it enough?

A further incentive to undertaking this book has been my sense of a widespread basic agreement with positions presented here—but which remains unarticulated, suppressed. An established Catholic publisher (after reading an early draft of the manuscript) expressed a favorable response ("you are dealing with a crucial issue in a responsible and constructive fashion"), but added that "we simply do not have the independence to publish freely on this topic." The same editor later wrote, "While no one, myself included, disagreed with the arguments in your book, the consensus of everyone was that in the *present ecclesiastical environment* it would not be advisable to publish such a book." I understood his position, and respected it.

The Catholic Voice on the Global Scene

Currently in Catholic circles few voices (beyond the Vatican) address the global population phenomenon. Many speak publicly of the birth control stance of the Church; countless others form their own consciences in private, properly their right and duty. But few Catholic voices specifically address the population phenomenon with its related controversies and ramifications. That too is a reason for this work. As of early 1998, I am aware of no single book by a Catholic author directly on this subject (Church-and-population), very few articles, plus an occasional welcome editorial.[9] In this post-Vatican II era when social justice issues have received greatly renewed attention, this oversight, this large gap, seems curious, indeed regrettable.

The Vatican and numerous local bishops, pastors, and others have repeatedly voiced the official message of *Humanae Vitae's* prohibition. Without hesitancy, starting from an ethical-moral teaching focused on the sexual exchange in marriage, they make the vast transition to the global sweep of humankind everywhere, in all circumstances. In the language and concept of universal principles, categorized as transcending all particular circumstances and situations, the official Catholic position asserts that neither local nor personal details of whatever sort can contravene the "intrinsic evil"—everywhere applicable—of artificial contraception. The same moral judgment is extended to sterilization and abortion.

I certainly do not ridicule this teaching, nor wish at all to caricature it. I understand its background and sources. I recognize it as reasoned, careful, and wholly conscientious. I also challenge it, respectfully, on the premise that Catholic theology has ever made its proper progress by challenge, by dialogue, exploration, contest, and candor.

It is my sense of it, moreover, that contemporary revisions of "natural law" thought (which in part undergird the *Humanae Vitae* prohibition) suggest new direction, new insights.[10] Indeed, our inherited, classical field of moral theology itself was named by the Second Vatican Council as in need of renewal.

> Special care should be given to the perfecting of moral theology. Its scientific presentation should draw more fully on the teaching of holy scripture, and should throw light upon the exalted vocation of the faithful in Christ and their obligation to bring forth fruit in charity for the life of the world.[11]

The pointed references to the utilization of Scripture as well as "fruit in charity for the life of the world" speak to our concerns in this book. Christ's message of love, compassion, and concern for the poor and afflicted, and his sense of common humanity shared globally, all deserve renewed attention, renewed application.

The impact of the Church on the overall population phenomenon is important—but perhaps on a global scale minor, one influence among innumerable others. Yet responsibility before God in this, as in all else, is not simply equated with the human scale of things. A veteran British journalist who has participated in several of Pope John Paul's trips abroad notes that the pope has encountered "some of the most wretched and overcrowded slums in the world." He then offers this assessment.

> Is it really "pro-life" to allow population levels to increase to such an extent that living systems in certain impoverished

> regions of the planet will never recover?... I am not
> suggesting that Pope John Paul is responsible for this
> worrying state of affairs, or even that his opposition to
> contraception is going to be decisive for the world's
> future...but his narrow interpretation of *Humanae Vitae* has
> boxed his church into a corner as far as the development of
> a coherent Catholic response to the population explosion
> is concerned.[12]

One does not wish, moreover, to overstress the Catholic position and testimony alone in an age that is religiously best when ecumenical. My own work has been as often with Protestants and Jews as with fellow Catholics. But clearly this problem has within it a particular Catholic factor, an intramural (as well as global) challenge that must be admitted openly and dealt with on its own terms. Ecumenism will be gladly served by turning often in these pages to non-Catholic sources—and inviting response from readers of other religious affiliations, or of no affiliation.

Recommended: the Culture of Listening

Perhaps we need to talk less, and to listen more. That advice was offered by Mary Robinson, President of Ireland and a graduate of Harvard Law School. In Washington (May 1993) to receive the CARE Special Humanitarian award for work for impoverished peoples worldwide, she stated,

> The suffering I encountered in Somalia offended all my
> inner sense of justice, a sense I acquired partly through the
> practice of law but mainly through a simple sense of what is
> right and fair as against what is profoundly unjust.... We
> need to stand back and reflect on whether our societies are
> properly nourishing the culture of listening...the *conditio sine*
> *qua non* of properly attuned institutional and governmental
> responses.... If we detach ourselves or turn away..., how can
> we escape a moral bankruptcy that must have a subconscious
> impact on social order in western societies? How can we
> celebrate human achievement and diversity of cultures if we
> disregard the life chances of men, women, and children in
> their thousands, in their millions?[13]

In London, 1987, a gathering of world notables launched a major report on "Environment and Development." They were addressed by a young woman from Indonesia, Jenny Damyanti, who had been invited to the event. She also spoke of listening:

> Please, presidents, prime ministers and generals, listen to the poor, to the voice of the hungry people who are forced to destroy the environment. Listen to the silent death of dying forests, lakes, rivers, and the seas, the dying soil of the earth, poisoned and trampled by human greed, poverty and inequality. We, the young, hear them loud and clear![14]

The "culture of listening"—and learning—should rank at least as high as the culture of pronouncement. Our Catholic Church, the cherished church of my youth and entire lifetime, has by no means caused or (in my view) shares major blame for the global suffering of a population "explosion," as some term it. And efforts at direct reproductive control, pro or con, can at best be only one remedial factor in a hugely complex picture, one way or the other. But the Roman Church has nonetheless a serious role and responsibility. Thus, on the population horizon, every possible remedial method needs painstaking assessment and reassessment—morally, theologically, religiously, and humanly.

It is no longer enough to pronounce. Listening, hearing, attending, respecting, responding, adjusting, and reassessing all deserve greater emphasis. Above all, those who bear the brunt of the suffering deserve not merely to be told—but to be heard as well.

Questions for Reflection and Discussion

1. Consider the opening quotation from Nathan Keyfitz. How long did humankind need to reach the level of 2.5 billion? Does it strike you as significant that the number was then doubled in about 40 years?

2. Is the purpose of this book legitimate within Catholic life and the Church? Are not decisions on such matters reserved to official levels—pope and hierarchy?

3. Concerning religious discussion and inevitable disagreements: evaluate the recommendations from the journal *Commonweal* (page 7).

Does controversy necessarily indicate basic or fundamental disunity?

4. R. J. Blackwell is quoted concerning the Galileo case. Evaluate his statement.

5. Vatican II, concerning moral theology: why and how does moral theology touch the "exalted vocation of the faithful"?

6. What does Mary Robinson mean by the "culture of listening"? How does it differ from a culture "of pronouncement"? How do they apply to the topic of this book?

What the World Expects from the Church—a Vignette

ONE COULD WRITE A SENTENCE—OR A BOOK—TO SAY WHAT the world at large expects from the Church. One could give a single lecture—or conduct a major conference—to address that issue. Pope John Paul II needed just twenty-one minutes in a prison cell to provide an eloquent response.

Some two-and-a-half years after a young Turkish gunman shot John Paul at point-blank range in St. Peter's Square (May 1981), the pope visited his assailant in Rome's Rebibbia prison.

> For twenty-one minutes the Pope sat with his would-be assassin, Mehmet Ali Agca. The two talked softly. Once or twice, Agca laughed. At the end of the meeting, Agca kissed the Pope's ring and pressed the Pope's hand to his forehead in a Muslim gesture of respect.[1]

The pope later disclosed that in fact he had forgiven his assailant immediately after the shooting, while suffering serious wounds. At the prison the Holy Father sat down, one to one, with a stranger of the streets, a man of alien culture and evil purposes. "I spoke to him as a brother whom I have pardoned, and who has my complete trust."

Popes, of course, are not the Church, but always its most prominent, personal, and formal sign. In a prison cell the spirit of Christ was richly real. A pope who has so often spoken of solidarity took a bold initiative of love, of compassion. He freely walked the extra mile.

This awareness of common humanity is what the world expects of the Church, because this is what the world saw in Jesus. The luminous prison episode provides a touchstone, a symbol and reference point, for the message of this book.

Part One
Population and
the Catholic Record—
Assessments and
Possibilities

CHAPTER ONE

The Church encompasses with love all those...who are poor and who suffer.

—VATICAN II[1]

Global sustainable development implies a long-term commitment to greater equity in access to resources and productive assets...above all a genuinely global approach to reducing both poverty and population.

—STATE OF WORLD POPULATION 1993[2]

Church and Population: Beyond Statistics

FROM THE VAST WASTELAND OF NETWORK TELEVISION EMERGES an occasional word of timeless wisdom. So was it when a commercial promoting a brand of margarine reminded us, over and over, that "it's not nice to fool Mother Nature." Disregarded or violated too long or in too gross a fashion, the natural world will exact a price, often severe.

Consider one example of a familiar sort. March 1992, USAir Flight 405, New York to Cleveland, departs from LaGuardia Airport under wintery nighttime conditions. Rolling swiftly, it lifts smoothly from the runway—to crash thunderously into Flushing Bay just beyond. Twenty-seven were killed, many injured. Investigators subsequently speak of ice on the wings, inadequately treated.[3] Result: catastrophe. Nature plays no favorites. Conform to the realities, or pay the price.

In recent years the sprawling metropolis of Los Angeles has experienced a major earthquake, rampant fires in residential hillside neighborhoods, several years of drought, and even more recent mudslides. One hardly blames earthquakes on the victims. But it is widely recognized that southern California, as well as many other areas, is now densely overpopulated in utter disregard of its natural environmental features and natural limits. Very likely future disruptions will occur, without regard for human convenience, with oversized populations predictably distressed.

If the phrase "not nice to fool Mother Nature" smacks of commercial whimsy, more sober phrasing comes from a Nobel Laureate, Henry Kendall. He warns that "people who take issue with control of population do not understand that if it is not done in a graceful way, nature will do it in brutal fashion."[4]

Robert Caplan writes similarly about his visit to a Third World capital.

> Cities keep growing. I got a general sense of the future driving from the airport to downtown Conakry, the capital of Guinea [Africa]. The forty-five minute journey in heavy traffic was through one never-ending shantytown: a nightmarish spectacle to which Dickens himself would never have given credence. The corrugated metal shacks and scabrous walls were coated with black slime. Stores were built out of rusted shipping containers, junked cars, and jumbles of wire mesh. Streets were one long puddle of floating garbage. Mosquitoes and flies were everywhere. Children, many of whom had protruding bellies, seemed as numerous as ants. When the tide went out, dead rats were exposed on the mucky beach. In twenty-eight years Guinea's population will double if growth goes on at current rates. Hardwood logging continues at a madcap speed, and people flee the countryside for Conakry. It seemed to me that here, as elsewhere in Africa and the Third World, man is challenging nature far beyond its limits, and nature is now beginning to take its revenge.[5]

The Church—and Those Who Suffer

Amidst such anxieties, some old and chronic, some qualitatively new, what does the world expect of the Church? What indeed does the Church, as articulated in the self-scrutiny of Vatican II, expect of itself? The following lines open the Council's magisterial document, *The Church in the Modern World* (no. 1): "The joy and hope, the grief and anguish of the people of our time, especially of those poor or afflicted in any way, are the joy and the hope, the grief and the anguish of the followers of Christ as well." The earlier *Dogmatic Constitution on the Church* (no. 8) spoke similarly: "The Church encompasses with her love all those who are afflicted by human misery and she recognizes in those who are poor and who suffer the image of her poor and suffering founder."

The "grief and anguish of the people of our time" has become a concern of the followers of Christ. Religion thus stands beyond some creed or code of private salvation. Somehow "grief and anguish" are factored into the perspectives of Christian life, faithful to the teaching of Christ himself. Challenged to summarize and characterize his message, Jesus himself did not point to creeds, propositions, or particularities of religious prescription or observance. Instead he pointed to "grief and anguish" in the person of a victim, a traveler on the road of life, beaten, disabled, and dying.[6]

Multiple Causes

Christ's unforgettable scriptural image of the beaten and disabled traveler (Luke 10:25–37) is today enlarged to include millions, indeed billions. Although it has been well said that nobody ever died of overpopulation, numbers beyond counting die daily from the ravages of malnutrition, water-borne disease, and sicknesses for which too often remedies are readily available in other sectors of the human family. Numbers of people beyond counting live lives of degradation, of grinding poverty, and of prostitution and labor indistinguishable from slavery.

Does anyone attribute all this to overpopulation? Perhaps some do. But today far more generally scholars of various disciplines see multiple interlocking causes at work, all exacerbated, however, by expanding populations, notably (but not exclusively) in Third World nations. This concise formulation of Norwegian Prime Minister Mrs. Gro Harlem Bruntland is typical: "Population is not about numbers alone; it is about the relationship between people and resources. It is about how resources are consumed, how wealth and opportunities are distributed, and how we can provide hope for the future."[7]

Throughout this book it will be evident that the global population phenomenon is considered a reality, a stern challenge, and—to state it negatively for the moment—a deeply complex reality by no means attributable to clear-cut, isolated reproductive causes alone. Nor are its causes to be found exclusively "over there," elsewhere, in Third World nations. The United Nations (Population Fund) quotation at the head of this chapter strikes that note—linking "access to resources and assets" to the reducing of *both* poverty and population.

The Population Phenomenon

Today's population phenomenon is abundantly documented in many sources and does not need validation or reformulation here. But some sketch or outline seems appropriate, either to remind or inform, as well as to contextualize our entire discussion. Michael Teitelbaum provides a succinct summary of an accelerating situation:

> Although the human species emerged perhaps 150,000 years ago, most of its growth in numbers has occurred in the last 40 years. It took scores of millennia to reach the first billion humans, around 1800; over a century to reach the second billion, somewhere between 1918 and 1927; about 33 years to the third billion, around 1960; only 14 years to the fourth billion; and 13 to the fifth in 1987.[8]

The 1997 United Nations Population Fund states that

> The world population in mid-1997 is 5.85 billion. Growth slowed to 81 million persons per year during 1990–95, compared to 87 million in the peak years of 1985–1990.... Long-range projections are lower: the world in 2050 is expected to have between 7.7 billion and 11.1 billion people, with the most likely projection considered to be 9.4 billion, nearly half a billion less than the 1994 estimate. Where the actual 2050 population will fall within this vast 3.4 billion range will depend largely on the actions or inactions of the world's nations in the next few years.[9]

Two points should be noted here: projections, as implied in the statement, are not predictions. They are real possibilities, contingent on many factors—some subject to human decision, some not. Second, reference to *growth* is net, not gross (i.e., the margin of excess of births over deaths).

Population concerns spring first from the sheer acceleration of growth, evident in Teitelbaum's summary of the historic periods of population growth:

1st billion—perhaps 150,000 years
2nd billion—just over 100 years
3rd billion—about 33 years
4th billion—about 14 years
5th billion—about 13 years

The increase, it should be noted, centers almost exclusively in the developing world, in areas often already severely stressed. In other areas fertility rates are in decline, even, in some areas, below replacement levels.

Population increase, moreover, produces its own momentum—an ever-widening number entering reproductive years, a dynamic factor resembling compound interest on a bank account or investment. More makes more, on an expanding base.[10] All this has been much influenced by improvements in medical science (and consequent decrease in mortality rates), improved agriculture, and numerous technological advances. More people live longer, and reproduce more. We celebrate this, but it also creates problems.

Concerns also arise from the relationship of human numbers to available resources. This relationship is often phrased as the "carrying capacity" of the earth. In an insightful analysis of that carrying capacity Joel E. Cohen spells out the enormous complexity of the challenge.

> The clear message is that people cannot forever continue to have, on average, more children than are required to replace themselves. This is not an ideological statement; it is a hard fact.... [Yet] "how many people can the earth support?" is not a question in the same sense as "how old are you?" It cannot be answered by a number, or even a range of numbers.... [It is] determined partly by processes

that the social and natural sciences have yet to understand, partly by choices that we and our descendants have yet to make.[11]

Cohen emphasizes that together we face choices, decisions. "Human choices, now and in the future, will determine where those limits fall." He spells out, as he sees it, several "thorny issues" that compose that "interplay of natural constraints and human choices." (We will return to these in the final chapter.) The book you are reading explores the Catholic participation in those choices.

Thus the population challenge is not merely statistical or demographic. It is human, political, economic, cultural, and philosophical—as well as profoundly ethical and religious.

Overwhelming, Disputed Data

For many of us a little of this data goes a long way. Even a little becomes quickly overwhelming, like astronomy when I hear of a star that is light-years away or other stars in the Milky Way distant by *thousands* of light years. "Such knowledge is too wonderful for me to attain" said the psalmist—about a good deal less information.

What am I to make of such overwhelming population data? What is the Church to make of it, to say of it? How should it respond to population perplexities? How draw any sensible or workable conclusions? In sympathy with such consternation Charles Mann asks, "How Many Is Too Many?" and spells out the conflicting interpretations of population data by economists versus biologists.[12] One says "up," the other "down." One shouts "white," another yells "black," bellowing past each other. In these population issues economists tend to trust the energies, initiatives, and ingenuities of a global marketplace; biologists, on the contrary, tend to count heads and probe the dynamisms of reproduction.

The feminist voice is another major advocate on the population scene, heard at various points in this book. This voice is sharply critical of "conventional population policy" emphasizing fertility control— which is often coercive, ignoring holistic health concerns as well as the larger socioeconomic realities within which these policies function. Ellen Chesler, director of the International Women's Health Coalition, stated this position in a published debate with a Princeton demographer and sociologist. "Traditional approaches," she said, "have for too long focused narrowly on distributing technology, and treated women as faceless demographic targets...[and] blamed women for having too many children while neglecting the larger framework of inequality and discrimination that governs their choices."[13]

These divergent "explanations" challenge and probably confound many who seek to get a handle on these issues. Thus while respecting the reality of a population dilemma, Charles Mann repeatedly cites counterbalancing studies where, remarkably, "increasing population has, if anything, raised land productivity." "Given half a chance," he adds, "people in Africa, like people anyplace, seem to make their own way."

But Mann also notes that what may be technologically or economically *possible* and imaginable may at the same time be politically most *unlikely*. He concludes his thoughtful essay with reflection on the increasing "disamenities," as he terms them, of his own New York City, "the hundred predicaments that population growth aggravates"— traffic, crime, dirty streets and parks, homelessness, deteriorating schools.

Consider a comparison. Must one be an expert or scientist to comprehend the principal characteristics of space flight—orbiting in a fabulously complex vehicle, extraordinary arrangements for food, breathing, and moving about, and for communication and navigation? Most of us have some correct sense of it, even if far short of a scientific, detailed grasp. One gets the general picture.

Similarly, some such basically correct grasp of population problems seems available even amidst the bewildering data. Two University of Michigan scholars, Bruce Oakley, biologist, and William Anderson, botanist, in an incisive article on population ask, "Is the earth overpopulated?"[14] To answer their own question they perhaps simply consulted the morning paper with its frequent news of destitute people in Somalia or Haiti, migrating and dispossessed populations, chaos in much of Africa—on and on. They then offer this trenchant observation: "It is difficult to fathom assertions that 'the world can support ten billion people,' when it is patently obvious we are already failing to provide humanely for half as many."

In other words it is one thing to amass abstract statistics and speculative studies that assess (in controverted form) the ultimate capacities of our physical, planetary ecosystems—as well as our political and socioeconomic systems. It is another thing altogether simply to look around the real world here and now, to witness the wretched facts of existence for multi-millions. Who can dispute the Oakley-Anderson assessment that "we are already failing to provide humanely for half as many"—a somber, realistic statement with weighty implications. One example: discussing declining global water resources, Sandra Postel notes that *more than a billion* members of our human family lack access to such a minimum of well-being as safe, reliable water,[15] while at least a billion try to get by on less than one dollar per day.[16]

Catholic Voices

But when Catholic voices, especially at official levels, turn to these issues suspicion is prominent. Imputations of ill-will, of disregard for spiritual values, of secular insensitivity, of data skewed to irreligious and materialistic purposes are emphasized. If experts in these areas discover data sufficiently compelling that they recommend control of population levels, should they be castigated for the logic of their findings? Does not the Church owe to others the same presumption of intellectual honesty and a sincere desire for human well-being that it expects to have exercised toward itself? Consider the following from Pope John Paul's Apostolic Exhortation *On the Family (Familiaris Consortio*, 1981):

> [Some] consider themselves to be the only ones for whom the advantages of technology are intended and they exclude others by imposing on them contraceptives or even worse means. Still others [are] imprisoned in a consumer mentality...whose sole concern is to bring about continual growth of material goods. The ultimate reason for these mentalities is the absence in people's hearts of God.... Thus an anti-life mentality is born, as can be seen in many issues: One thinks, for example, of a certain panic deriving from the studies of ecologists and futurologists on population growth, which sometimes exaggerate the danger of demographic increase to the quality of life. But the Church believes that human life, even if weak and suffering, is always a splendid gift.[17]

Granting various merits in the pope's comment, nevertheless, on what basis, concretely, does he detect an "anti-life mentality" here? These are observations of appalling poverty, chronic destitution, in which clearly the *ratio of human numbers to actually available, here-and-now resources* (food, water, fuel, land, plus medical, educational and hygienic services) constitutes the very reality itself. Is it "anti-life" to notice, to care, to report?

Oakley-Anderson report that, "Every day thousands of children die of malnutrition-related disorders. Of the 5.4 billion people alive today the bottom billion can't get the nourishment necessary for good health and vigorous work." Is such an observation "anti-life," or an expression of "panic"? Is it not rather a statement *on behalf of* the "splendid gift" of life?

True, every knowledgeable person today hears the constant application of statistics in our society to every conceivable political, economic, and social cause, pro and con. If the devil can quote Scripture, he has become equally at ease with statistics. Yet it seems established beyond statistics that human numbers are growing enormously, with severe suffering and impoverishment steadily aggravated as a consequence. In fact, as appears in the next chapter, the official Church itself, and scholars of the Church's academic community, have acknowledged this fact repeatedly.

Much of the global reality and challenge is encapsulated in an episode told by Claudia Ford, a trained midwife who has spent fifteen year in Asia and Latin America in health, family-planning, and human rights programs.

> I remember being in an extremely remote village in Bangladesh, a place it took a couple of days to reach, crossing many rivers and walking several miles. We talked with an obviously malnourished woman there who had five kids and was using modern contraceptives. We asked her, "Why are you using family planning?" "I'm tired," she said, "I have many children and I don't want to have any more. I have this much rice and I have to feed this many people. If I have more people to feed, then I have to have more rice and I can't see where more rice is going to come from. Our community is very crowded. And there are too many people." This was an illiterate, poor woman whose childbearing decisions didn't have anything to do with sophisticated policies.[18]

This, then, is not primarily a theoretical dispute about the ultimate "carrying capacity" of the earth. It is not a theoretical dispute about evaluating the present level of global population as "overpopulation" or otherwise. It is a de facto observation about horrendous, massive suffering in the human family, about injustice, about portentous political and economic instabilities, about vast human need already present today—and more tomorrow. Those in varying scholarly disciplines who report on the situation, who submit their data to public assessment, are not categorically "anti-life." In fact, just the opposite is as likely the case. They deserve a hearing by all who care about God's human family. This is essential to that "culture of listening" of which the President of Ireland spoke (Introduction).

An Afterword on Population

Discussion about "global population" must include recognition of the diversity within the overall picture. In many developing nations fertility has declined rapidly with the increase of contraceptive use and family planning. In some developed nations fertility rates are below replacement levels, which could eventually affect economic, cultural, and political stability. (Note, fertility rates can decline while absolute population continues to increase because of large numbers entering reproductive years.)

A 1997 report from the Johns Hopkins University Population Information Program provides a partial summary:

> Since the 1960s the rate of population growth has slowed. In what demographers have termed a reproductive revolution, fertility has declined as contraceptive use and family planning has risen.... The world now contains 400 million fewer people than it would have otherwise.
>
> World population is growing by 1.5% per year today compared with 2% per year in the 1960s. In some developing countries, however, primarily in sub-Saharan Africa, population is still growing at 2% to 3.5% per year, rates at which populations would double in 20 to 35 years. Even rates of 2% or less create a powerful momentum for future population increase, particularly as they are applied to ever larger numbers of people.[19]

A further point will be emphasized in this book. Whereas family planning programs are effective in the short range, long range stability requires social justice alleviation of severe poverty, of gross levels of unequal distribution of basic necessities. It works both ways: alleviation of poverty influences a fertility decline—which tends in turn to reduce poverty.

Questions for Reflection and Discussion

1. The opening quote (and others) from Vatican II connects the Church and suffering. What is the foundation for such a connection? How does that relate to a discussion about global population?

2. ("Multiple Causes") Mrs. Bruntland sees population as "not about numbers alone." Is she right or wrong, in your view? Why?

3. How much is a billion? How would you explain a billion (of anything) to a fifth-grade student? (Suggestion: how many miles from the earth to the Sun? How many round trips to the Sun would be needed to reach a billion miles?)

4. Joel Cohen ("Population Phenomenon") says that the question, "how many people can the earth support?" can't be answered with numbers. Why not?

5. How does the Oakley-Anderson statement throw light on the discussion? How does it shift the emphasis away from statistics?

6. Is advocating constraint on population growth "anti-life" (in a religious or moral sense)? Is such an advocacy morally wrong?

CHAPTER TWO

I do believe that the Second Vatican Council was a great council whose effects are not nearly at an end, a council that began a new era in the Church...a council that will never allow the Church to return to the way she was.

—KARL RAHNER[1]

Life is a fountain, not a kitchen tap, and the movement for reform and renewal cannot be turned off.

—THOMAS O'DEA[2]

Population: The Catholic Record— Acknowledgment and Awareness

IN THE SECOND VATICAN COUNCIL (1963-65) THE GREAT historic Church turned a corner, entered a new era, began a new chapter in its long record. For a Church with two thousand years of history the relatively brief period since the Council ended constitutes merely a *beginning* of that new era. But Catholics today find themselves, inescapably, in a long era of adjustment—with some tension and some struggle.

Theologian James Bacik tells of a professor teaching a course on sexuality who sums up the Christian contribution as "No, no, and no."

As a lifelong Catholic I regret this "no and no" image often associated with the Church, especially in sexual issues. At the same time I behold the moral and sexual chaos in the contemporary world—AIDS, other sexually transmitted diseases, increasing unwed pregnancies, children without parents, family breakdown, and so on. Sexual wisdom and balance are rare. The Church deserves credit for taking these issues seriously and for, by and large, offering careful argumentation in support of the stands it takes.

Moreover, moving beyond essential core areas of personal spiritual values—of articulating a meaning for human existence, addressing the total pattern or context under God within which life and death, suffering and striving occur—the Church in the last century has increasingly explored the broad "social issues" of humankind. This Catholic "social teaching" includes war and peace, nuclear weaponry, the environment, economic justice, marriage and the family, the dignity and rights of labor, and the divine call for a solidarity that transcends the multiple barriers of race, gender, and nationality in the human family. It also includes population, as an emerging concern.

In this chapter we (selectively) survey the Catholic record on global population; our goal here is primarily factual—with assessment reserved for subsequent chapters. That Catholic record of explicit attention to population is still in a formative stage, still a fairly slender body of material. Nevertheless, even if fairly slender, official Catholic sources have acknowledged that the population phenomenon exists at disturbing, formidable levels. Such acknowledgment—seemingly little noticed by the general public, Catholic and otherwise—is itself significant.

We will discuss papal statements on population, Vatican II, Vatican diplomatic action, particularly in the United Nations, and statements by both North American and South American episcopal conferences. In addition, a very limited but significant body of academic, theological commentary deserves attention. Indeed, placing the relevant theological comment alongside official Catholic sources promptly illustrates the classic tension existing between these intramural, family centers of religious life. The official or institutional Church is devoted to that which is authoritative and directive; the Church's academic community more often looks to exploration, critique, and (as deemed appropriate) doctrinal development. The former perennially seeks a more conforming, subservient role from the latter, with limited success despite persistent efforts.

We will also discuss (and place considerable emphasis upon) Catholic social action in many parts of the world. In so doing we will see that global population problems are deeply intertwined with human realities beyond numbers, beyond contraception and "population control."

Catholic "Social Teaching"

Catholic social teaching is customarily dated from Pope Leo XIII's encyclical on labor (*Rerum Novarum*, 1891). It is, of course, overwhelmingly evident that the gospels—the necessary and wholly indispensable source of *all* Christian living, individual and social—were written nineteen centuries earlier. The gospels, in turn, stand within the broader context of the entire biblical outlook and message. So in a full and proper sense "social teaching" is as old as Christianity and the Bible, influenced as well by the tradition of postbiblical centuries. Thus, later chapters (Part II) will consider particularly how the life and message of Jesus affects the population issues under discussion here. This has been done far too little, hardly at all.

In looking at "social teaching" we meet at the outset a puzzlement, a theological twist. Pope Paul VI's encyclical *Of Human Life* (*Humanae Vitae*, 1968) dominates the official Catholic position concerning global population.[3] Yet that encyclical is not generally regarded as "social teaching"; its message, significantly, emerges rather in the perspectives of individual conduct, individual (or individual married couple's) decisions.

Social teaching, on the contrary, refers to social or society-wide issues, to economic, political, and cultural issues, affecting whole groups, whole nations, even the international community. But with *Humanae Vitae* a fundamentally moral pronouncement at the *interpersonal* level has become in effect a major *social* pronouncement, for better or for worse, properly or improperly. This moral pronouncement, promulgated in terms of universal applicability ("intrinsic evil": for *all* times, places, persons, circumstances, without exception) has become a central determining factor in the Church's stance vis-à-vis global population issues.

No one denies the importance of moral values in social teaching. But moving from personal and interpersonal conduct to social conduct—to decisions by millions of people or affecting millions of people in widely diverse circumstances—is not simple, but complex and risky. In the same way, the transition from individual conduct to state, community, or political conduct also is not simple, but complex and risky. The community can tax, can arrest and imprison, can call the citizen to risk life and limb in military service, and can require that you halt your car at the next red light. It can exact a fine if you burn your leaves in autumn or dispose of garbage improperly. No individual is entitled to impose any such behaviors or constraints on another individual citizen.

Nevertheless, one way or another, along this road or that, the Church contributes a spectrum of positive values to population realities and their related controversies. Official church voices have increasingly and explicitly admitted the reality and gravity of the population phenomenon. And *many aspects* of Catholic social teaching and social action *indirectly affect* population dynamics, although largely without recognition or acknowledgment as such. Some of these will be spelled out in this chapter.

Two Popes: The Second Vatican Council

Writing prior to Vatican II, Pope John XXIII devoted fifteen paragraphs to "Population Increase and Economic Development" in his encyclical *Mother and Teacher* (*Mater et Magistra*, 1961).[4] He admitted that "the question often is raised how economic organization and the means of subsistence can be balanced with population increase, whether in the world as a whole or within needy nations" (no. 185). Pope John was optimistic, seeing "in science and technology...almost limitless promise" (no. 189). He upheld the Church's birth control prohibition, and stressed the serious need for international cooperation (no. 192).

Pope John XXIII's famed document *Peace on Earth* (*Pacem in Terris*, 1963) carries only the brief statement, "Everyone certainly knows that in some parts of the world there is an imbalance between the amount of arable land and the size of the population" (no. 101).[5] Themes of human dignity, rights, and an equitable social order occur throughout the document, themes characteristic of this great pope's administration.

Pope John XXIII convened the monumental Second Vatican Council (1962-65). In its *Pastoral Constitution on the Church in the Modern World* (*Gaudium et Spes*, 1965), the Council turned to the major problems of the times, including "the special problems arising out of rapid increases in population...[for which] international cooperation is vitally necessary" (no. 87). "Some men today are gravely disturbed by this problem; [the Council hopes] there will be Catholic experts in these matters, particularly in universities."[6] The traditional prohibition concerning birth control was retained (because reserved to a special papal commission; see below), but the Council urged that people be "informed of scientific methods of birth regulation...in conformity with the moral order." Parents were encouraged "to cultivate a genuinely human sense of responsibility which takes account of the circumstances of time and situation" (no. 87).

Another section of the same major document (no. 50) has great importance, a quiet revolution in Catholic thought. Here the purposes inherent in marriage were conceded for the first time at this official level to include "true married love and the whole structure of family life," education of children, "reading the signs of the times and their own situation on the material and spiritual level and an estimation of the good of family, of society and of the Church." "Marriage is not merely for procreation...[but also for] the mutual love of the partners, [and] a whole manner and communion of life." The Catholic heart and mind were thus, theologically, newly oriented to wide, complex, and diverse horizons.

With the death of John XXIII during the Council, leadership passed to Paul VI. But not long before his death, despite the optimism on population issues previously expressed, Pope John established a "small and confidential international commission to consider the threat of overpopulation." Paul VI retained and enlarged the commission to a membership of sixty-six.[7] He told the continuing Council that the issue of contraception would be reserved to this commission and papal decision.[8]

After the Council, but prior to his *Humanae Vitae,* Paul VI issued his widely respected *On the Development of Peoples* (*Populorum Progressio,* 1967),[9] characterized (in 1978) by the distinguished British economist Barbara Ward as "prophetic wisdom...there is not a page which is not relevant to where we are now."[10] In that letter Pope Paul states,

> It is not to be denied that accelerated demographic increases too frequently add difficulties to plans for development because the population is increased more rapidly than available resources so that all solutions seem to end in a blind alley. (no. 37)

The pope adds this significant comment:

> It is finally the right of parents having completely examined the case to make a decision about the number of their

children; a responsibility they take upon themselves keeping in sight their duty to God, themselves, the children already born, and the community to which they belong, following the dictates of their conscience instructed about the divine law authentically interpreted and strengthened by confidence in God. (no. 37)

Even in the ever-controverted *Humanae Vitae* Pope Paul, before reaffirming the traditional teaching on birth control, gives early acknowledgment to "the rapid demographic development. Fear is shown by many that world population is growing more rapidly than available resources, with growing distress to many families and developing countries." He further grants that modern conditions "often make the proper education of a larger number of children difficult today" (no. 2). The document has eloquent reflections on human love, family life, the Church—and all of these as existing in and affected by civil society.

The Latin American Bishops

Merely one month after *Humanae Vitae,* Pope Paul opened the Second General Conference of the Latin American Bishops, Medellín, Colombia, termed by Philip Berryman as "The Magna Carta...of applying Vatican II to Latin America." Paul's opening address spoke of "the law we have reaffirmed" that does not however prompt "a blind race toward over-population, does not diminish the responsibility or liberty of husband and wife, nor forbid a moral and reasonable limitation of birth."[11]

Among the conference commissions at Medellín was "Family and Demography."[12] The report from this body acknowledged complex demographic problems—both "rapid population growth," and also that "the majority of our countries are under-populated." The bishops supported *Humanae Vitae* while pointing to the "responsibility and freedom of married couples," as acknowledged by the pope himself.

The bishops quoted Pope Paul's October 1965 statement before the United Nations: "The problem, in fact, is not to decrease the number who eat, but rather to multiply the bread." The bishops "wish to confront the challenge of demographic problems with an integral answer focusing on development." Special support is pledged "for [married couples] who try to attain the ideal set forth [in *Humanae Vitae*] despite difficulties."

The United Nations

Beginning in 1946 (long before *Humanae Vitae* in 1968), the Vatican asserted its adverse position on contraception and population through the U.N. When early plans, deliberations, and activities of the World Health Organization (a U.N. agency) relative to population planning encountered strong Vatican opposition, millions of people not of the Catholic faith were in some measure affected. Milton P. Siegel, first Assistant Director General of WHO, affirms that Catholic authorities, from Rome and from Catholic nations, blocked contraception and population issues from the new body's agenda—throughout an estimated seven- to nine-year period. The Vatican took the position that contraception and family planning were political, not health issues. This impact on the U.N. was, says Siegel, "clearly the result of the very effective job done by the Vatican and its representatives."[13]

At the U.N. Conference on Population (Bucharest, 1974) the Vatican as a member state vigorously criticized heavy consumption patterns in the developed nations, as affirmed by the consensus of the conference delegates. The Vatican delegation, however, dissented from the unanimity of 135 nations supporting (in the Vatican's critical description) "indiscriminate recourse to means of birth prevention." [14]

Later in 1974 the U.N. World Food Conference in Rome was addressed by Pope Paul himself.[15] While advocating broad economic development for the poor nations Paul struck bluntly at contraception:

> It is inadmissible that those who have control of the wealth and resources of mankind should try to resolve the problem of hunger by forbidding the poor to be born.... Is it not a new form of warfare to impose a restrictive demographic policy on nations, to ensure they will not claim their share of the earth's goods?

Dissent

Since the Church is *all* of the Church, the pilgrim people of God, we note as part of the Catholic record that a sizeable segment of Catholic laity as well as clergy have in repeated polling expressed dissent toward the teaching of *Humanae Vitae*. Some thirty episcopal conferences (i.e., national groupings of bishops) issued statements at the time of its publication, voicing a wide diversity of reaction—by no means a reception without reservation.[16]

Evidence for such dissent is abundant and continuing.

•A 1994 *Los Angeles Times* poll reported that, of priests and nuns surveyed, 44 percent regard birth control as seldom or never sinful.[17]

•A *New York Times*-CBS poll in 1986 reported that 68 percent of American Catholics (all ages) favored the use of artificial birth control.[18]

•In 1989, 163 European theologians issued "The Cologne Declaration" objecting, among other matters, that the pope "draws upon the concepts of 'fundamental truth' and 'divine revelation' in order to defend a highly particular teaching [i.e., artificial contra-ception]...grounded neither in Holy Scripture nor the traditions of the church." This Declaration was subsequently supported by an additional 130 French, 60 Spanish, 63 Italian, and 431 American theologians.[19]

•A respected Catholic family magazine editorialized on the twenty-fifth anniversary of the encyclical that while specialists continue "to argue the merits and demerits of the teaching" most married couples have long since made their own decisions; for them "the question is practically moot."[20]

These opinions and tensions do not directly focus on population but indeed form part of the Catholic record, shaping fundamental perspectives that apply to population concerns.

In 1994, however, highly visible dissent did emerge (by Catholic laity primarily), occasioned by the Cairo population conference. On the opening date of the U.N. conference a full-page ad appeared in *The New York Times*, a startling addition to the Catholic record. Headlined "An Open Letter to Pope John Paul II on the Question of Contraception," the ad was sponsored by the Catholics Speak Out organization,[21] with thirteen co-sponsoring groups—plus a fine-print, eye-dazzling mass of individual names from the U.S. and abroad. Speaking as "faithful Catholics" the authors acknowledge papal efforts for "overall development," for human dignity, and the papal challenge to affluent nations. But, they add, "We say to you simply, on the issue of contraception, you are wrong"—particularly in the impact of that stance on population issues, ignoring the "vast majority of faithful, practicing Catholics." Before and throughout the Cairo conference another lay organization, Catholics for a Free Choice, was also notably articulate and dissenting.[22]

Pope John Paul II

The current Holy Father, John Paul II, has, if anything, been more vigorous on the contraception issue, seeming to raise it ever closer to a central point of Catholic belief. Some feel it has become a veritable test of orthodoxy. Thus the issue now stands increasingly and intensely associated with papal authority itself on the one hand—while inextricably and continuingly related to the population phenomenon on the other.

In his *Splendor of Truth* (*Veritatis Splendor,* 1993, 179 pages, 40,000 words) Pope John Paul II has moral teaching as his focus, especially the concept of "intrinsic evil" (actions *never* morally justifiable):[23]

> The *negative precepts* of the natural law are universally valid. They oblige each and every individual, always and in every circumstance. It is a matter of prohibitions that forbid a given action *semper et pro semper,* without exception, because the choice of this kind of behavior is in no case compatible with the goodness of will of the acting person, with his vocation to life with God and to communion with his neighbor. It is prohibited to everyone and in every case—to violate these precepts. They oblige everyone, regardless of the cost....(no. 52)

> Each of us can see the seriousness of what is involved, not only for individuals but for the whole of society, with the *reaffirmation of the universality and immutability of the moral commandments,* particularly those that prohibit always and without exception *intrinsically evil acts.* (no. 115; italics in original)

Population is not mentioned, contraception not emphasized. But the message is clear.

In an earlier powerful encyclical, *On Social Concerns* (*Sollicitudo Rei Socialis,* 1987), the pope did mention population briefly: "One cannot deny the existence especially in the Southern Hemisphere of a demographic problem which creates difficulties for development." He protests the coercion that has sometimes accompanied (and corrupted) efforts at population control.[24] (See my Chapter One for comments on Pope John Paul's *On the Family.*) In travels to over ninety nations this pope has forthrightly, often courageously, addressed social justice for the poor, dispossessed, powerless, and disenfranchised.

The following items also appear in the public record under Pope John Paul II:

News report: "In Burkina Faso [the pope] spoke out against contraception, pointedly contradicting the policies of those African governments that view unbridled population growth as a major cause of poverty."[25]

News report: "On one visit to South America the pope used the word 'contraception' no less than sixty times in ten days of public speeches."[26]

News report: William Wilson, U.S. ambassador to the Vatican during the Reagan administration, states that "American policy (foreign aid for family planning) was changed as a result of the Vatican's not agreeing with our policy." Ambassador Wilson personally accompanied State Department officials to the Pontifical Council for the Family in Rome. The United States "finally selected different programs and abandoned others as a result of this intervention." These relationships also involved contacts between the Apostolic Delegate to Washington, Pio Cardinal Laghi, with William Casey, Director of the Central Intelligence Agency. *Time* connects this Vatican-U.S. activity with "one of the great secret alliances of all time" aimed at the dissolution of Communist rule in Eastern Europe.[27]

News report: The U.N. Population Fund Executive Director, Dr. Nafis Sadik (a Pakistani gynecologist who administered her nation's family planning), tells the Associated Press: "All mention [of population and family planning issues] has been removed (Earth Summit agenda, Rio, June 1992) at the very active participation of the Vatican and one or two governments, the Philippines and Argentina."[28]

In March, 1994, Pope John Paul met personally with Dr. Sadik—a meeting reportedly sought by Dr. Sadik two-and-a-half years earlier. At the time of the meeting the Vatican had been protesting aspects of the U.N. preparations for the International Conference on Population and Development in Cairo (September, 1994), charging the absence of a "coherent moral vision."[29]

In his address to Dr. Sadik the pope referred to population and development as "a topic of vital importance for the well-being and progress for the human family...a very complex global population situation...[involving] essential decisions for the future of our society...[in which] at stake is the very future of humanity." He emphasized that "a population policy is only one aspect of an overall development policy," and that "truths about the human person are the measure of any response to...demographic data." He outlined a sharp negative critique of U.N. proposals for the forthcoming conference, citing an absence of adequate acknowledgment of family, acceptance of abortion and sterilization, and other issues. Catholic objection to the "imposition of limits on family size and to the promotion of methods of limiting births which separate the unitive and procreative dimensions of marital intercourse" are reiterated.[30] (In Chapter Four below, see further extended comment on the papal address to Dr. Sadik.)

From the Theologians—a Remarkable Symposium

Although the Catholic theological and general intellectual community has given vigorous, if not excessive, attention to the contraception controversy, explicit consideration of related population aspects has been meager.

One remarkable exception stands out. The prestigious Jesuit quarterly, *Theological Studies,* in 1974 devoted an entire issue, eight articles, to marking the U.N. World Population Year.[31] This particular issue of the quarterly was a year in preparation, including consultations with U.N. personnel and other agencies. Twenty-five years later much of the material retains vigor, pertinence, and sharp challenge (inadequately reflected in my selected summaries of authors McCormack, Murphy, Henriot, Hehir, Thomas, Mazelis and Hurley, following).

Rev. Arthur McCormack ("The Population Explosion"), missionary, consultant at Vatican II and delegate to the U.N. Population Commission, strongly affirms the reality of the population crisis in many areas.[32] He cites the experience of Jamaica where a tourist boom plus the discovery of bauxite produced economic progress—with consequent governmental attention to social programming. But measured over a decade all progress was nullified by population increases.

Urging that the Church has a significant contribution to make, McCormack offers this advice:

> If the Church wishes to be authentic in this field, the first question to ask is what are the facts? It has the obligation to study the whole complex subject carefully, scientifically, without prejudice, without bias, as objectively as possible. This does not mean that one should abandon Christian

principles, but it does mean one should not let them affect factual study or cause one to close one's eyes to the truth for fear of doctrinal difficulties.

Rev. Francis X. Murphy ("The New Population Debate"), then professor at Johns Hopkins University, moral theologian, and noted author, sees population "as an area of fundamental moral responsibility." Urging the "communitarian vision of world society" proper to Christianity, Murphy notes that fertility control alone will hardly solve the world crisis. While "need for highly responsible fertility control" remains, nevertheless "the ethos of consumerism prevailing in most developed societies...has maximally contributed to the pollution of air, water, soil, and exhaustion of natural resources." U.N. declarations, he notes, "acknowledge a legitimate variety of goals in population policies," for example, lowering of mortality rates, immigration and emigration control, ecological balance, and elimination of discrimination against minorities.

Murphy's strong analysis of "the new population debate" fully acknowledges the gravity of the crisis in population and food and the importance of a response from religious bodies—ranging from parishes to worldwide institutions, plus the individual and the family. Such informed witness and comment, along with others in this collection, is a rich and unique theological resource.

Jesuit Peter Henriot ("Global Population and U.S. Policy") similarly emphasizes the "relationship of population growth to economic growth in developing nations" as well as the "impact of consumption patterns in the developed nations." Henriot sees the need for "a domestic population policy" in the United States, a consideration rarely encountered then or now. He points to Paul VI's *Populorum Progressio,* the 1971 Roman Synod's *Justice in the World,* and the 1973 American bishops' statement on population (see below) as evidence of Catholic concern for issues of population, all with an *internal* development emphasis.

Rev. J. Bryan Hehir of the U.S. Catholic Conference ("Church and Population: A Strategy") comments on how it is easier to speak to Americans about contraception than about "contraconsumption." He asks if the world can afford the reproductive habits of the Third World—*and* the consumption habits of the First World. Hehir emphasizes the crucial distinction of abortion from contraception; opposing them equally on both the national and international scene, he says, blurs the morally qualitative difference between them. Such blurring weakens the contribution of Catholic thought. Political implications (and risks) are richly developed in Hehir's remarks.

The specialization of the late John L. Thomas as a noted Jesuit sociologist of family gives distinctive coloration to his treatment of the Catholic role in population realities ("Family in a Contraceptive Culture"). He examines connections of family well-being, population, and Catholic social teaching.

Each person's given sociocultural setting or system, says Thomas, affects every human being and family profoundly, inescapably— influencing and limiting their behavioral options. Thus we can be critical of a given culture or society, while sympathetic with persons living within it. For Thomas contraceptive practice plays a key role in balancing high fertility potential with mounting socioeconomic constraints. Failing to use such a key social mechanism (contraception), larger family values will be imperiled, "trapped in a series of contradictory expectations, needs, and requirements."

Thomas asserts that "responsible thinkers must recognize that the Church's official stance...is a feasible solution only under conditions of high infant and maternal death rates." He calls for "a long overdue critical re-appraisal of the specifically Catholic approach to sexuality."

Significantly at a time when feminist values were still emerging, *Theological Studies* included a laywoman (a U.N. human rights officer and political science doctoral candidate). Irma Garcia De Mazelis ("Housewives and Mothers in Development") explores the question that, fortunately, has come increasingly to the fore in population discussion: "Is there a causal relationship between higher status for women and lower fertility rates?" Responding affirmatively, she does not, however, discuss Catholic impact on that question.

The symposium concludes with Denis E. Hurley, the widely respected (now retired) Archbishop of Durban, South Africa, addressing "Population Control and the Magisterium." This forthright prelate states, "By insisting that moral standards be preached in impossible situations, Church leadership could be guilty of a double injustice: to the poor who are supposed to live up to these impossible standards and to pastoral clergy supposed to preach what they know very few of their hearers can practice."

Hurley wishes to disengage a Catholic "absolutist mentality" from "authentic moral values." He regrets the following confrontation: (a) the Church's traditional moral system mainly concerned with absolute unchangeable principles, the traditional Catholic "essential" approach—*confronting* (b) scientifically assembled facts of a human situation in which those principles have to be lived, the "existential" modern approach.

Hurley's article, and the symposium, concludes on this note: "We must avoid at all costs incurring the reproach of Jesus, 'You load on men burdens that are unendurable, burdens that you yourselves do not move a finger to lift'" (Luke 11:46).

Let us pause to summarize common elements in this 1974 *Theological Studies* collection.

1) All the authors regard the population phenomenon as real and serious; none attempts to "argue it away"—but several see the official Church as defensive or minimizing toward it.

2) None explicitly calls for a repeal of the *Humanae Vitae* prohibition; however, Hurley, Thomas, and McCormack are notably uneasy with it.

3) None characterizes *Humanae Vitae* as a *positive* contribution to the global situation, as a step forward.

4) All regard Catholic social doctrine as possessing crucially important contributions to the problem. (This fourth point provides the basis for extensive reflection in our next chapter—the Catholic contribution in population aspects beyond and other than sexual morality.)

The writings of Rev. Charles Curran must be briefly noted here. Curran is one of the few moral theologians to address population. Discussing "Population Control: Methods and Morality," Curran states that much of Catholic moral theology assumes a basic harmony and order in the world, with a bias toward the "controlling power of reason."[33] He suggests that such a bias expresses itself in an excess of optimism, which, *if incautious,* minimizes difficulties, obstacles, and oppositions confronting real people in real life. On the contrary, Curran urges a greater acknowledgment of the tragic and chaotic in human affairs—war, famine, ethnic divisions, environmental degradation, economic greed and exploitation, and the ever-present consequences of human ignorance and shortsightedness. "There are more tensions and possible sources of discord in our world than [the traditional Catholic] approach is willing to acknowledge." His is not a counsel of despair, but of caution and gravity, with Christian hope.

Curran discusses the freedom of married couples, which, while crucial, is not absolute, and subject to limitation if necessary. He distinguishes the basic right to procreate—from a "right" to any personally preferred number of offspring. Curran urges caution with demographic data: "Population growth is not the only problem, nor the cause of all the problems, nor the major obstacle to the solution of all problems." His well-known dissent from the official Catholic teaching on contraception is again respectfully stated; his entire article deserves careful study. As with the other theologians above, his nuanced views suffer in summation here.

The Synod of Bishops, 1980

As Vatican II drew to a close Pope Paul VI initiated a new "collegial" consultation format for the world's bishops with the pope, every three years. More exactly, elected representative-bishops and some additional observers were to assemble in Rome with the Holy Father, who would receive their observations and issue a subsequent pronouncement on the topic of the consultation.

The sixth of these consultations, or synods, gathered in Rome in 1980 to consider "Christian Families in the Modern World." The unscheduled topic of population—an uninvited guest at the dinner party—surfaced early.

The speech of Archbishop John Quinn of San Francisco, while denying that he advocated a change in *Humanae Vitae,* brought basic demographic data of world population into the synodal spotlight. Quinn pointed to the net increase of 150,000 new human lives on earth each day. "He suggested that certain nuances and clarifications could amount to a development of doctrine [i.e., in *Humanae Vitae*]." Quinn recalled instances of such evolution, concerning sacred Scripture and toward human rights, in the work of Vatican II. "This speech electrified the synodal hall."[34] Several Third World bishops arose to support Quinn's position. Others spoke to affirm the official church position, emphasizing First World blame in population problems—and an Irish bishop, Dermot Ryan, cautioned that "the Synod cannot substitute compassion for moral principles."

Later in the synod Archbishop Denis Hurley, South Africa (quoted above), stated that even very dedicated couples increasingly "find it extremely difficult to accept" the Church's official teaching. He then added that the Church's historic acceptance that "in certain circumstances a person may kill, as in self-defense or in a so-called just war" seems to make the exceptionless, absolute prohibition against contraception an inversion of values—to stand moral theology on its head. Hurley's remarks were omitted in the press synopsis of the meeting.

Jesuit reporter Thomas Reese further notes that "the final message ignored the population crisis"—which surely was discussed with considerable, if unwelcome, vigor.[35]

The American Catholic Bishops

In this necessarily selective survey of the Catholic record concerning population issues we finally note the 1991 statement on the environment by the American bishops, *Renewing the Earth*.[36] Granting that "rapid population growth presents special problems and challenges," they wisely place six paragraphs of discussion on population within a substantial and generally impressive document of five chapters on the environment. (The religion-environment relationship as applicable to population will be explored in Chapter Eight.) It also appears to be part of the broad Catholic record that this statement has generally received slight pastoral attention.

Eighteen years earlier, in their 1973 annual meeting, the American bishops issued an excellent statement on the forthcoming U.N. Population Year.[37] Drawing on Pope Paul's *Development of Peoples* they stress a broad developmental approach, insisting that "population discussion cannot be reduced to simple discussion of demographic facts."

The bishops (1973) clearly reflect Vatican II, acknowledging the Church's serious role, encouraging (in their "Conclusion") "our Catholic people to take a positive approach to the question of population, and [establish] research and educational efforts in Catholic educational institutions."[38] Decisions about family size and frequency of births belong to parents, not governments—whereas "parents should take into account their responsibilities before God, children already brought into the world, and the community to which they belong."

Conclusion

In conclusion I return to the wealth of useful comment in the 1974 *Theological Studies*. Peter Henriot comments on a certain Catholic reluctance to deal with population issues.

Because the "population movement" has frequently been characterized by positions at variance with Church teaching—e.g., abortion—Catholics have tended not to talk about population problems. But such silence today would be totally irresponsible. The facts must be faced squarely and appropriate responses readily endorsed.[39]

Archbishop Hurley makes a similar observation, that "the population problem has not received from the Church the attention it merits, for obvious reasons"—namely, Catholic doctrinal conflict with enormously difficult demographic data.[40] Arthur McCormack makes a similar observation.

Interestingly, a Presbyterian minister, president of Eastern College (St. Davids, Pennsylvania), more recently expressed a similar lament: "I have never been in a church discussion on population issues.... Perhaps underlying our anxiety is a question, 'Isn't it a devaluing of family and children?'"[41] On the broad Christian front the task of an adequate response still lies ahead, it seems.

So in this chapter we've sampled both the good news and the bad news on the Catholic church-and-population record. Good news: the issue has been confronted; concern has been demonstrated. Bad news: the record remains very limited, often contentious, intellectually occasional, and overall surely still inadequate.

Note: Vatican responses to the 1994 population conference at Cairo (both before and during) constitute an important part of the Catholic record on population issues. The papal address to Dr. Sadik is discussed above; further aspects will be discussed in later chapters.

Questions for Reflection and Discussion

1. Prior to the Second Vatican Council two horrendous world wars, a global economic, and continual technological change occurred. Does a changing world influence change in the Church? How was Vatican II part of such change?

2. What is the meaning and purpose of Catholic "social teaching"? Of what value is it? How might such "teaching" exist in a fixed, final form?

How might it be progressive, evolving? How might it apply to population issues?

3. Because Vatican City is a sovereign state the Roman Catholic Church has a real (although limited) role in the United Nations, and maintains formal diplomatic relationships with most nations. What in this chapter helps you evaluate the Church's role in international relationships?

4. Is dissent, as discussed in this chapter, simply disloyalty, disobedience, or insubordination? Or even heresy?

5. Several theologians discussed the Church's role and stance in population issues (*Theological Studies,* 1974). Which of their comments strike you favorably or unfavorably?

CHAPTER THREE

Action on behalf of justice and participation in the transformation of the world fully appear to us as a constitutive dimension of the preaching of the Gospel....

—Synod of Bishops, 1971[1]

I was deeply impressed to find the clergy, particularly in Latin America, ranging themselves so unequivocally on the side of the poor and the weak... [and] the bishops of North America presenting their pastoral message of an "option for the poor."

—Willy Brandt[2]

The Catholic Stance: Strength, Achievements

NOW AND AGAIN POPES ISSUE THEIR MOMENTOUS DOCUMENTS, encyclicals, often lengthy and dense in style, rarely bestsellers. Some prove significant, others less so. Regardless, Al Smith, a Catholic campaigning as Democratic nominee for the presidency in 1928, was asked his opinion of a notable encyclical of that time. It is reported that Smith replied, "Will somebody please tell me what in hell is an encyclical?"[3] Not all Catholics, it seems, keep abreast of these theological refinements.

Despite unparalleled throngs that papal tours and visits often attract, popes, as well as the Church generally and Catholic doctrine, are often targets of the "slings and arrows" of modern critics. When Pope John Paul II's encyclical *Veritatis Splendor* (1993) reasserted the moral doctrine of "intrinsic evil" (applicable to artificial means of contraception), the Washington-based Population Institute newsletter ran a six-panel cartoon depicting the pope instructing a dismayed woman. The cartoon pope's comment: "No abortions, no pills, no IUDs, no condoms, no diaphragms, no foam, no gel, no artificial birth control, no pro-choice, you must have the baby." Then the smiling pope-figure concludes, "I love family planning." An accompanying editorial, less derisive, was equally adversarial.[4]

Nevertheless, beyond barbs and brickbats (and legitimate criticism), much of the official Catholic stance vis-à-vis population actually harmonizes with advanced thinking in this much-controverted field. The point is that, factually, the Church is far more than a nay-sayer. In his widely respected *Earth in the Balance* Al Gore (senator, later vice-president) remarks, "Many environmental theorists who think of the Catholic Church only long enough to complain bitterly about its opposition to birth control (which many Catholics, in fact, use) might be surprised to read the pope's powerful and penetrating analysis of the ecological crisis and recognize him as an ally."[5] (Gore refers to Pope John Paul's strong 1989 statement,[6] one of many positive Catholic contributions to environmental and population concerns discussed—selectively, not exhaustively—in this chapter.)

The Church: More Than Pope and Vatican

An important distinction must be recalled early in this discussion: for Catholics "Church" includes the Vatican, popes, and hierarchy, but the Church is far more than the Vatican and popes. The Church as institution possesses structure and a history, but the Church is far more than an institution. The Church, as Vatican II made clear, is the *entire* "People of God" (in the phrase of Vatican II), female and male, laity and clergy, poor and rich, educated and uneducated, existing in unnumbered cultures and conditions—in response to Jesus Christ and his first disciples.[7] We follow Christ, but we are inescapably as well followers of the followers of Christ, heirs of that rich (also flawed, compromised, and checkered) tradition. In Karl Rahner's words, "The historical continuation of Christ in and through the community of those who believe in him, and who in a profession of faith acknowledge him explicitly as the mediator of salvation is what we call *church*."[8]

In a more whimsical mood—which happens even to theologians—Rahner compared the Church to a chess club.

> The situation in the church is really like that of a chess club. Those who really support the club and give it its meaning are the members to the extent that they play chess well. The hierarchy of the club leadership is necessary and appropriate if and as far as it serves the community of chess players and their "hierarchy," and does not think it is identical with the latter or that it can play chess better simply in virtue of its function. So too office (authority, governance) is to be respected in the church; but those who love, who are unselfish, who have a prophetic gift constitute the real church and are far from being always identical with the office-holders.[9]

Hence, pope, Vatican, and hierarchy are no more wholly the Church than president, congress, and the political establishment are wholly the United States. In his now-classic *Models of the Church* Avery Dulles highlights five "models"—community, herald, sacramental, servant, and institutional—and allows for many more. Of these, adds Dulles, only the institutional "cannot properly be taken as primary. Of their very nature, I believe, institutions are subordinate to persons, structure subordinate to life."[10]

This distinction underlies the approach and understanding of this book. While respecting positions of high authority and responsibility, nonetheless I affirm a consciousness of *responsibility shared* in Christ's kingdom. We are all the Church, all sinful, all striving, all responsible, albeit differing in roles. Thus when I speak of the Church's role, or record or stance I by no means focus exclusively on official levels of Catholic life.

Catholicism on Sexuality and Birth Control: An Appreciation

One can appreciate and dissent simultaneously. We do it often. I approve of my family, and am deeply grateful—but sometimes disagree within my family and household. I am glad to be a U.S. citizen, but am surely critical of much in U.S. life—culturally, politically, and otherwise. I firmly espouse democracy, but see flaws in it at the same time. I am deeply committed to the Church, but that very commitment leads me to seek reform, renewal, and improvement, according to my limited knowledge, experience, and conviction. But it is no surprise when others view the same reality differently. How often have I walked slowly around a free-standing sculpture, noting how variously the same object appears from different angles, different perspectives. Is just *one* of those perspectives true?

So with official Catholic teaching on sexuality: I dissent, partly—but I appreciate, largely.

Of course, this book has its focus on global population issues in relation to the Church. This is not a generalized discussion of sexuality or contraception, either to explain, defend, or refute. But Catholic moral teaching on sexuality has been dominated in the public mind by the din and clamor (and vituperation) over contraception and abortion. In fact, there's much more to it than that.

The Catholic view of sexuality derives from a religious view of human existence itself. In the deepest possible sense ours is a created world, a world that belongs to the Creator, and to whom each of us also therefore belongs. David Steindl-Rast, author and monk, in his dialogue with physicist Fritjof Capra, puts it this way:

> Long before we are even theists or non-theists we all experience in our best, most alive moments that we belong. The notion of our ultimate belonging implies that to which we ultimately belong.... If we belong to God, God belongs to us; we're in a relationship. This is mysticism, of course, but anyone of us can experience it daily.... God has to be personally related to everything and in the most intimate depths.[11]

Here is the basis of Christian environmentalism, a theology of existence and great nature itself—"related to *everything.*" Implied here is personal worth, human dignity and destiny, a depth of wonder and meaning—however ignored and disfigured in actual living, as indeed it often is. *Everything* thus becomes part of a context of meaning, in God, in belonging, sexuality included—however ignored and disfigured in actual life, as indeed it often is.

Vatican II spoke richly of the vocation of marriage, family, and responsible parenthood.[12] One has only to survey momentarily the pain and sorrow we see around us, in families and the lives of children, between spouses, in countless relationships—with no assessment of blame—but with compassion for wounds, loss, and frustration. The message of the Church offers a sorely needed and inspiring corrective, not magic but orientation, direction, some sense of meaning.

Within this setting of endowed meaning and purpose in a valued life, sexual relationships and intercourse fit and function *purposefully.* There is no Catholic exhortation "to have as many children as you can." Responsible, loving parenthood and marital partnership are stressed. The traditional (official) prohibition against artificial means of preventing conception interprets the choice of such means as illicit manipulation and deliberate frustration of our God-given, life-giving, and love-sharing powers and signs.[13]

This teaching is neither frivolous nor casual, a mere preference or assumption, lacking foundation. Hence, it is not surprising that we encounter opposition within the household of the faith tradition when we advocate change. In the next chapter we will discuss a rationale for proposed *moderate change* and development in this doctrine. It is sufficient here to acknowledge a tradition of great dignity.

Population: More Than Contraception

Recall the six-panel cartoon described above, critical of papal moral teaching. By emphasizing a variety of contraceptives it suggests that population problems today are best if not exclusively combated by such means. That may or may not be the policy of the sponsoring population agency. But such political artwork hardly specializes in subtlety. The Church is taken to task for its stance on artificial means of contraception. But Church policy—and the actual centuries-long Catholic record of service—in fact is considerably more nuanced, more comprehensive, more incisive than our artist-critic allows or likely realizes.

While protesting artificial contraception in principle, the Vatican has further vigorously criticized *coercion*—pressure in campaigns promoting contraceptives and sterilization. When "target populations" of such campaigns are illiterate, impoverished people, the potential for abuse is enormous. If, moreover, the functionaries of such campaigns work toward quantified goals with continued funding or their own jobs at risk, the potential for abuse only grows.

These promoted interventions in human lives and sexuality—which affect women more directly and drastically—are inextricably related to health care. Yet *attention to that link* is very frequently absent. Pills, intrauterine devices, surgeries (sterilizations, abortions), to say nothing of the processes of pregnancy and birth, are bodily issues, intensely significant health issues (for better or for worse). Hence "services" touching all these should be, insofar as possible, delivered in conjunction with careful medical assessment or counsel, with awareness of, and concern for, overall health.

Yet some observers see Vatican protests against coercion or pressure only as signs of ultra-conservatism. In fact, abuses have occurred. Consider the following from India:

> Under foreign advice, family planning targets were set, with financial incentives and cash awards proffered for meeting them. This brought corruption in the health care services as figures were concocted to assert—with fanfare—the number of tubectomies performed. Health workers became increasingly identified as the government's family planning target chasers, employees who viewed women not as human beings but as "tubes and wombs and targets" with whom financial incentives were linked…. There was little concern for their health needs, and interest was shown only in those who accepted permanent methods.

> In a social context where little change was attempted in other areas, coercion was the one stick seen as a means for beating the growth rate…. Female literacy, an assurance of minimum wages, social and political awareness are far more important determinants in opting for a small family.[14]

Vatican protests against coercion are not without justification. At the theoretical, policy, and operational levels, ethics scholar Sissela Bok notes that "short shrift has often been given to crucial ethical considerations."[15] Betsy Hartmann adds:

> Even if one accepts that, broadly speaking, incentives and disincentives are justified—that there must be limitations to personal liberty for the good of the community—another question arises: Just *who* defines what is in the public

interest? Who designs the tax system? Who decides that population control must be a priority, instead of women's rights, land reform, health care and education? Those who hold the reins of power, of course.

In many, if not most, countries, poor people are cut out of the political process.... They are not the ones designing family planning incentive schemes in the capital cities of the Third World, or in AID, or the World Bank's offices in Washington. Their definition of the public interest differs fundamentally from that of the politicians, technocrats, and generals who rule *over* them, not *for* them.[16]

Coercion is a top-down phenomenon, deserving the critique and opposition the Church offers to it.

The Church and NFP

Church promotion and support for one particular mode of conception control, "natural family planning" (NFP), is also often dismissed as irrelevant, ineffective, or again merely expressive of ecclesial conservatism. But in fact impressive medical testimony supporting NFP as *one* form (not the *only* form) of contraception is emerging. Not entering the medical debate, I simply note credible sources engaged in serious medical research of NFP, hardly viewing it as irrelevant or ineffective.[17] Official Catholic support for NFP is based on Pope Paul's *Humanae Vitae,* which in turn derives from certain perceptions of moral principle (noted above, and further discussed in the next chapter)— *plus* assertion of NFP's medical acceptability. The latter, independent of the former, appears increasingly well established while, of course, open to debate and continued research.

Creditably, in its services the Church acknowledges an awareness and concern for population problems. In 1988 *Time* reported that the Missionaries of Charity, coworkers of the revered Mother Teresa in Calcutta, had taught NFP to some 64,000 women.[18]

Again, Betsy Hartmann, citing varying rates of NFP effectiveness in Third World settings, further notes that it is inexpensive, has no side effects, and requires no continuing source of supply. She adds:

Like barrier methods, NFP...provides an important

> alternative to hormonal and surgical forms of birth
> control.... An estimated seven percent of contraceptive
> users worldwide employ some technique of natural family
> planning.... In addition to support from more traditional
> advocates of natural family planning, today support is also
> building among women disillusioned with the side effects
> of other contraceptives and interested in a more holistic
> approach to birth control, in which a woman's knowledge
> of her own body and male co-operation are key. Such
> advocacy could help change the tenor of NFP, so that it is
> more acceptable and accessible in the future.[19]

Such comment is not cited as in some way definitive, the last word,
but rather as representing in fact one professional viewpoint in the field.
As a non-Catholic observer, Hartmann's testimony resembles official
Catholic positions. She also adds that "NFP's success...largely depends
on training, motivation, and cooperation between partners"—complex
variables sometimes feasible, oftentimes not, throughout humankind's
unimaginably diverse circumstances.

I make no effort to evaluate NFP, a modality to which the official
Church has been attracted first of all for doctrinal rather than medical
or demographic reasons. That in itself is not unreasonable, nor by itself
persuasive.[20]

The Church, Development, and the "Demographic Transition"

Driving the expressways everyone now and then encounters a
construction zone, a slowdown area. A worker stands in the roadway
waving a large red flag to catch the attention of oncoming drivers. At
this point in our discussion, behold, a large red flag—drawing attention
to this special term, "demographic transition." In population literature
it carries a crucial (and, not surprisingly, controverted) concept. That
concept connects with poverty, with economic development, and with
sustainable development. I wish further to connect development to
Church policy in this area.

Today a substantial consensus in population studies emphasizes
development as the most promising, most effective check on rampant
population growth. The Church concurs. Under the label of
"demographic transition" populations are assumed to decline, to move

toward stabilization, toward that desired and necessary balance of reproduction and mortality—when (and if) brutal pressures of hand-to-mouth existence, of destitution, hunger, and gross insecurity, are first diminished and then removed. In official policy the Church concurs and contributes.

Noted sociologist and population scholar Nathan Keyfitz comments on the importance and the mysteries of the demographic transition.

> One of the most universally observed and least readily explained social phenomena of modern times is the demographic transition: the fact that with industrialization both death and birth rates fall to new low levels.... Whatever the mechanisms, it is certain that birth rates in the less developed countries will decline as the countries develop.[21]

Keyfitz attributes no automatic magic to this "transition" process, which at best is difficult and gradual. He asserts (as do most other observers) the need for the additional direct intervention of birth-control programs. Susan Bratton, one of the few explicitly Christian authors to address these issues, also warns against assuming that *only* by economic growth does such demographic transition occur. "If we assume this," she states, "then we must immediately concede that any conscious governmental or social attempt to influence population structures is worthless."[22]

Pope Paul VI remains linked in the public mind to his stand on birth control. But speaking to the World Food Conference in Rome (1974), predictably critical indeed of "an irrational and onesided campaign against demographic growth," Paul strongly supported economic development, especially in the agricultural sector amidst rural populations. He was, however, skeptical of the "accent placed on the quest for mere economic success deriving from the large profits of industry, with a consequential almost total abandonment of agriculture." He pointed as well to "a crisis of solidarity" that refuses to see humankind as a family in the widest sense, and interdependent. He sought to encourage "the notion of integral development embracing the whole man and all men...[including] the progressive reorientation of production and distribution."[23]

In *On the Development of Peoples* (1967) the same pope had stressed that "development is synonymous with peace," infusing the entire document with this theme of development.[24] His vision in this encyclical is global, confronting the enormous phenomena of poverty, structural injustice, and inequity in trade relations. He proposes worldwide society as a reality and unity under God, and the elemental purpose of the goods of the earth to nourish *all*—not merely *some*.

"Development" here represents more than an expanded GNP (gross national product), the capitalist golden idol that too often measures the enrichment of the already well-off—leaving the less fortunate to the erratic dynamisms of trickle-down market theory. The pope rather looks to "development" as holistic (i.e., more than merely economic) well-being, a realization gaining ground among some economists, ecologists, and observers in the United Nations Development Programme (UNDP; see *Human Development Index,* below). The much-discussed "demographic transition" (a fertility decline) appears substantially encouraged by broad-based societal development.

Noted demographer John Bongaarts states that "investments in family planning programs produce larger reductions in unwanted fertility when social conditions such as education and gender equality are favorable."[25] Jennifer Mitchell adds, "The demand for large families is so tightly linked to social conditions that the conditions themselves must be viewed as part of the problem."[26] Fertility does not function in a social vacuum.

Economic development itself is encouraged by a fertility decline. The energy flow is reciprocal; it works both ways. Thus, to the Church's credit, by promoting development the Church's social theology supports incentives to fertility decline—and the latter in turn facilitates development.

Unregulated fertility, however, can neutralize or in effect cancel development. Recall from Chapter Two: an economic boom in Jamaica, fueled by tourism and newly discovered mineral deposits, sparked expanded social welfare programming. But population increases over the same period nullified any per capita improvement—the frustration of running harder to stay in place.[27] (In 1960-1994 Jamaica's population rose from 1.6 million to 2.4 million, projected to 2.6 million in the year 2000. Jamaica, a Caribbean island, has a population density of 2256 persons per 1000 hectares, compared to 275 per 1000 hectares in the United States.[28] Populations expand, islands do not.)

Thus direct reproductive control appears necessary as a complement to, and component of, a demographic transition, along with sustainable development. Nathan Keyfitz comments on this connection: "Regardless of the deeper origins of low birth rates, abundant evidence shows that information about birth control and access to contraceptives have been major causes of declining fertility in all countries."[29] Even this persuasive double formula (economic development, fertility control) says little about the demographic impact of social justice or "human rights" factors (discussed later in these pages), whether by presence or by absence. We may quite properly assume justice as necessary for development to be truly "sustainable," but it is hardly a widespread assumption, perception, or concern.

The *Human Development Index*

The Church's linking of development and justice has much in common with the refinements to the concept of development made by the aforementioned UN Development Programme's innovative *Human Development Index* (HDI), produced annually since 1990. The HDI is a direct challenge to the inadequacies of GNP alone as a measurement of human and national well-being. The 1993 Report states, "By combining indicators of real purchasing power, education (literacy), and health (life expectancy), the HDI offers a measure of development much more comprehensive than GNP alone."[30] Typically, the 244-page 1997 report renders this data with stunning analytical specifics.

In a radio interview, Mahbub ul Haq (from Pakistan, originator, chief architect of the Report, former Special Advisor to the UNDP Director) emphasized a positive, even optimistic interpretation of the Report's overall message—hedged with considerable caution. Ul Haq sees positive signs in the "developing world."

> Developing nations in the last thirty years on the human side set a level of progress in health, education, nutrition, in children's welfare, in mortality, *three times as fast* as the industrial nations had achieved in the previous one hundred years.... Yet we cannot become complacent. There is a very long agenda of human deprivation.... [But] pessimism is a luxury we cannot afford. It paralyzes the ability to change. There's no excuse today that nations have gleaming F-16 fighter planes on their runways when people are sleeping on their pavements.[31]

Commenting on the 1993 Report, Mary Jo Griesgraber of Washington's Center of Concern ("working to develop and renew Catholic Social Thought") indicated assets as well as deficiencies. She concludes, "The *Human Development Reports* have gone a long way in setting out an alternative model of development that is sustainable, equitable and participatory for all peoples."[32]

Development, Sustainable and Otherwise

It is also important to note that development itself, both as concept and as process, increasingly comes in for reassessment. Today the ecological demand is for development that can be *sustained*, in balance with natural resources, with the environment. Imagine, as a comparison, a corporation that, in a five-year burst of profit-making, exhausted its personnel, product inventory, equipment, and sources of supply—then collapsed! Would you recommend such an investment to your mother?

The word and concept of *sustainability* is crucial. Development alone, on the Western industrial, capitalist model, may well end up as an ecologically fatal strategy. The operation was a success; the patient died. Or, the proverbial Pyrrhic victory: with one more such "triumph" we're finished. *Sustainability* is an essential component in development, a *sine qua non.*

Lester Brown comments on sustainable development:

> At the heart of reshaping the global economy is the establishment of new goals centered on sustainability. "Economic growth" as measured by the GNP, continues to be our key indicator of "progress" even though it is steadily destroying the natural systems that are its foundation.

> Likewise, we persist in equating economic growth with "development," even when the poorest of the poor end up worse off. A revamping of economic rules and principles is essential to make them serve rather than subvert the fundamental aim of shaping a better future. National accounting that subtracts for the depletion or destruction of natural resources, decision-making techniques that value future costs and benefits more thoroughly, and investment criteria that stem the loss of natural capital are among the reforms vitally needed.[33]

At the time of the Rio "summit" conference (June, 1992) "sustainable development" came to the forefront. *Business Week* headlined a pre-conference issue: "Growth vs. Environment—The Push for Sustainable Development," characterizing sustainable development as a sharp challenge to "the purposes of society, relationships between humans and nature, requiring social justice and equity." A tall order by any measure![34]

Thus the demographic transition of populations *based on development*—a theoretical construct founded initially on the industrialization history of western Europe—becomes not less but more complex, itself more problematic both as process and as guiding theory.

There is, therefore, a serious need to see economic development in close relationship with ecology, with environmental sustainability. The Catholic Church (in admirable if belated concert with many churches and world religions) is responding to the ecological crisis, in which population holds such a central role. The strong statement of Pope John Paul II, while not explicitly using the code term of "sustainability," points to that factor—and goes beyond it to the moral crisis.

> People are asking anxiously if it is still possible to remedy the damage that has been done. Clearly, an adequate solution cannot be found merely in a better management or a more rational use of the earth's resources, as important as these may be. Rather, we must go to the source of the problem and face in its entirety that profound moral crisis *of which the destruction of the environment is only one troubling aspect.*[35]

The pope's full statement along with that of the American bishops (1991)[36] provide two insightful analyses of the ecological challenge (although one could not further point to widespread parochial awareness of them). It is moreover of much interest to note Max Oelschlaeger's carefully argued hypothesis that the major religions can, should, and are beginning to exercise a uniquely significant role in ecological awareness and renewal. He adds, "One doesn't have to be a genius to know that unless we can defuse the population bomb we have little chance of resolving the ecocrisis."[37]—a sober responsibility and challenge, indeed, a long road and a steep climb, just barely begun.

On Balance, The Church's Meritorious Role

We return to our first focus, assessing the role, stance, and record of the Church from the positive side (the human side, as Mahbub ul Haq recommends). It becomes overwhelmingly clear that population issues and crucial population dynamisms extend far beyond specific reproductive factors—the neuralgic area in the Catholic position. To focus on these, to make them the measure of all else, is by no means the consensus impression one gathers from the population and global development literature at this time.

Joel Cohen, head of the Laboratory of Populations at Rockefeller University, New York City, notes that "in largely Catholic Latin America, fertility has been falling rapidly." Cohen sees an important, indirect Church role in such decline. "By promoting literacy for adults, education for children, and the survival of infants in developing countries, the Church has helped bring about some of the social preconditions for fertility decline."[38]

In strongly promoting development, now increasingly understood as one key to the crucial demographic transition, the Catholic role worldwide is meritorious, though far from perfect. The point is not to assert the Church as an unsurpassed leader in this field. But who keeps score? Who knows? In compassionate attention to human well-being much in harmony (for example) with the UNDP perspective, the Church has worked and struggled throughout the centuries—long before demographers came on the scene with their own valuable contributions.

Repeat: the Church record is flawed, as all things human under the sun, with excesses of conservatism and obscurantism, too frequent favored status for the privileged and powerful, politics instead of prophetic courage, on and on. All true, but not the *whole* truth, happily. Again, who keeps score? Many may volunteer as scorekeeper, but few are qualified. Theologian Karl Rahner, commenting on a world in which "the human race is growing gigantically and at a terrifying rate" states modestly that today's Christian

> makes no pretense of knowing some prescription, ready-made or even better than the non-Christian, for each and every problem that arises merely on the grounds that one knows that this world is encompassed by the power and

compassion of the incomprehensible mystery we call God, and dare to call Father. The Christian knows as well as anyone else that this world is caught up in a movement the effects of which in terms of concrete living no one sees clearly, since all calculations serve only to increase the element of the incalculable.[39]

It is the position of this book that contraception has an important, valid role in dealing with population pressures. Thus I propose the Catholic Church can and should reassess its position toward the reproductive aspects of population issues. Its own solid tradition of development in doctrine (to be explored in Chapter Four) renders such reassessment a theologically authentic prospect. But direct reproductive controls nonetheless remain only one part of a very large and deeply perplexing population picture, a part easily and often overemphasized. Because of such overemphasis, assessments of the Catholic contribution are commonly distorted; such distortion tends moreover to an over-simplification of the population perplexity itself.

"On the Fate of the Poor..."

We turn to reflection on the world's absolutely poor, to their position in the population problem, and the relationship of the Church to them. The *Human Development Report* states that, "More than a billion of the world's people still languish in absolute poverty, and the poorest fifth find that the richest fifth enjoy more than 150 times their income."[40]

Frances Moore Lappé and Joseph Collins (co-founders of San Francisco's Institute for Food and Development Policy) concentrate the poverty, population, and accompanying hunger problem into two terse sentences. They insist, "We must face the evidence telling us that the *fate of the world hinges on the fate of the today's poor minorities.* Only as their well-being improves can population growth slow"[41] (italics added). They add that "to attack high birth rates without attacking the cause of poverty and the disproportionate powerlessness of women is fruitless." (Demographers would likely reply that the sought-for "answers" can only be found by action in *both* directions: poverty reduction contributing to fertility decline, and fertility decline facilitating the relief of poverty.)

The world's poor to whom these authors point have no advocate on the world scene more effective, organized, or persistent than the

Catholic Church. Pope John Paul II—in encyclicals on labor (*Laborem Exercens*), on social concerns (*Sollicitudo Rei Socialis*), on the one hundredth anniversary of the first major social encyclical by Pope Leo XIII (*Centesimus Annus*), and consistently on trips abroad—has been an eloquent and analytical spokesman for that concern.

Concern for the poor is further implemented in countless Catholic ways around the globe. If alleviating poverty contributes to improved conditions of life, is intrinsic to development, which in turn promotes reproductive constraint—then by its historic contributions to those factors of well-being (newly emphasized in UNDP's *Human Development Index*) *the Church is a major factor.* Consider the following evidence, randomly selected.

• In Latin America under Church encouragement "hundreds of thousands of grassroots communities have sprung up," base communities, an "instrument by which social and political change necessary to combat poverty and oppression could be helped." How so? "Bible study punctuated by discussions on severely practical matters like dealing with sanitation and drinking water...organizations where the poor find equality, understanding and true Christian solidarity, instead of being encouraged to suffer in silence."[42]

• Archbishop Oscar Romero (March, 1980), six Jesuit priest-professors (November, 1989), the four heroic churchwomen (December, 1980) and unnumbered others in El Salvador—why *murdered?* The obvious, incontrovertible answer: governing and land-owning elites saw in their advocacy of the poor a clear threat to privilege and power.[43]

• The Institute for Rural Education (Puno, Peru) visited by author Tina Rosenberg in her study of violence in Latin America. IRE, founded by the Church some twenty-five years earlier, is "a network of campesino federations that provides training and credit to peasants, and organizes rural unions." She found IRE the major reason local peasants were unreceptive to the terrorist Sendero Luminoso movement then so powerful in Peru.[44]

• Visiting impoverished sugar workers on the island of Negros (Philippines, 1981), Pope John Paul II stated, "The Church will not hesitate to take up the cause of the poor and to become the voice of those not heard when they speak up, not to demand charity, but to ask for justice." His speech infuriated local planter-owners whose customary mode of control has been as often murder and violence as economics.[45]

Lappé and Collins emphasize that the "fate of the world hinges on the fate of today's poor." By no means is the Catholic Church alone in working for and with the poor; perhaps in many times and places it is outdone by others. Many churches and heroic agencies share that mission. But the Catholic contribution remains weighty, real, and historic. One can also point to discrepancies, to conflicts and contradictions within the Catholic record itself, granted. But in the spirit of its holy founder who was poor, walked with the poor, lived poor, and died poor, a central albeit imperfect fidelity to his teaching and example lives on, ever an unfinished task.

A Brief Summary

After recalling that the Church is more than popes and Vatican we have considered points at which Catholic policy at an official level as well as Catholic action amongst people, particularly Third World poor, are clearly positive, progressive, and contributory. The premise: the *"population problem" is fundamentally embedded in massive poverty.* Concerning "demographic transition," sustainable development, the U.N.'s *Human Development Index*: the Church responds with its own intensive and supportive modern record, ever imperfect, of realistic concern for, and involvement with, the poor, worldwide, appreciating economic factors but also emphasizing other factors beyond economics—education, health, human rights, and spiritual as well as bodily hunger.

Admitting family planning and conception control as important, the Church promotes "natural family planning," which is increasingly respected. But no birth control in whatever form will alone provide the profound social reforms needed to alleviate destitution. That need must be faced, grasped, and dealt with—in the "developed nations" with our mindless, destructive consumption, but also in "developing nations" with political corruption and favoring of wealthy elites.

Some Catholics, of course, see the Catholic opposition to artificial birth control, sterilization, abortion, and various direct efforts at population control as itself a major contribution to human dignity and integrity worldwide. I respect that claim, but emphasize rather a need to reassess that opposition in terms of the Church's own tradition and theological resources—discussed in the following chapter.

Finally, A View from Colombia

Working amidst the impoverished Paez Indians in Caloto, Colombia, Father Antonio Bonanomi is only one recent admirable example of fidelity to Christ's mandate. In a recent interview this priest-anthropologist (whose life has been threatened and house burned down because of his work with the poor) recalled his earlier years as a professor in Rome, coming later to Latin America.

> I lived my whole life in Rome, directing a seminary and teaching. I was absorbed in that world, and thought I was a good Christian. But when I came to Latin America I realized the Gospel is something else. Here [Colombia] God's word is not in books; it is alive.... In Rome I thought going without food for one day was heroic. I learned, though, that hunger is daily bread for the people here. Nowadays, many documents of the Church make me laugh. Oh, I believe in social doctrine, but here it all seems like a superstructure. Here, living alongside this or that person, you come upon Jesus with very few intermediaries. I have found Jesus Christ as a human being; He has become a person for me. Before, I believed everything about Jesus was true, but now I don't believe it anymore—I experience it.[46]

Thus at least a partial accounting of the credits of the Church and Catholic people facing today's global population challenge.

Questions for Reflection and Discussion

1. Summarize the purpose or general line of reasoning in this chapter.

2. Concerning the opening, much-quoted statement from the Synod of Bishops: *justice* and the "*transformation of the world*" are a "constitutive dimension" of the Gospel. What does that mean? In fact, Jesus never mentions justice. Do justice and transformation, from the Gospel message, connect with religious action and attitudes toward population problems? If so, how?

3. What are the positive qualities of the Catholic teaching on sexuality?

4. What is "sustainable development"? How does it affect the growth or decline of population?

5. The Catholic Church is a church, not primarily a vast social agency. Yet Pope Paul VI, for example, strongly advocated "development." Why?

6. Jesus "walked with the poor, lived and died poor." What meaning does this have for the Church's role in population issues?

CHAPTER FOUR

Somehow, Church leaders do not appear to "get it"—that is, get the often desperate situation in which women, and especially poor women, find themselves—a situation where biology is destiny, where they are powerless and "have no choice." It is as if "openness to life" happens in a vacuum, apart from enabling conditions....

—DAVID S. TOOLAN, S.J.[1]

The question is how the Church's ban on birth control accords with its larger social doctrine.... The left hand takes away what the right hand gives, and the policy does not cohere.

—DAVID S. TOOLAN, S.J.[2]

The Catholic Stance: Evaluating the Present— Looking to the Future

AT THE AGE OF EIGHTY, THE VERY MONTH OF HIS DEATH IN what was probably the last of innumerable interviews, Karl Rahner looked back—and forward. The high point of his life? "The real high point is still to come," he said. "I mean that abyss of the mystery of God, into which one lets oneself fall in complete confidence of being caught up by God's love and mercy forever."[3] Never losing his appreciation of the past along with an instinct for the future, Rahner in this as in so much else has a lesson for the Church. On what basis before God does an individual, a nation, or the Church itself ever assume that where one now stands is best and final, to be tenaciously maintained? Life pulls us forward.

Six years earlier Rahner reflected on the enormous expansion of knowledge just within his own lifetime. "If one adds up what a scholarly theologian must ideally know today," he said, "after forty years of my theological work I have become ten times dumber. Forty years ago the ratio between what I knew, and the problems, available information, and methods was maybe one to four. Today it's more like one to four hundred."[4]

For Rahner this expanded ratio was significant, with much implication for theology today. Indeed such recognition of vastly expanding knowledge is now a commonplace, is it not? Hence in this chapter we will consider the likelihood, reasonableness, and probable necessity of further accommodation, of adjustment, of development in our Catholic response to a dynamic world.

Catholic theology and the historic belief system that it serves— sometimes by challenge—do not exist in some ethereal, timeless realm detached from the realities of the world around it. In acknowledgment of that, the Second Vatican Council spoke not only on the Church (*Lumen Gentium*, November 1964) as one would expect—but also, in its longest proclamation, on the Church in the modern world (*Gaudium et Spes*, December 1965). This latter was a highly significant, unprecedented, extended meditation on the interactions of Catholicism and society. In short, it proclaimed that what happens in the world at large affects theology, affects religion, and affects the Church—sooner or later. And the Church in turn affects the world. It has always been so; we are now more aware of it, and receptive to it.

In that context we turn now to evaluate further the official Catholic position concerning population on the global scene (with a reminder of several evaluations expressed earlier in these pages[5]). For that purpose this chapter has two sections. In Section One we consider and assess a meeting between the pope and the population executive of the United Nations—specifically the pope's own statement, which encapsulates the present official Catholic position. In Section Two we ask if, how, and why the *present official position might undergo change*—possibly the next historic instance of Catholic doctrinal development.

Section One: Evaluating the Present— a Papal Statement

The Pope Meets the U.N. Population Executive

Pope John Paul II's address to Dr. Nafis Sadik, director of the United Nations Population program, in their meeting at the Vatican, provides a focal point both fair and authentic—the pope's own summary of his and the official Catholic position on population issues.[6] His statement runs approximately 2800 words, twenty-two paragraphs, with these six subdivisions: Basic ethical principles; Human development and the family; Responsible parenthood; Status of women and children; Valid implications of population growth; and Moral Significance of (the forthcoming) conference issues. He begins with a greeting:

> I greet you, Madame Secretary General, at a time when you are closely involved in preparing the 1994 International Conference on Population and Development, to be held in Cairo in September. Your visit provides an occasion for me to share with you some thoughts on a topic which, we all agree, is of vital importance for the well-being and progress of the human family.

Clearly the pope takes the issue seriously. He accepts the gravity of the problem and its reality, although his statement is temperate, certainly not alarmist. Too often, it seems, persons concerned to support the Church's position seek to minimize if not deny the problem itself. The pope himself does not do so.

The pope goes on to say that "The Holy See has carefully followed these matters, with a special concern to make accurate and objective assessments of population issues," and has been active in U.N. preparations for the conference—voicing substantial dissatisfactions (reviewed toward the end of his presentation).

In his address the pope further states that "in accordance with its specific competence and mission, the Holy See is concerned that proper attention should be given to ethical principles..."(no. 2). He presents four such principles, "certain basic truths" on which "the Holy See seeks to focus attention…truths about the human person [which] are the measure of any response to demographic data"(no. 2).

> That each and every person—regardless of age, sex, religion or national background—has a dignity and worth that is unconditional and inalienable; that human life itself from conception to natural death is sacred; that human rights are innate and transcend any constitutional order; and that the fundamental unity of the human race demands that everyone be committed to building a community which is free from injustice and which strives to promote and protect the common good.(no. 2)

Highlighting these strong principles or criteria the pope then in effect adds further criteria by comments on "the family [as] an institution founded on the very nature of the human person," by advocacy of "responsible parenthood" and the welfare of women and children.

Jesus—and "Natural Law"

Let us stop here for a moment and consider the tone of the pope's address. By way of comparison, anyone familiar with the famous "pastoral letters" of the American bishops on peace (1983)[7] and economic issues (1986)[8] will recognize in the papal address to Dr. Sadik a similar philosophical tone, the prominence given (as the pope says) to "authentic human values recognized by peoples of diverse cultures, religions, and national backgrounds"(no. 2). When speaking to a broad audience—Dr. Sadik and beyond—the phrases of the Bible obviously do not provide a common language; hence the search for common ground is necessary and admirable. Yet in their two "letters" the American bishops use *two* languages—that of philosophical discourse, reasoning alone, in addition to strong use of biblical and gospel resources. The pope himself commonly does the same, elsewhere—but here much less. *Jesus Christ is never mentioned.* God, Church, the pope's own writings, yes; the gospels and Jesus, no. In a Christian context, this is surely questionable.

The fact is, or sorely seems to be, that Jesus Christ is rarely brought to bear on doctrinal reflections originating in natural law. That omission does not invalidate such reflections. But when suffering and poverty are so profoundly interwoven in the realities at issue, one would hope and expect the Church to place its scriptural Lord and scriptural accounts in a high place of honor, witness, reference, significance, and emphasis.

The omission suggests that in fact Christ has come very little into all of this, that the Catholic position heavily derives from philosophical principles of natural law, itself useful and holding an established role in Catholic thought. But perhaps now that role is overplayed, overemployed, and over-relied upon to the point of distortion.

Population and Environment

Continuing his address to Dr. Sadik, the pope links population with environmental issues.

> The study of population and development inevitably poses the question of the environmental implications of population growth. The ecological issue too is fundamentally a moral one. While population growth is often blamed for environmental problems we know the matter is more complex. Patterns of consumption and waste, especially in developed nations, depletion of natural resources, absence of restrictions or safeguards in some industrial or production processes, all endanger the natural environment. (no. 9)

One might ask the Holy Father at this point a question concerning his reference to "the environmental implications of population growth," ethically and theologically considered. Ought not he and we include a principle such as the following, candidly acknowledged: *Population growth may in some times and places be such that self-imposed restraints should be actively encouraged, and facilitated by appropriate health and family planning services. Moreover, reproductive restraint can in such instances be legitimately portrayed as morally prudential, even obligatory for the sake of individual family welfare as well as the broad common good.*

The pope refers to "the ecological issue...patterns of consumption...depletion of natural resources"—truly crucial aspects of the problems under consideration. But the question is thus raised concerning the Church's own record in promoting consciousness of this "fundamentally moral" issue. The answer, to my awareness, is *little and late*. Although the relationship of Church, population, and environment will be explored in Chapter Eight, the pope's own comment here reminds us that he himself did not speak forcibly on this "fundamentally moral" issue until late 1989[9]; the American bishops said little until 1991.[10]

The point deserves emphasis. Here is a positive, extremely important, pastoral aspect of the population problem and human welfare broadly—where the Church could and should be positively engaged. In the U.S. the environmental movement—i.e., attention to consumption patterns, pollution, wasteful life-styles—has held increasing prominence at least since the publication of Rachel Carson's *Silent Spring* (1962) and "Earth Day" (1970). Yet Catholic involvement has been sparse, almost invisible. This record itself suggests a narrow moral focus by the Church, a myopia that overlooks the elephant in the front room. It is altogether proper that the pope raises this issue with the United Nations, emphasizing the moral implications of the environment-and-population relationship. It would be equally appropriate to admit the Church's own remiss record in this regard, and to implement serious administrative and pastoral measures *now* to make up for seriously lost time.

Indeed, monumental ("fundamentally moral") environmental issues have enjoyed little prominence in the official (and pastoral) Catholic agenda. One hopes and senses now, slowly, a welcome change. Pope John Paul's comment to Dr. Sadik is one indication.

Responsible Parenthood—and "Public Authorities"

Discussing "responsible parenthood" with Dr. Sadik (no. 5) the pope asserts, certainly correctly, that the Church does not encourage "unlimited procreation." He gives four characteristics of responsible parenthood, adding that "all propaganda and misinformation directed at persuading couples that they must limit their family to one or two children should be steadfastly avoided, and couples that generously choose to have large families are to be supported." Is it so likely that efforts "at persuading couples" can be dismissed as "propaganda and misinformation" (while surely *some* are)? Can the Church offer ethical criteria to discern when family limitation would *be wise and right*—and hence reasonable efforts at such persuasion commendable?

Pope Paul VI previously addressed this delicate issue of public campaigns concerning population—seeming more sympathetic to the legitimate role of "public authorities." Pope Paul VI stated,

[When] the size of the population increases more rapidly than available resources...public authorities can intervene within the limit of their competence, by favoring the availability of appropriate information and by adopting suitable measures...in conformity with the moral law... [respecting] the right and freedom of married couples."[11]

I have seen no data on Dr. Sadik's response to Pope John Paul II (despite efforts to obtain such from her office). However, an article published at that same time carried a comment of hers concerning the Vatican in U.N. population issues.

When I talk to the Vatican, I tell them that when they call for abstinence, I don't know what kind of world they are living in. How many women can tell their husbands that, when they have no power? We have to realize that in many parts of the world, women want [birth control] methods they can hide from husbands and families. Many of them are desperate, saying, "Can't you give me an injection, or a pill, because I don't want to be pregnant again." Women in developing countries have lives that are pre-decided. Their role is to be married off. Anyone who says the reproductive role of women isn't the most important in the emancipation of women doesn't know what really goes on in our countries.[12]

"Unitive and Procreative Dimensions"

Pope John Paul's statement is rich in many respects, contributing ethical observation at the highest level of international comment and dialogue. That religion speaks and is heard at this level is itself seriously welcome and an important achievement. But the statement also seems basically resistant, more negative than positive or supportive, unready to concede or commend the good will of colleagues addressing an enormous, common global conundrum. The adversarial implications of *Humanae Vitae* have high priority in Pope John Paul's statement:

In defense of the human person the Church stands opposed to the imposition of human limits in family size, and to the promotion of methods of limiting births which separate the unitive and procreative dimensions of marital intercourse, which are contrary to the moral law inscribed on the human heart."(no. 5)

The pope, not surprisingly, tightly connects (a) "defense of the human person" with (b) objections to "methods...which separate the unitive and procreative dimensions of marital intercourse." Many in the Church, who otherwise share the pope's fundamental values and perspectives of human existence and destiny, dissent here. They simply disagree that "marital intercourse"—sexual union itself—is alone the ultimate norm and expression for the "unitive and procreative dimensions" of married life. Rather they would point to the totality of the living marital relationship, day in and day out, year in and year out, in sickness and in health (of spouses, of children), in good times and bad, in bearing and sharing joys and burdens, in decision making, in sacrificing for each other and the children. If fidelity, love, and responsible sharing characterize this totality, this entire marital spectrum, then they would never concede that an act of contraceptive sexual intercourse somehow cancels all that reality, outweighs it, or negates it. In fact, the decision for contraception may well—indeed likely (in *that* context)—be motivated as a *preservative* of all that reality, *a positive contribution* to it. The "defense of the human person," so admirable in the Catholic agenda, would simply not require or be implemented by this prohibition.[13]

As an expression of the totality of married life, recall the rich musical drama *Fiddler on the Roof,* based on the folk tales of Sholom Aleichem.[14] Watching three daughters defy tradition by choosing to marry "for love," Tevye, the peasant-father, confused, asks his wife about love. "Golde, do you love me?" Her reply is equally eloquent and unromantic (she attributes his question to indigestion). "Do I love you? For twenty-five years I've washed your clothes, cooked your meals, cleaned your house, given you children, milked the cow.... For twenty-five I've lived with him, fought with him, starved with him, for twenty-five years my bed is his. If that's not love, what is?"

Golde answers by concrete details of their total life together. Similarly, when two Jesuits wrote a scholarly defense of the official Catholic position on contraception, a husband responded with echoes of Golde.

My wife and I could never figure out her ovulation (hence

ten pregnancies, seven births)…. I don't know either of these gentlemen [the authors], but feel pretty sure, having been around Jesuits for more than 60 years, that they don't go without regular meals, have clean sheets, and do no heavy lifting. Neither do they have to worry about sick children, mortgage payments, school fees, insurance premiums, income taxes and car breakdowns, as the rest of us do. So scholastically their procreative argument is fine; practically, it imposes almost impossible burdens. About married life they don't have a clue.[15]

If that rings true in middle America, how much more so for families and married couples in Bangladesh or the teeming shantytowns of Jakarta or Conakry?

Continuing Controversy

While the pope speaks to Dr. Sadik in absolute categories, a mere three months previously the German Bishops Conference issued *Population Policy and Development: A Clerical Contribution to the Debate.* Emphasizing the established preference for "natural family planning" the German bishops say the Church "also has to help those, especially women, who feel their living conditions do not allow for the practice of this method. The Church does not exert pressure in questions of family planning and has to respect responsible decision-making by couples."[16] Citing the problems of AIDS, abortions, teen pregnancies, and single mothers, the bishops respond to the suffering involved. "It is a moral duty to prevent such suffering, even if the underlying behavior cannot be condoned." At the very least this German statement has subtle but significant differences from the papal position.

When the dean of American (Catholic) moral theologians, Jesuit Richard McCormick, published a generally negative appraisal of the central doctrine of *Humanae Vitae* he included this observation:

It certainly is true that a teaching can be correct even when the reasons are faulty. But it is quite a different thing to propose a teaching of natural law as certain when, after many years, most theologians can find no persuasive reasoning to support its absoluteness.[17]

In response to McCormick's article and subsequent debate with two fellow Jesuits,[18] Bishop Thomas Gumbleton (Detroit) wrote this supportive observation.

> I can vouch for the fact that very many bishops share the same conviction. However, sadly enough, fewer and fewer are willing to say this publicly.... I hope some day we will have a church willing to allow open discussion of controversial issues, including even the issue of contraception.[19]

Bishop Kenneth Untener (Saginaw, Michigan), writing at the same time, quoted his own earlier words to fellow bishops at their national conference (November, 1990).

> [The Church's official teaching on birth control] is not compelling to people in general..., not compelling to the Catholic laity..., to many priests..., to many bishops. When we know this, and don't say it, many would compare us to a dysfunctional family, unable to talk openly about a problem everyone knows is there.[20]

Clearly, indisputably, substantial controversy continues here. To speak to the world at large in language of absolute certitude on behalf of the Church or its tradition or body of doctrine, when in fact such certitude is not shared, not supported by many Catholics of unquestionable loyalty and credentials, seems itself questionable. Pope John Paul II appears to have so spoken to Dr. Nafis Sadik.

It is beyond the scope of this book to assess the U.N. positions on these global issues. But as an authorized participant in the U.N. process the Holy See has the right to speak, to criticize. As a church it has both the right and the duty to formulate and enunciate a moral critique. Nor can the Vatican position be faulted because it is, insofar as it is, adversarial or unpopular. But what is seriously questionable is the disallowance of substantial discussion within its own circles, permitting the continued perception that in a global problem of severe extremes of human suffering and privation the church of Jesus Christ can ever say that the dimensions of its charity, love, and compassion are fixed and defined by its interpretation of "natural law."

In the 1980 bishops' synod in Rome (see Chapter Two) when discussion turned to population, an Irish bishop, ironically a Scripture scholar, was reported saying, "In expressing sympathy with those who experience difficulty in their married life, the synod cannot substitute compassion for moral principles."[21] For the Christian *can these be opposed?* How so? Is it so clear that a human interpretation of "moral principles" in application to unimaginably diverse, anguishing, and complex circumstances (which remarkably apply most often to *someone else, far away*)—deserves priority over compassion? Why so?

The problems at issue here should not, of course, be formulated only in terms of compassion (see Chapter Five). In the serious interpretation of many, fundamental disruptions of planetary ecosystems are at risk (an ultimate call for ultimate compassion). Even the pope's own words to Dr. Sadik and in his 1989 statement do not dismiss this possibility, a possibility that "endangers the natural environment" (no. 9).

Dramatic Symbolism

In the conclusion to his address to Dr. Sadik, the pope recalls several reservations already expressed in U.N. discussions by delegates of the Holy See. Nevertheless in Rome, in this meeting, the distinguished spokesman for one of the world's oldest, most venerable traditions addressed a spokeswoman for one of the world's youngest traditions—together facing a common challenge. One can see in Dr. Sadik, a highly respected Pakistani gynecologist, a representative of that world that the Church in the Second Vatican Council pledged to serve. In this conference Church and world were face to face as colleagues, not as teacher and disciple, or superior and inferior. In this context one might recall the British moral theologian John Mahoney reviewing Vatican II's contributions to moral theology. He selected "a single conciliar sentence summing up the general tenor of the Council's thinking"[22]—from the *Pastoral Constitution on the Church in the Modern World:*

> The Church safeguards the deposit of God's Word, from which religious and moral principles are drawn. *But it does not always have a ready answer to individual questions, and it wishes to combine the light of revelation with the experience of humankind in order to illuminate the road on which humanity has recently set out.* (no. 33, italics added)

That sentence from Vatican II urges that we Catholics—since we surely don't have all the answers—bring ("combine") the "light of revelation" into dialogue with "the experience of humankind." For what purpose? "To illuminate the road on which humanity" walks, works, and struggles. In the 1994 meeting of the pope and Dr. Sadik of the U.N. one could see that exhortation of Vatican II partly implemented (by the very fact of the meeting itself), and partly ignored (by the seeming dominance and self-assurance of the Vatican voice—more speaking than listening, more instructing than learning).

Section Two: Looking to the Future— "Development of Doctrine"

> *It is from the continuing dialectic, for the Church as for all believers, between belief and experience, that there results what theology has come to term the development of doctrine.*
>
> —JOHN MAHONEY, S.J.[23]

John Mahoney speaks of a "continuing dialectic"—a dialogue, a respectful exchange, mutual exploration, interaction, meaningful conversation, a reciprocal and cooperative effort to find new truth. I recall from my Jesuit days a rule or counsel urging that disputes or disagreements—personal or intellectual—be conducted "not for the purpose that either party may appear to have the upper hand, but so that the truth may appear." That is dialectic, ideally.

This particular "dialectic," says Mahoney, is "between belief and experience," as much for the Church at large as for individuals. In other words, the formula and statement of faith as our tradition now phrases it—assessed carefully (and prayerfully) against contemporary life, contemporary *experience*. Example: our understanding of the biblical creation account has been both modified and enriched by contemporary discoveries in biology, geology, astronomy, cosmology, linguistics, archaeology, ancient literary genres, and other areas.

One major challenge to faith and belief today comes from the vast expansion of human population. Whether or not present numbers constitute "overpopulation" or a "population explosion" is not the point, theologically. The fact of vastly and rapidly expanding population is soundly documented. Similarly, the destitution of at least one fifth of the earth's population—a billion human beings, our sisters and brothers under God—is observable, uncontested fact. Has this global circumstance any significance for Catholic thought, teaching, and theology? Is this global circumstance adequately addressed today by the official Catholic policies of faith (documented in previous and following pages)? This too is a call to dialectic.

Mahoney further states that this encounter, this confrontation of faith with our contemporary experience, can produce "what theology has come to term the *development of doctrine.*" Such development provides the controlling idea for this section of our study as we look ahead. *Can* the Church change (in this area)? *Should* the Church change (in this area)? That's the dialectic we undertake here, at least in preliminary form.

We will briefly consider four areas of contemporary theological activity: (1) "development of doctrine," (2) "signs of the times," (3) new theological appreciation of the impact of experience ("history") in human lives, and (4) liberation theology. None explicitly pertains to population. But all carry implications for positive development in the Church's official response to the challenge of expanding populations. Comments from authors John Noonan and Karl Rahner will conclude the section.

1. "Development"—Change and Growth

"A power of development is a proof of life.... A mere formula either does not expand or is shattered in expanding. A living idea becomes many, yet remains one," wrote John Henry Cardinal Newman (1801-1890), celebrated English convert, author, preacher, and theologian (whom many expect one day to be canonized). He sought to understand the fact of growth and development in religious doctrine—dogmas appearing in later Christianity that were not evident in earlier Christian eras (e.g., Trinity, seven sacraments, doctrines of Mary, primacy and prerogatives of the bishop of Rome as pope, and others).[24] The point had been little explored before Newman's *Essay on the Development of Christian Doctrine* (1845), which remains a landmark, a major source and reference point for much discussion today.

Newman emphasized that growth is inevitable and normal in life and thus, like astronomers calculating the presence of an unseen planet, he expected and justified such growth within a dynamic church. As Christianity grows into a philosophy or system of belief, under varying and expanding circumstances, "old principles remain under new forms. It changes with them in order to remain the same. In a higher world it is otherwise, but here below to live is to change and to be perfect is to change often."

Will the global population phenomena of our times encourage a change, a development in the position of the official Church concerning artificial contraception (and related reproductive issues) with its concomitant impact on population issues, major or minor? Why not? One can be sure, looking back, that historically all such developments seemed unlikely—perhaps impossible—at first. But the unlikely has often occurred. John Mahoney summarizes some of that unlikely history.

> There cannot be any doubt, however, that the Roman Catholic Church's teaching over the centuries and in recent decades has changed markedly in many respects— as in the field of biblical studies; in the possibility of salvation for believers outside the Catholic Church; in ecumenism; in the matter and form of the sacrament of Orders; in recognizing the moral possibility in marriage of birth-control through periodic abstinence from intercourse. That in recent years such changes appear to have become recognized as legitimate in so short a time is not necessarily to be seen as simply reflecting the accelerating rate of change in society at large, but at least equally as indicating that many such changes were long overdue in the Church.[25]

The term "development" requires attention here. In this context "theological development" refers to the gradual achievement of a new consensus in the faith community at large. This historical process finally includes official affirmation—producing a doctrine that thereby replaces or displaces a prior consensus and affirmation. The new *is related to the former*, similar in subject matter, but dissimilar at least in emphasis or in rendering explicit what was previously only implicit.

Theoretically the new is a *development* of the old, as the bloom is a development of the seed, or an adult a development of the child. A *development*, however, is not usually a flat reversal or rejection; however, actually demonstrating this orderly, organic relationship may sometimes be problematic.

Few changes in Catholic life have impressed me as personally and directly as that which we now call "ecumenism." For all the earlier half of my life the phrase and the notion of "no salvation outside the church" was commonplace, taken for granted—despite its murky quality if one stopped to think about it. The phrase itself emerged in the third century, holding unquestioned sway over the centuries. But the doctrine formed at a time when geographical and historical knowledge of humankind was severely limited. Eventually we became better informed; we changed. The doctrine still stands, but generously modified, amplified enormously in realism, understanding, and sensitivity.[26]

Karl Rahner remarks that substantial changes in theological thought often occur so gradually as to be largely unnoticed.

> Even the most conservative theologian thinks and writes nowadays in a different way than, let's say, thirty years ago. Take the latest document of the pope, *Salvifici Doloris* [1984]. When has there ever been a papal document in two thousand years that even vaguely suggested our Semitic roots? Even for the most conservative representatives of the Church much has changed in mentality and practice.... [The pope has] spoken about the "Yahwist"—one of the sources of Genesis. If he had said that, let's say, as archbishop of Cracow under Pius X, he would have been removed from office. The history of ideas advances in unreflexive ways.[27]

Scripture scholar John McKenzie notes that the New Testament itself shows how the early church "modified or even created sayings of Jesus to answer questions that he had never answered. The life of a Christian in a large Hellenistic city presented problems which the Palestinian Christian did not experience."[28] What about Christians in New York or Bombay?

Another biblical scholar, Carlo Maria Martini, Cardinal-Archbishop of Milan, former rector of Rome's Gregorian University, recently commented on doctrinal development and the Church's current situation.

> I don't know what the development will be regarding contraception, but I believe that the Church's teaching has not been expressed so well. The fact is that the problem of contraception is relatively new; it was only possible with new techniques in the past forty years or so. The Church on the other hand thinks very slowly, so I'm confident we will find some formula to state things better, so that the problem is better understood and more readily adapted to reality. I admit there is a gap and this bothers me, but I'm confident it can be overcome.... I'm sure the Holy Spirit will guide the Church to overcome the question as the Church has overcome other moral problems in the past. Usury was an almost unsurmountable impediment in the 14th century, but little by little we began to see the problem in a different light.[29]

2. "Signs"—More Than "Nice Messages"

Scene: husband at the wheel of the car, his wife consulting a large road map. She reports, "I think we're lost." He replies, "What's the difference? We're making great time!" But, of course, motion without direction is chaos; "we're lost." Similarly on the larger roads of life exact maps and reliable signs are scarce, often unclear.

Thus Vatican II at several points encouraged us to look for the "signs of the times."[30] Pope John XXIII who convened the Council, in his historic encyclical *Peace on Earth* (*Pacem in Terris*, 1963), concluded each of its four major sections with reflections on "signs of the times." Such "signs," it seems, carry hints for us, guidance on the way, directions for the road ahead. Apparently God speaks in these signs. Discussing "a theology of the signs of the times" Gerald O'Collins states that they "are more than nice messages to be deciphered.... Phenomena which touch great sectors of the human race are seen as more than sociological changes of far-ranging impact. They serve as indicators of divine designs."[31]

Dennis McCann states that these "signs" reside in and emerge from "the main features of the modern world as characterized by profound changes in society, politics, and the moral and religious dimensions of cultural values." Without the Council's appeal to the "signs" numerous "questions prominent in all postconciliar theologies of social praxis could not have been formulated, let alone answered."[32]

Jesus urged his followers to read the signs of the times (Mt 16:2–4). Could one even interpret Christ's parable of the Good Samaritan as such a "sign," *in microcosm*? Was not the lonely victim along the road a sign, a summons, a revelation? What then are today's millions of wounded travelers—ever more populous—along the global highways, rural byways, and urban back alleys?

From personal history I reflect that in my own lifetime global population has risen from about two billion, and now approaches six billion. I ponder in faith the meaning and implications of such signs of our times, my times. This book is a modest effort to respond to my own question.

3. Experience, Circumstances, History— New Appreciations

Another present-day evolution in theological thought applies here: recognition of the deep influence of history, of human experience, of life's real circumstances. Surveying the "signs of the times" Vatican II acknowledged that "ours is a new age of history with critical and swift upheavals spreading gradually to all corners of the earth.... And so mankind substitutes a dynamic and more evolutionary concept of nature for a static one."[33] These few words carry a powerful charge.

"A dynamic concept of nature" refers, of course, to human nature, replacing a "static," or fixed or unchanging concept of human nature. Obviously certain fundamental human characteristics do remain universal over the globe and throughout time—human bodily structure and needs, basic sociability, the distinguishing quality of self-reflection, abstract thought, religious sensibility, and so forth. But the Council acknowledges a new realization of the *differences* produced in human lives by the specifics of social and economic circumstances, by material advantage or privation, by the experience of supportive nurture (both psychologically and physically)—or on the contrary the prevalence of domination, violence, great stress, and similar oppressive conditions. Poverty, illness, exploitation—all have impact, all make a difference, all must be taken into account and accorded serious weight.

Shortly before Vatican II (foreshadowing its treatment of experience, and "history") Karl Rahner spoke of development of dogma, comparing the Church to this dynamic quality of human nature. The human person "is not like a [merely passive] photographic plate." On the contrary each person responds actively, in dynamic fashion. "In order to understand what he sees or hears the human being must react, take up a stand, *bring the new experience into connection with what he already knows or has been affected by or dealt with, the whole historical sum of his experience....* He can never abstract...from his ever new, changing historical reality."[34]

The Church, composed of human beings under God, must do similarly, says Rahner. The person retains identity, but changes. The Church too has identity, its inherited formulae of belief, inherited from yesterday's best perceptions.

> The mind of humanity, and even more the Church, has a "memory." They change while they preserve, they become new without losing anything of the old. We today have our own philosophy, while we still philosophize with Plato.... Still more we have our theology, which bears the undeniable stamp of our time, while we continue to learn anew from Scripture, the fathers, the scholastics. If we fail either to preserve or to change, we should betray the truth, either by falling into error or by failing to make the truth our own in a really existential way.

In its currently adamant stand on population issues, what truth does the Church propose and defend? Is it not *ultimately* the sacred quality of each of us, of life received from God, lived in God's presence and context, radically intimate with God here and now, responsible before God, with God as both source and absolute future, alpha and omega? Our ultimate truth is not sexual—neither genital nor reproductive—or even interpersonal or communal, vital as all these are. Rather our first level is created and dependent existence itself, each of us a person oriented essentially to God "in whom we live and move and have our being." The truth of this most fundamental faith-level underlies all principles concerning conduct in general, including reproductive behavior in particular.

Today "development in doctrine" calls for the humble, human acknowledgment of finitude by the Church, acknowledging new demographic awareness simply not available yesterday—with all the social, political, economic, scientific, spiritual, and psychological implications entailed. This call and challenge confronts the official Church in our day. Rahner states that

> Realities, truths, which had not been seen explicitly in the earlier formulation...[now] make it possible to see the same reality from a new point of view, in a fresh perspective....[35]

Thomas Aquinas touched the issue long ago, in his philosophical principle, "Whatever is received is received according to the manner of the one receiving it."[36] A "static" understanding, on the contrary, would instead insist that a human person is just that, a human person, whenever or wherever. Differences in circumstances are considered minor, secondary—or at least not entitled to consideration as a primary influencing factor.[37]

Theologian Mary Elsbernd, however, provides a detailed, insightful study tracking the theological emphases of Pope John Paul II; she shows him moving *steadily away from* a wide acceptance of *historical development* as a factor in Catholic social and moral teaching. Elsbernd begins with the *Octogesima Adveniens* of Pope Paul VI (1971, notably no. 4), which (along with emphases from Vatican II) was then "heralded as a central expression of an historically conscious methodology" in papal teaching. The present pope *reduces and finally reverses* such historical acknowledgment and sensitivity. Rather, "timeless" transcendent principles under the custodianship of the papal magisterium are now presented as dominant, sufficient, and obligatory. "A shift took place from an ecclesiology which saw the Church as a pilgrim people in the world to...the Church as guardian of truth which it dispenses to the world." One wonders, incidentally, to what extent the Holy Father has himself been historically influenced in his own theological shift.[38]

4. A Theological Upsurge

Also increasingly prominent in the life of the Church is today's theological and pastoral upsurge known as "liberation theology." Partly a theology properly so-called, and partly a pastoral-folk movement impressive in numbers and authentic participation, this phenomenon originated in Latin America, but is not confined thereto. It is precisely an upsurge, an upwelling, schematically "from below," from the proverbial grassroots, not imposed or delivered from above by hierarchy, clergy, or intellectuals. Roger Haight states that liberation theology is "a continuous development of the spirit and teachings of Vatican II...an attempt to interpret Christian doctrine in a way responsible to the universal problems of human suffering manifest in the social repression of today's world."[39]

Liberation theology is not first of all an abstract set of principles formulated in a tight, conceptual system—and then concretized in deduced applications. This new mode of theology takes seriously—and recovers—the immeasurable involvement of Jesus Christ with the poor, with the world's powerless, while remaining cognizant of a divine will for the salvation of *all*. Philip Berryman comments on the "relatively small group" of theologians associated with the movement.

> Most of them spend some of their time working directly with the poor themselves. The questions they deal with are those that arise out of this contact with the poor. In fact, liberation theology is an interpretation of Christian faith out of the experience of the poor. It is an attempt to read the Bible and key Christian doctrines with the eyes of the poor. It is at the same time an attempt to help the poor interpret their own faith in a new way.[40]

A Pause, a Summary

A short summation may help to connect these four theological sketches, asking how they apply to our topic of population. We have sketched (1) development of doctrine, (2) "signs of the times," (3) a new appreciation of human nature as affected by circumstances of life, "whatever is received...," (4) liberation theology, the recovery of the importance of the poor, allowing theology itself to be influenced by the experience of people in their existential struggles. Population issues—demographically and statistically as well as politically, economically, and internationally—confront all of these, call out to them, challenge and engage them. Each of these four theological initiatives surely applies to population questions—justifying and indeed requiring reevaluation of the Church's contemporary official stance.

The four "new" understandings—each a modest, limited step or set of steps forward—is a thoroughly valid exercise of theology. The eventual maturation—or diminution, even disappearance—of each will be revealed in due time. Meanwhile, each—and others not discussed here—functions as a challenge, raising questions just as does "the new" in every field. Karl Rahner was quoted earlier as considering himself "ten times dumber"—a gracious overstatement, but with a grain of truth nonetheless. Rahner acknowledged the pertinence of the new "secular" insights and discoveries for theology; he did not seek to discount them, fend them off, somehow to marginalize them (as too often occurs in theology, and not only in theology). These new discoveries, new explorations, new products of human ingenuity constitute cumulatively a demand to be heard, to be respected, and to be integrated. Theology is by no means exempt.

Evidence of the complexity that calls for attention today can be found in Arthur Dyck's article on "Population Policy" in the *Westminster Dictionary of Christian Ethics.*[41] Dyck concludes with references to *sixteen* other entries in the *Dictionary:* abortion, contraception, coercion, economic aid, environmental ethics, fairness, family, hunger, oppression, parenthood, poverty, procreation, sexual ethics, sex discrimination, sterilization, status of women. Numerous others could be added. Has the Vatican (or anyone else) reached a definitive integration of these issues, and can consequently instruct everyone everywhere on the conduct most suitable before God?

Finally, two additional contributions assist here—John T Noonan's comments on "Development in Moral Doctrine,"[42] and Rahner's comments on "Church and World."[43]

Noonan: Development in Moral Teaching

John Noonan, an unusual figure in Catholic scholarship, holds a doctorate in philosophy from Catholic University, and a federal circuit judgeship in the U.S. Court of Appeals. He is a professor (emeritus) of law—and a noted author on moral issues. In his "Development of Moral Doctrine" he surveys four areas of major transition in Catholic moral teaching over the centuries: usury, marriage, slavery, and religious freedom. "Wide shifts in the teaching of moral duties, once presented as part of Christian doctrine by the magisterium, have occurred. In each case one can see the displacement of a principle or principles that had been taken as dispositive.... What was forbidden became lawful."

Noonan devotes careful attention to Cardinal Newman's "highly influential theory" of development in theology. He cites the Vatican II document on revelation (*Dei Verbum*, especially no. 8), which recognizes historical progress in doctrine as legitimate. The changes produced by Vatican II, says Noonan, were founded on broad societal experience. For example, the Church's ultimate repudiation of slavery by Leo XIII (1890) after centuries of toleration and acceptance, followed "only after the cultures of Europe and America changed through the abolitionists' agency and the law of every civilized land eliminated the practice." He emphasizes the impact of (secular) experience.

Noonan further notes that the literature on development has largely concerned formal theological dogma rather than "mutations of morals." It is time, he asserts, for new candor and new courage in the realm of moral teaching: "Must we not, then, frankly admit that change is something that plays a role in Catholic moral teaching?"

Interestingly Noonan—who has written extensively on the moral doctrines pertinent to contraception and abortion—mentions neither (nor population) in this article. In an address celebrating the 25th anniversary of *Humanae Vitae,* moral theologian Kevin McMahon cites Noonan as regarding that encyclical as now "a given of Catholic doctrine," with the time for debate past.[44] Personal correspondence from Judge Noonan cites his *Contraception* (Harvard University Press edition, 1986, appendix) as indeed referring to *Humanae Vitae* as a "given but [I] argue for an interpretation of it different from that given by many theologians. My understanding of it does not exclude development." And there's surely no development possible in this or any area without debate, dialogue, and serious reassessments.

Rahner: On Church and World

Rahner's own essay in the *Encyclopedia of Theology: The Concise Sacramentum Mundi*, published under his editorship, is typical in sustained, penetrating analysis coupled with direct affirmation and emphasis. No more than Noonan's article does it pertain explicitly to population. But by implication it illuminates issues under discussion here.

Looking at Vatican II's *Pastoral Constitution on the Church in the Modern World* Rahner points out that the topic here is *not* the familiar church-state issue—but church and *world*, substantially (though not totally) different. Without employing the term "development of dogma" (although his *Encyclopedia* has an essay under that title by another contributor), Rahner observes *changing awarenesses* in Christian life.

> The Church only slowly learns fully to appreciate the freedom of the individual and human groups, or to value the unity and multiplicity of the many churches which the one Church comprises and also their basis in natural and secular history (cf. Vatican II: decrees *On The Catholic Eastern Churches, On Ecumenism*). The Church only slowly came to acknowledge the relative autonomy of secular sciences and the potential variety of social, political and economic organization of human groups…. The Church is slowly attaining a more unconstrained, comprehensive and personal appreciation of human sexuality.

Slowly! These are all aspects of the "world" to which the Church inescapably does and must relate, for better or for worse. But the Church's response has evolved, changed, developed *slowly*—but surely. Rahner fully acknowledges the vast complexity of today's world, respecting as well the human efforts to cope, to improve if possible— people struggling even merely to survive, to engage enormous problems and challenges. In all this the Church has a vital role, but *cannot dictate or assert a greater certainty than she in fact possesses*. "The Church must really make clear the difference between Christian principles and the concrete decisions which cannot be deduced from them alone, so that the limits of the possibilities open to the official Church are plain."

He further expresses concern for any Church use of pressure in "institutional contacts with the world…in order to attain its legitimate aims…. For to do so would mean that the Church was having recourse to something other than men's free, unforced obedience in a faith which has to be perpetually exercised anew." One can apply this comment to the Vatican record with the World Health Organization, with behind-the-scenes action with the Reagan administration concerning birth control, and at the Rio Summit concerning population issues on the conference agenda.[45] The question: are such "diplomatic" policies and their political implementation appropriate expressions of Christ's commission to his church?

Of course, nothing becomes true merely because a Karl Rahner or any other commentator says so, or even because popes or high churchmen or councils so speak. One looks for internal plausibility, for a coherence between their words and one's own experience, usually voiced with some degree of support from other qualified, credible sources. Authority can impose and speak with a large public audibility and visibility unavailable to others, but credibility remains weak in the presence of contrary experience. It is troubling to many, for example, to hear today's papal voice enunciating principles of moral conduct widely unsupported within the pope's own communion and almost totally unsupported in major Christian churches beyond his own. Does this prove the pope to be *wrong?* Hardly. But it does seem to justify calls for review, for reassessment, for a degree of reserve and even circumspection not now in evidence. Even in the Church "it takes many to be intelligent"—simply another way of stating the theology that underlies the tradition of the great councils in historic conjunction with the papacy.

A Final Thought

Before God and the world in the Second Vatican Council the Church elaborately and eloquently pledged a new richness of servant-relationship with the "world." That pledge has been honored, enacted in countless times and places, usually far from spotlights and headlines, often at enormous risk and high personal price. Toward the further honoring of that pledge this discussion of assessment, possible renewal, and development is dedicated.

Much more could be said and deserves to be said. Theological movements and initiatives have been only sketched, others omitted. But the goal has been at least to indicate energies percolating within the life of the Church—and to place them in tentative relationship to the population issues of our times.

The goal has been to demonstrate how much in the Catholic intellectual and pastoral life of our day applies to population concerns. So, as we look to the future, "signs of the times" may be only signs, only pointers. But they do exist both inside the Church and outside. Signs and maps provide no transportation; they actually move you nowhere. But they do point to roadways that, if traveled, can mile by mile lead to distant, even unlikely destinations.

Questions for Reflection and Discussion

1. Karl Rahner commented (note 4) on the enormous expansion of knowledge in his lifetime. What impact does this expansion have on theology?

2. How would you (a) summarize and (b) evaluate the pope's address to Dr. Nafis Sadik—favorable points, unfavorable points?

3. Concerning John Mahoney's choice of a summarizing statement from Vatican II (note 22): how do you understand that statement?

4. Part II of this chapter nominates four contemporary theological areas or emphases as important for the study of population issues. Although none of the four explicitly speaks of population what connections or relationships do you see?

5. John Noonan cites "four areas of major transition in Catholic moral teaching over the centuries." In what ways does such "transition" show strength or weakness, growth or deterioration?

6. This chapter deals extensively with the relationship of Church and world. Vatican II had a major document on that subject. Is that relationship important? If so, why? Summarize what that relationship is, or ought to be. How does it tie in with a study of Church and population?

Part Two
Reflections on
a Pastoral Theology
of Global Population

Whether it is congenial or uncongenial, in spite of all complaints that we are rendering many people in the Church insecure in their moral conscience, it must be said that there are not a few concrete principles and patterns of behavior which formerly—and quite rightly in the circumstances—counted as binding, concrete expressions of the ultimate Christian moral principles, but today are not necessarily binding always and in every case.

—KARL RAHNER[1]

Knowledge is much more a task than an accomplishment. It is something that is real, but it is also something partial. A little humility is going to have to be an increasingly prominent characteristic of theological reflections and discussions. And the topic of natural law is no exception.

—TIMOTHY O'CONNELL[2]

Population and New Vistas in Theology

IN THE WORDS OF A FOLK ANTHEM OF THE 1960s, "THE TIMES, they are a changin'." True then, and still true. Not even the ancient and venerable Church is insulated. Timothy O'Connell, quoted above in his noted text of moral theology, remarks that moral theology itself is in a time of historic transition, "a moment of beginning."[3] This book aspires modestly to be a small part of that "beginning," a "critique from the inside."

In this second part of *Global Population from a Catholic Perspective* we place less emphasis on the Catholic record (although that record necessarily remains our continuing context), shifting now toward Catholic alternative perspectives and possibilities in this area of humanity's challenge. What do we find, selectively, in our enormously rich Catholic heritage that (at least implicitly) applies to global population trends, challenges, and needs?

In the very exploring of such a question we participate in a noble tradition. Even the earliest Christians faced questions that the venerated founder never discussed. Christ had, however, bequeathed to them a body of intensely pregnant perspectives and principles by his living, by his very person, by the Jewish tradition he observed and respected, by his way of relating to others, by his teaching, and by his death and resurrection.

Thus our enormously rich theological heritage embodies and continues those studious collective efforts of the first Christians, ongoing through the centuries, to apply his teaching to contemporary questions and challenges. Now it's up to us.

Within that Catholic theological tradition this book specifically touches two major areas in more or less equal measure: moral theology, and Catholic social theology (commonly named as "social thought" or "teaching, or "social ethics"). In moral theology personal, individual moral conduct has held center stage. Sexuality has been a major emphasis.

But social theology by definition looks to human activity in community—family, civic, national, international—the individual in his or her communal opportunities, responsibilities and, indeed, vulnerabilities. Social theology also looks to the relationships and responsibilities of groups and organizations, one to another. It considers law and politics, commerce, those areas of powerful social structures— the fixed economic, cultural, and political arrangements that affect millions, in fact everyone.

Of course, these two areas with two names—moral and social—are not in reality separate at all. They fuse, interact, slide back and forth into and within each other, and frequently collide.

Addressing modern population phenomena and concerns, official Catholic participation—pope, Vatican, hierarchy—touches both areas of reality, private *and* social, drawing upon both areas of theology. This proves sometimes rich and helpful, sometimes confusing and distressful.

Moral Theology: Selected Factors

Assessing the official positions of the Church on population issues, we must, of course, single out and evaluate those particular elements of traditional moral theology on which official positions are largely based, without digressing into a full-scale discussion of moral theology (available elsewhere[4]). Some of these elements have been discussed earlier, some will be discussed in chapters following. In a final chapter these traditional positions will again be reviewed in comparison and contrast with proposed revised positions.

Following, then, are nine key factors in Catholic moral theology that influence official policies and perspectives on population issues, briefly sketched.

1. Natural law. Natural law is considered to emerge from the evident, intelligible meaning of nature itself. For example, the human reproductive system is clearly intended by the Author of nature for the purpose of reproduction. That fact becomes a norm, a law: conduct in accord with that purpose is right; conduct not in accord with that purpose is wrong. At the same time natural law, enormously influential in Catholic moral and ethical reflection, is subject to multiple interpretations.

2. Intrinsic evil. This term refers to conduct that can never be justified under any circumstances. Murder, distinguished from killing (as in self-defense), is always wrong. Kidnapping, child abuse, leading someone into drug addiction or prostitution is always wrong, evil intrinsically.

3. Modes of reasoning: deductive, inductive. Deductive reasoning starts by developing or discerning a principle of conduct. For example, the very purpose of human speech is truthful speech. Lying perverts this purpose. Hence such conduct is wrong. Deductive reasoning applies a principle to specific instances and reaches an ethical or moral decision or evaluation.

Inductive reasoning is exemplified by the familiar murder mystery process—detectives first pull together the available evidence. They then reason to whatever conclusion the evidence indicates. The physical sciences employ inductive reasoning.

Catholic moral theology has drawn heavily on deductive reasoning (which fits coherently with concepts of natural law and intrinsic evil).

Present-day emphases in moral theology give much greater weight to circumstances (often new, unique, ambiguous, or opaque) that confront actual moral decision making. This requires the inductive approach.

4. Basic methods in moral decision making. These methods are commonly described in three categories.

(a) Goal-oriented approach ("teleological"): strong emphasis on the human orientation to God, God's law, and an eternal destiny. This is largely the natural law method.

(b) Rule-oriented approach ("deontological"): centered on law, on commandments, on rule provided by authority, divinely sanctioned.

(c) Relational/responsibility approach: an emphasis on the social nature of the human being, inserted by the Creator into here and now relationships, responsibilities, within communities.

Theologian Edmond Dunn, surveying new trends in Catholic moral theology, notes that "official teaching of the Catholic church on human sexuality is rooted in the goal-oriented approach"—whereas, in contrast, the Church draws on the relational/responsibility "approach in formulating its social teaching."[5] Consistence suggests that a reappraisal is in order. In this book I favor the relational approach, while seeing values to be retained in the other two approaches, surely.

5. Consistence. A norm that stands outside of theology, but provides an inescapable criterion nonetheless. Inconsistency or outright contradiction within a body of thought, opinion, or teaching signals a need for reappraisal.

Timothy O'Connell states, "Radical respect for life, what is called 'a *consistent* ethic of life,' in the end presents itself to us not only as an interesting ethical focus, but also as the fundamental basis for Christian morality, indeed, as nothing else than a more specific formulation of the very identity of the ethical task."[6] (See Chapter Six.)

6. Truth, fixed or evolving? Two positions are prominent. Official Catholic positions strongly favor a "classical" or traditional position that considers truth fixed and unchanging. What is true today is true tomorrow, necessarily. Present-day emphases in moral theology give greater weight to "history" and circumstances, to truth seen as evolving, emerging. In favor of the latter position, noted moral theologian Joseph Fuchs states, "Mutability belongs to the human person's immutable essence."[7]

The New Dictionary of Catholic Social Thought notes that "the historically conscious model is much in evidence in recent documents on Church social teaching but that in official documents on sexuality and bio-medical ethics a classicist methodology is still evident."[8]

7. Scripture. Catholic moral theology before Vatican II gave minimal attention to Scripture. As this changes, a counterbalance to natural law occurs. Ethicist William Spohn states that "natural law and tradition have so monopolized Catholic moral reflection since medieval times that it has virtually ignored scripture."[9] This attention to Scripture is more than an embellishment and can be expected to exert a truly significant influence. (See Chapter Five.)

8. "Preferential option for the poor." In the gospel pages Jesus clearly stands with and amongst the poor and disadvantaged. This fact is central, neither peripheral nor incidental. It is a major credit of liberation theology that the role of humankind's underprivileged has again been centralized, made a focus of serious reflection and reappraisal.

9. Conscience. The individual in her or his particular circumstances is the ultimate moral actor, responsible before God. "Conscience" names that fact. The Church has long acknowledged this in theory, but tends strongly to obscure or compromise it by heavy stress on the role and weight of ecclesial authority.

These necessarily brief sketches are also necessarily selective, by no means the only elements of moral theology operative here. They simply single out certain factors in moral theology that assert themselves— loudly call attention to themselves—as one looks at global population concerns from a Roman Catholic standpoint.

The Next Steps
In Part II, these discussions:

Chapter Five: compassion for those who suffer acute deprivation, an emphasis derived from Scripture.

Chapter Six: abortion, the Church's position assessed by a "consistent ethic of life."

Chapter Seven: science, a key source of population data, offers a challenge to the Church—which in turn challenges science.

Chapter Eight: the Church's emerging stand on environmental issues inescapably confronts population realities.

Chapter Nine: report of an interfaith approach.

Chapter Ten: summary of the present Catholic stand compared and contrasted with new emphases emerging from its own contemporary moral theology.

Two Further Notes

1. For readers less familiar with religious terminology, a comment on "pastoral" in the title of Part Two, "A Pastoral Theology of Global Population," may be helpful, The term is more general than precise, but "pastoral theology," as used here, points to theology and the life of the Church in relationships with the everyday world—politics, economics, married life, community life, intergroup and interpersonal dynamics, and so forth. It consists, as used here, in efforts at understanding these relationships, at new insight, at exploration and probing, at dialogue.

2. It needs to be acknowledged that the topics we explore in this book may be of as little interest to the average churchgoing Catholic as, say, the foreign policy of the United States toward Kenya or Honduras is to the average U.S. citizen. Yet the government maintains embassies and ambassadors in both nations. The very issue of global population, whether viewed in its moral, economic, political, or theological aspects, generally attracts meagre interest. Yet, foreign policy issues for a nation surely are consequential—and how the Church declares and exercises itself on the global scene also matters. The pope's innumerable visits around the globe (and the popular response evoked) amply dramatize this.

We spoke in the Prologue of Pope John Paul's visit to the man who sought to kill him. The Holy Father provided thereby a singular example to a world where vengeance, retribution, and competitive advantage often reign supreme. The pope walked the extra mile, as Jesus asked, and as Jesus did.

As Christians, as Catholics, as Church, as sisters and brothers in God's one family, let us look at today's population challenge—of national and international dimensions, and let us ask, what is the "extra mile" today?

Questions for Reflection and Discussion

1. The opening quotes from Rahner and O'Connell point to change in Catholic moral theology. Do you agree that theology can change? Are not Catholic doctrine and theology timeless, insulated from change?

2. How does moral theology differ from Catholic social teaching or theology, as two fields or areas? Do they connect with each other in any way?

3. Nine points of moral theology are noted as particularly pertinent to population issues. Pick one and suggest how it might relate to population realities, or to the Catholic stand on such issues.

[For Jesus] the focus of his preaching and ministry...the keynote in all of it was clearly compassion. Jesus enters progressively into the dilemma of the human situation and into the greatest suffering and rejection that the social sin of the human community can inflict upon the unfortunate.... Jesus crucified is a naked man among the stripped and unprotected of the world who cannot clothe themselves in the privileges of power. And that is his last word to us. He died as he lived, among the poor and disregarded and underprivileged by his own choice.

—MONIKA HELLWIG[1]

Christian spirituality [has] often lacked a keen sense of the importance of compassion as a practical response to suffering and to the consequences of social evil and sin.

—MICHAEL DOWNEY[2]

Scripture, Compassion— and the Population Challenge

IN THIS CHAPTER WE REFLECT DIRECTLY ON SACRED SCRIPTURE and the compassion of Jesus Christ, the prime exemplar and norm of Christian living. We ask to what extent such compassion has seemed to influence official Catholic policy on population—and recommend new pastoral approaches.

In Fredericksburg, Virginia, stands a unique battlefield monument. Usually at such Civil War locations one sees statuary of generals on horseback, soldiers posed defiantly with rifles, or the like. Fredericksburg honors a memorial to compassion. The inscription:

> *In memoriam:* Richard Rowland Kirkland, Co. G, 2nd South Carolina Volunteers, C.S.A. [Confederate States of America]. At the risk of his life this American soldier of sublime compassion brought water to his wounded foes at Fredericksburg. Fighting men on both sides of the line called him "The Angel of Marye's Heights."

Atop a large base, the sculpture shows soldier Kirkland bent above a prostrate form, holding a canteen to the fallen man's mouth. After terrible slaughter by Confederate troops well entrenched on Marye's Heights in early winter (1862), the field that night was littered with Union dead and wounded. Soldier Kirkland, himself later killed in battle, distinguished himself forever, going out among the wounded— the extra mile of compassion.

Scripture—and Moral Theology

Compassion as a Christian mandate originates in Scripture, not in natural law. In the previous chapter we discussed the pope's address to Dr. Nafis Sadik (United Nations), observing in his address an absence of all explicit reference to Christ, to the gospels, to the biblical message generally. One does not wish or ask for some token scriptural reference—simply legitimating a message by connecting it to a veneer of scriptural sources. Rather one evaluates the emphasis. What gets emphasized? What is set forth as the groundwork, the basic perspective and foundation of the position proclaimed? Natural law has its honored function in Catholic intellectual history, continuingly. But it is not the heart of the matter, not now, not ever.

Discussing "The Use of Scripture in Catholic Social Ethics," Jesuit ethician William Spohn begins with this observation: "Critical reliance on biblical materials marks a fundamental change in the method of Roman Catholic moral theology. No longer the most neglected source of moral theology, Scripture increasingly grounds the discussion of moral questions in the gospel and person of Jesus Christ."[3] That observation is certainly not verified in the Vatican documents on population (discussed later in this chapter), even when oriented to "pastoral work."

Spohn elsewhere states that today "Christians turn to Scripture to discover more than the right thing to do; they want to act in a way that responds to the God of their lives."[4] This new scriptural emphasis responds to the call of Vatican II (*Decree on Priestly Formation*, no. 16) that moral theology's "scientific exposition should be more thoroughly nourished by scriptural teaching." Significantly this new emphasis is intended "to bring forth fruit in charity for the life of the world."

The field of Catholic moral theology today experiences strong currents of revisioning, based on numerous themes of Vatican II— including (but by no means confined to) the indicated return to Scripture. This book aspires to contribute to such revision. But in the opinion of a former president of The Catholic Theological Society of America such revision and renewal is far from complete.

> Today, some decades after the conciliar observation [above], I believe the call for the renewal of moral theology [concerned with the practical implications of Christian faith for ideals, values and behavior] still stands in need of fulfillment. Considerable progress has been made, but the discipline is not yet sufficiently integrated with biblical spirituality, nor is it adequate to the needs of today's world.... Moral theology is being called, on the one hand, to foster a more radical trust in God and, on the other, to foster a more radical and thoroughgoing ethic of justice.[5]

The Scriptural Christ

In *Jesus, The Compassion of God* Monika Hellwig searches for that characteristic of Christ that most incisively expresses his meaning and relationship to today's world. While never mentioning population concerns, she emphasizes that "the following of Jesus in our times confronts us constantly with human suffering on a massive scale, caused by structures of society...."[6]

Vast population phenomena today, as best we can comprehend them, place millions, perhaps billions of God's one family at enormous risk. Earlier (Chapter One) we quoted scientists Oakley and Anderson asking how we reasonably expect to provide even minimally decent living for substantial increases of humankind's populace when we fall drastically short of that measure for half as many *now*.

Hellwig, concerned that Christianity respond worthily to the suffering of our day as Jesus did in his, reminds us that Christian belief sees in Jesus more than heroic moral example. Rather, we see in Christ the very expression of God's presence and divine concern, divine articulation— however such reality exceeds our efforts at exact explanation or formulation. She reminds us that theology, however scholarly, remains closer to art than science, closer to Beethoven and Shakespeare than to Einstein.[7]

So Jesus appears in the gospel pages and Christian experience as God's own compassion, carried out, enacted, embodied, personalized, rendered real, historic, and cultural—Jesus fully human, incandescent with God, wholly compassionate, and vulnerable. A few glances at the gospel pages may serve to recall this quality in Jesus.

•"'Lord, remember me'.... Jesus said to him...'today you shall be in paradise with me.'" (Lk 23:42–43)

•"Whenever you did this for one of these brethren of mine you did it for me." (Mt 25:40)

•"Woman, is there no one left to condemn you?... Well, then, I do not condemn you either. Go...." (Jn 8:10–11)

•"Forgive them, Father, they don't know what they are doing." (Lk 23:34)

•Jesus "stood up to read the scriptures...[choosing] 'The Spirit of the Lord is upon me.... He has chosen me to bring good news to the poor...sight to the blind...to set free the oppressed.'" (Lk 4:16–18)

•"As he walked along he saw a man who had been born blind...he rubbed mud on the man's eyes... [who] came back seeing." (Jn 9:1,7)

•"Whoever gives even a cup of cold water...." (Mt 10:42)

•"Jesus saw the large crowd, and his heart was filled with pity for them...like sheep without a shepherd." (Mk 6:34)

•"I am the good shepherd...." (Jn 10:14)

•"There was once was a rich man who dressed in the most expensive clothes... [and] Lazarus, full of sores... [at] the rich man's door." (Lk 16:19–20)

•"'Love your neighbor as yourself....' 'Who is my neighbor?' 'There was once a man going from Jerusalem to Jericho, and robbers attacked him... a Samaritan came along....'" (Lk 10:25ff.)

Numerous other passages, equally eloquent, could be included. These few serve as samples.

A Contemporary Compassion

No single or monolithic description ever does justice to the complex reality of a human being, least of all Jesus Christ. Scripture and subsequent Christian reflection portray what Paul referred to as "the infinite riches of Christ" (Eph 3:8). But Hellwig opts for compassion as the most comprehensive characterization of Christ's life and ministry appropriate to our time. Compassion, if synonymous with pity, goes beyond it.

> [Compassion] implies a movement toward the other to help, but also a movement into the other to be present in solidarity and communion of experience. It implies sensitivity, vulnerability to be affected by the experience of the other…[also] remedial action against suffering and oppression. Most of all…involvement in the situation.[8]

This compassionate Jesus dominates the gospel pages. He dominates as well the hearts and minds of martyrs, saints, and holy common folk known to us in daily life and in our congregations—but is regrettably and conspicuously absent in official Catholic policy statements today on population. Population concerns—let us never forget—are preeminently concerns of poverty, suffering, deprivation, gross indignity, exploitation, and oppression. As a noted Evangelical journal states editorially, "Where people are malnourished and resources stretched thin, adding more people makes the suffering worse."[9]

(I wish explicitly to affirm that in Pope John Paul II personally I see a man of intense Christian compassion; his concern for suffering and poverty is very real, often expressed. It is thus the more regrettable that this largely disappears [or is muted] in his statements on population, and in other Vatican proclamations on these issues. One can also ask of John Paul if his intense concern for fundamentally abstract doctrinal consistency does not at times conflict *seriously* with his concern for human suffering.)

Jesus Recommends a Pariah

In these difficult questions it is not only useful but imperative to recall a luminous passage in Luke's gospel (10:25–37). Jesus, asked by a lawyer or teacher of the law about the key to eternal life, gives an unforgettable response: "Love the Lord your God…and your neighbor as yourself." Then to illustrate and concretize, Jesus tells of a compassionate Samaritan.

In the *New Jerome Biblical Commentary* Franciscan Robert Karris remarks that in the story of the Samaritan, "the law-observant people do not aid the stripped and apparently dead man for fear of defilement." Jesus, Karris adds, calls us "to imitate the conduct of a pariah, a Samaritan"—who was compassionate.[10]

In his study of compassion (using his scientific research of related attitudes) sociologist Robert Wuthnow repeatedly encountered the Good Samaritan parable, even where explicit religious consciousness was absent. "The Good Samaritan is a common feature of our collective tradition…one of those ancient myths that embodies the deepest meaning of our culture. In learning it and reshaping it we define what it means to be compassionate."[11] Wuthnow has the following thoughtful description of compassion, *including* individual value but *adding* social or societal value.

> There is a great deal more to compassion than just helping the needy…. Compassion is a value, a means of expression, a way of behaving, a perspective on society…. It holds forth a vision of what a good society can be, provides us with concrete examples of caring we can emulate, and locates us as members of the diffuse networks of which our society is woven.[12]

Compassion thus means far more than "kindness," more than pity or "feeling sorry for," ethically more than an impulse to do the generous thing. Compassion activates Judeo-Christianity's basic mandate—love of "neighbor," so variously and richly urged in Scripture. "The only obligation you have is to love one another. Whoever does this has obeyed the Law" (Rom 13:8).

Compassion and solidarity, compassion and the broad common good of essentially social human persons: these connections (although violated grossly and daily) characterize our very humanness. Hence the compassion for which we argue is validated not only in the benefits to the recipient (as the victim along the scriptural road to Jericho), but in the fulfilled humanity of the compassionate (in Christ's paradigm, a Samaritan).

Finally Judeo-Christianity reveals the presence of God in the neighbor. Pope John Paul II states it this way:

> One's neighbor is then not only a human being with his or her own rights and a fundamental equality with everyone else, but becomes the living image of God the Father, redeemed by the blood of Jesus Christ and placed under the permanent action of the Holy Spirit.... Beyond human and natural bonds, already so close and strong, there is discerned in the light of faith a new model of the unity of the human race, which must ultimately inspire our solidarity.[13]

At the heart of this vision lies more than a call. There resides here a moral mandate—as much incumbent on the Church itself as on all others. As in the human hand—when the index finger is pointing out to others, three other fingers point back to self, to the Church, to each of us.

Population: a Vatican Pastoral Document

In Chapter Four we looked at Pope John Paul II's address to Dr. Nafis Sadik and noted the heavy emphasis on philosophical language and natural law. If the pope's emphasis might be explained as a message couched in terms more intelligible, more acceptable to a secular or at least non-Catholic audience, let us turn to another Vatican document, same time period (1994), same topic: *Ethical and Pastoral Dimensions of Population Trends* (*Instrumentum Laboris*, from The Pontifical Council for the Family).[14]

Explicitly this is an instructional message, official in source, "to guide pastoral work in the area of demography because population questions affect the family with regard to the freedom and responsibility of married couples in their task of transmitting life."[15] At least here the religiously alert reader expects a pastoral framework and perspective of gospel values. As a concrete index, then, consider this sixty-four page booklet's seventy-seven footnotes (source references). The indicated sources on which the text draws are these: Pope Paul VI, ten references; Pope John Paul II, twenty-eight; Vatican II, five; other Vatican statements, seven; Christian Scriptures (New Testament), one; Hebrew Scriptures (Old Testament), none.

This important Vatican document quotes papal and other Vatican sources fifty times, the New Testament once (from Corinthians, note 70), the Hebrew Scriptures not at all (other sources pertain mostly to demographic and United Nations materials). Christ receives the first and only mention in footnote fifty-one.

Does this pattern of omission vitiate or cancel all value of *Ethical and Pastoral Dimensions?* No. It remains useful, sometimes insightful, sometimes questionable, always at least addressing and thus acknowledging a monumental global issue. But it is inadequate "to help form guidelines for the Church's pastoral work." As one who has engaged in a considerable quantity and variety of that pastoral work I see the text as somewhat informative, but academic and oblique, not pastoral.

Among the praiseworthy facets of this compact, complex document (three chapters, eighty-nine sections) two can be singled out. First, indicating the vast network of causes underlying population phenomena, thirteen "internal causes in developing countries" are noted: bad political administrations, foreign debt, unequal access to property, military budgets, and others (no. 18). Second, the document certainly demonstrates and acknowledges Church awareness of population as a serious problem on the world scene:

•"With realism, the Church recognizes the serious problems linked to population growth...."(no. 3)

•"During this century the world population has grown steadily...estimated for 1993 at 5.5 billion."(no. 4)

•"The world population has doubled between 1950 and 1991." (no. 5)

•(Quoting Vatican II) "International cooperation is vitally necessary... arising out of rapid increases in population." (no. 43)

•(Quoting Pope John Paul II) "The Church... recognizes the serious problem of population growth in the form it has taken in many parts of the world."

Although occurring in a document generally skeptical and adversarial, these acknowledgments nullify any impression that the Vatican denies the reality of the population challenge.

A Significant Contrast

As we saw with the pope's address to Dr. Sadik, it is instructive to compare and contrast the Vatican priorities in the indicated population pronouncements with two other major ecclesiastical documents from American sources: the bishops' "pastoral letters" on peace (1983) and economic justice (1986).[16] These remarkable, extensive statements addressed both a Catholic constituency and the nation at large, each the result of approximately three years of consultation and nationally circulated drafts, on enormously complex social issues.[17] In the former, explicit scriptural reflections cover nine pages (paragraphs twenty-seven to fifty-five); in the latter, sixteen pages (paragraphs thirty to sixty-one). Despite subsequent lukewarm appraisals by some Scripture specialists, clearly a serious effort and a scriptural consciousness are evident. Granted also, both documents are more extensive than the Vatican items under comment here—but that hardly seems sufficient to explain the scriptural vacuum in the Vatican statements.

Both American documents deal with formidable contemporary social problems; both use considerable philosophical (natural law) argumentation as well as data from relevant areas of political and intellectual activity. The statement on economics is notably a vehicle of compassion; while acknowledging certain human benefits accruing from capitalism, it nevertheless offers a candid, forthright critique of evils, burdens, and the competitive disregard inherent in capitalism. Pope John Paul himself has spoken similarly, particularly in his encyclicals on labor (*Laborem Exercens*) and on social ills (*Sollicitudo Rei Socialis*), among others.

Priority of Values?

But what of the Vatican's *Ethical and Pastoral Dimensions of Population Trends?* Official Catholic teaching on population appears (appearances that matter enormously in global political perceptions) to subordinate compassion for suffering and gross deprivation in favor of insistent moral strictures concerning the means of controlling reproduction. Such insistence no longer bears the characteristic stamp of Christ's compassionate identification with the poor—despite claims to the contrary.

In the summer of 1994 the African nation of Rwanda underwent a crucifixion of unimaginable proportions resulting from tribal hostilities, from power struggles, from the remnants of colonial exploitation, from (as the Vatican's "pastoral" document incidentally points out) "a very strong concentration of population caused by immigration to a fertile region and maintained by a high rate of procreation."[18] All this— massacres, dispossession, famine, and mass flight to neighboring nations—occurred in a country already classified in the "Extreme Human Suffering" category of the *International Human Suffering Index.*[19] The Population Reference Bureau (a source also used in the Vatican publication) put Rwanda's population, 1993, at 7.4 million—with a projected doubling time of thirty-one years.[20] Can a global Church of the compassionate Christ respond to such suffering by a focus on means of reproduction? Granted, that emphasis is certainly not the only emphasis in the Vatican documents nor in Catholic action generally, but it is assuredly one strong emphasis underscored repeatedly in confronting and protesting United Nations efforts to deal with such problems.

Granted, moral consideration and moral precept have a relationship to compassion, to a religious response to the well-being of others. This is the Vatican intent, deserving respect. But lesser values—themselves under considerable dispute within the Church broadly—appear to have taken center stage, prioritized over greater values. George Howard, psychologist at Notre Dame University, reviewing population data, states that "one of the few humane, effective means we have for combatting such mass human suffering is the use of artificial means of birth control. The Jesus I meet in the gospels, I believe, would not have aligned himself against these methods of preempting human suffering."[21]

Compassion as Policy?

Compassion, of course, is a rich, diverse reality, hardly susceptible of exact definition. In his *Acts of Compassion* Robert Wuthnow states that the Bible speaks of compassion forty-one times, of kindness forty-five times, and of love 450 times. But in our era of varied biblical translations merely consulting a scriptural concordance under "compassion" will not disclose the true scope of this theme. Indeed the magisterial six-volume *Anchor Bible Dictionary* under "compassion" simply says, "See love." "Love" in turn covers twenty pages.[22] Love, pity, mercy, charity, compassion, involvement, solidarity—these connected, reciprocal realities of attitude, appraisal, and action toward our fellow human beings are at the very core of the biblical message.

But as the Church looks at a secularized world, at population, at "population control" programs with which it officially disagrees, can *compassion* realistically be recommended as a *policy*? Is not compassion (et al.) rather an ever-accepted, ever-commended virtue—but hardly a policy stand? Perhaps the institutional Church assumes that in denouncing population control programs as immoral it exercises "tough love," a stern rigor and realism in discharge of its prophetic, critical duty. The Church thus seeks to protect from sin, from compromise, from corruption and moral decline. Is that not compassion—at its best? Many think so.

Yet two national bodies of bishops—those of Latin America (1968

Medellín and 1979 Puebla conferences) and the United States (1986 pastoral letter on the economy)—explicitly espouse as Church policy a modern form of compassion: "a preferential option for the poor."[23] Georgetown theologian Anthony Tambasco writes that "this theme has attained wide acceptance in biblical scholarship, as well as being emphasized by liberation theologians, and thus has been adopted by the [U.S.] bishops." Tambasco adds that for the U.S. bishops "the hermeneutic perspectives of liberation theology were certainly no small influence in recognizing increasing inequality as the overriding problem of our times" (an observation surely applicable to population issues). The option for the poor, states Tambasco, is far more than "a pious sentiment of charity toward the unfortunate."[24] Apparently some major ecclesiastical bodies therefore do regard such compassion as appropriate, realistic policy for the Church today.

The Poor, the Pope, and Population

The poor are central in Scripture and theology; for the recovery and reemphasis of that truth we are heavily indebted to liberation theology. Thus in *Theology and the Option for the Poor* John O'Brien includes the following among his conclusions:

> The massive catastrophic suffering of whole peoples in poverty and marginalization is more than a theological theme. Since salvation in Jesus Christ is historically mediated through the achievement of a new quality of human solidarity of which the poor are the privileged architects, involvement in the struggle of the poor is a condition of the lived faith, which seeks self-understanding in theology.... The acquisition of the option for the poor is not a substitute for theoretical rigor in theology but, rather, is theological theory's practical rootedness and goal....[25]

Vatican enthusiasm for liberation theology and theologians has been uncertain, to say the least. Nevertheless, in the Philippines (1981), for example, Pope John Paul spoke blunt words to the landowners and planters on the island of Negros. Throngs of peasants—an estimated half-million—"marched for days in the tropical sun from the far south" to see the pope in the city center of Bacolod and to hear him say,

> The Church will not hesitate to take up the cause of the
> poor and to become the voice of those who are not listened
> to when they speak up, not to demand charity but justice....
> Landowners and planters should not be guided in the first
> place by the economic laws of growth and gain...but by the
> demands of justice and by the moral imperative of
> contributing to a decent standard of living...for the
> workers.... To all the sugar cane workers I say...never forget
> the great dignity God has given you... It has been the
> constant teaching of the Church that workers have a right
> to organize....[26]

That same night after hearing the pope the president of the planters'
federation, infuriated, phoned the bishop, Antonio Fortich. "So you
want war, do you? Well, we'll give you war, all-out war—if that's what you
want."[27]

Not because he so incensed the rich elite, but because he spoke to
and for the voiceless, the pope and the Church spoke for Christ—a
shining hour, a worthy stance.

I make no effort to appraise or finally characterize the work of a
complex pope whose pontificate continues as this is written. Much is
admired, much is controverted.[28] The quoted statement bears no
reference, of course, to population. But it provides ample evidence of
(a) the intense social concern typical of the present pontiff, and (b) the
international character of that concern. The question remains: is more
needed? Is it enough?

But when is enough—enough? The pope's words in the Philippines
(quoted above) are admirable and courageous. But are they *enough* in a
Philippine nation with a population of 65 million (from 28 million in
1960), with a doubling time of 28 years, a projected 101 million in 2025?
The Catholic hierarchy there, in a nation where Catholics are 83 percent
of the population, has staunchly opposed government efforts at
population control—despite Vatican acknowledgments that "the Church
recognizes the serious problems linked to population growth."[29]

Does the pope listen when, for example, Peter Henriot, the director
of the Jesuit Center for Theological Reflection in Lusaka, Zambia, states
that important values in Catholic social teaching—family, rights of
parents, social justice—are "sometimes overshadowed by the insistence
on adherence to its strict teaching on artificial contraception.

Promotion of 'natural family planning' is important...but can it be and should it be the *only* approved method?"[30]

Henriot situates "the heart of the difficulty...[in] the failure [of Catholic social teaching] to come to grips realistically with the rapid population growth in the South. Africa's growth rate of over 3 percent annually means a doubling of the population every 20 to 25 years with staggering consequences." (Historian Paul Kennedy notes that in 1950 Africa's population was half of Europe's; by 1985 it had drawn level— about 480 million each.[31]) What lies ahead? Pastorally, theologically, is something missing in our Catholic response, in the face of "staggering consequences"? Is the pope's social concern *enough*?

A Congruent Analysis—a "Secular" Source

While many population specialists and organizations feel that direct measures at fertility control are urgently needed, others view such measures (especially implemented alone, in isolation) as less effective— if not downright futile. For example, the Institute for Food and Development Policy (San Francisco) has specialized in the study of hunger (therefore poverty and population as well) on the global scene. In *Taking Population Seriously* the Institute's Frances Moore Lappé and Rachel Schurman outline a program that one could confidently recommend to Catholics—scholars, officials, and laity—for careful study, for further assessment, analysis, and development.[32] It is more explicit, more probing, more oriented to population than anything thus far from Catholic sources. With a strong social justice component, it contains many echoes, many points of resemblance to contemporary Catholic social criticism, not least of all from the liberation theologies.

Lappé and Schurman articulate a power-structure perspective on population issues, congruent with much in Catholic social teaching—also as implied by Pope John Paul above. Lappé and Schurman place "power as a critical variable in both political *and* economic affairs as well as in social and cultural life." The poor are powerless, structurally cut out and cut off, marginalized, disenfranchised, landless, without ownership. In Brazil, for example (as reported in 1988), large farms owned by a mere 224 families equalled lands held by nearly two million peasant families.[33]

Why do the poor so commonly have many children? "High fertility can best be understood as a response to anti-democratic power structures within which people are left with little choice but many births.... [These structures] perpetuate conditions keeping fertility high."[34] Consequently, as a formula it could be stated simply: *no change in social structure = no change in fertility.* Admittedly oversimplified for emphasis, that formula nonetheless expresses a provocative point.

Lappé and Schurman outline five components of a society that encourages—provides realistic and sustainable incentives toward—a moderated fertility.

> 1. Enhanced power of women—through basic literacy, education, and employment.
>
> 2. Heightened power of peasants to provide food and income for themselves because reforms have widely dispersed access to land.
>
> 3. Bolstered power of consumers to secure adequate nutrition where deliberate policies have been implemented to keep basic food staples within reach of all.
>
> 4. Enhanced capacity of people to protect their health as medical care becomes accessible for the first time.
>
> 5. Heightened power of women to limit their births through birth control.[35]

Could not such a program be proposed and supported as (in religious terms) *a modern compassion*—a programmatic compassion, responding to the "signs of the times"? Would not the implementation of such a program, incrementally, articulate the compassion of Christ sensitive to the historically changing circumstances within which we live?

Lappé and Schurman provide a "schematic representation of some of the many arenas of human relationships in which decisions are made which directly and indirectly influence fertility" (see Figure 1).[36]

Four levels or "arenas" appear—broadest on top, descending to the most localized domestic level at the base. The pressures move downward. Each arena experiences pressure and influence from all levels above. The schema is not proposed in my pages here as an analytical *fait accompli,* but rather as a matrix for reflection and observation, further analysis and questioning. The schema offers a broad systems perspective and analysis as an approach to population issues, globally *and* locally.

Figure 1
Arenas of Decision-Making Power Influencing Fertility

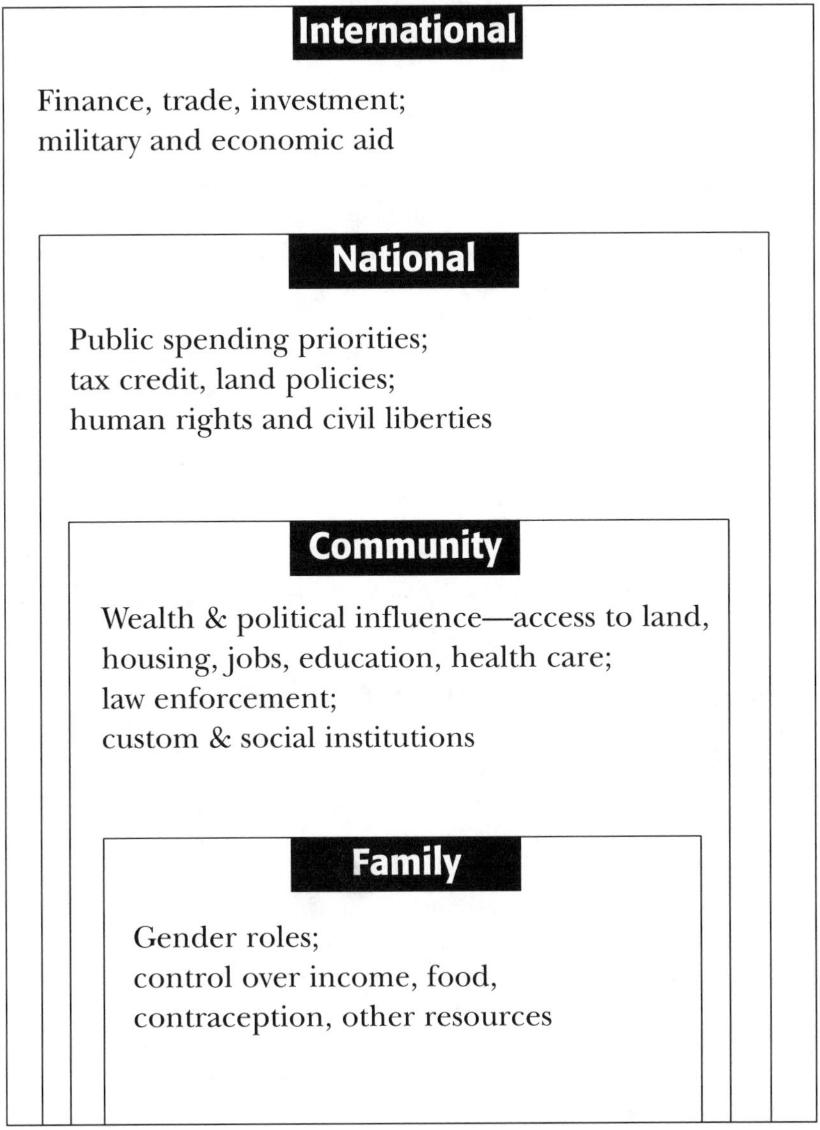

International

Finance, trade, investment;
military and economic aid

National

Public spending priorities;
tax credit, land policies;
human rights and civil liberties

Community

Wealth & political influence—access to land,
housing, jobs, education, health care;
law enforcement;
custom & social institutions

Family

Gender roles;
control over income, food,
contraception, other resources

From: Frances Moore Lappé, Rachel Schurman, *Taking Population Seriously*, Food First Books, 398 60th St., Oakland, California, 94618 (1988). Reprinted with permission.

Their analysis confirms, but also contrasts with, official Catholic positions. Both identify social justice, or social injustice, as central; Lappé and Schurman assert that "rapid population growth is a *moral* crisis because it reflects the widespread denial of essential human rights to survival resources—land, food, jobs—and the means to prevent pregnancy." Vatican emphases are similar.

But the official Catholic stance places heavy emphasis on protesting coercion and programs deemed contrary to Catholic moral teaching. Lappé and Schurman also acknowledge and protest coercion, but carefully relate coercion to structural, societal dimensions, much beyond specific population-control programs. The authors state, "*Ignoring the social roots of hunger* while trying to reduce birth rates leads almost inexorably to more coercive birth control technologies and programs that jeopardize people's health and self-determination" (italics added). Their analysis further diverges from Vatican emphases by seeing contraception as "critical to the goal of greater human freedom—especially the freedom of women—as well as essential to halting population growth."[37] Vatican emphases appear to locate *freedom* primarily if not indeed exclusively in relation to coercion. Does the elementary distinction apply here: not only *freedom from* (coercion) but also *freedom for* (conscience, choice, response to actual circumstances)?[38]

Perspectives on Compassion: Summary, Conclusion

This chapter nominates compassion as characteristic of Christ's ministry, an appropriate call to the Church today. Christ's compassion is a powerful element in the Christian heritage, but today appears muted and subordinated in official Catholic positions concerning population. The Vatican's *Ethical and Pastoral Dimensions* was cited and analyzed in this regard. Admirable in several respects, Vatican emphases gravitate strongly toward moral denunciation at the large cost of losing richer, more helpful, more positive factors.

By comparison, analyses of the American bishops were considered; their study of the economy demonstrates a more scripturally sensitive compassion as a realistic religious policy recommendation. Pope John Paul himself has often spoken similarly.

Authors Lappé and Schurman provide a credible interpretation of the population challenge that coincides with much in the Catholic social tradition—food for thought from the Institute for Food and Development.

To conclude, some of Catholicism's finest modern exemplars are heroes of compassion: Mother Teresa of Calcutta, Dorothy Day, Archbishop Oscar Romero of El Salvador. The martyrdom of Romero (March 24, 1980) at the hands of anonymous "security forces" shows how bitterly the powerful cling to privilege if and when challenged. His death symbolizes and exemplifies the severity of today's structural divisions of advantaged and disadvantaged, the global "haves and have-nots," worldwide, which are manifested in population problems.

In one of his final homilies Romero directed this reminder to the Church itself: "Critics should always be ready in turn for criticism. If the Church denounces injustices, she should also be ready to listen to criticism and be ready to convert. The poor are a constant cry that denounces not only social injustice but also the lack of generosity in our own Church."[39]

Not merely poverty itself but the overt oppression of the poor was Romero's constant theme, shocking to El Salvador's wealthy who had assumed him to be "one of their own." In one of those final Sunday homilies broadcast to the nation he stated,

> The poor have marked out the way the Church should go…. The key for understanding the Christian faith is the poor…. Our Salvadorean world is not an abstraction; it is a world mostly made up of poor and oppressed men and women. In this world, the poor are the key to understanding the Christian faith, the political dimension of that faith, and the Church's action. The poor tell us what the world is, and what service the Church can offer the world.[40]

One month later, celebrating Mass at Divine Providence Hospital in San Salvador, Oscar Romero was assassinated.

Questions for Reflection and Discussion

1. Isn't morality primarily rules and commandments, "do's and don'ts"? If so, why does Vatican II encourage attention to Scripture in moral theology in order "to bring forth fruit in charity for the life of the world"?

2. How does a book about global population problems connect with moral theology? Are they not "apples and oranges"?

3. Each of the briefly indicated scriptural texts occurs, of course, within larger passages or contexts. Select one or two to see if and how it relates to compassion. If Christianity concerns salvation, how does compassion fit in? (p. 108)

4. Robert Wuthnow says, "Compassion is a value, a means of expression, a way of behaving, a perspective on society." Do you agree, or disagree? (p. 110)

5. "The poor are central in Scripture and theology." Really? Is that true? Does it matter? And what has it to do with attitudes toward population problems and pressures? (p. 115)

6. Compare the population analyses of authors Lappé and Schurman with the official Catholic stance. What are the strong points and weak points of each?

CHAPTER SIX

The "consistent ethic of life" should be taken seriously.... [Hence] abortion should be viewed within the larger context of other life-and-death issues, such as capital punishment and warmaking.

—RICHARD MCCORMICK, S.J.[1]

When the Church recognizes that abortion is as complex, as social, and as conflictive of rights as the issues of war or hunger, then perhaps we, the Church, can address abortion with more even-handed compassion, and war and hunger with even more rigor.

—CHRISTINE GUDORF[2]

A "Consistent Ethic of Life": Abortion and Population

TO OPEN OUR DISCUSSION OF ABORTION ON THE GLOBAL scene look momentarily at one Third World nation. Consider Nepal, high in the Himalayas, where "most of the women in jail are there on sentences related to abortion"—often from ten to twenty years. Dr. Aruna Upreti, maternal and child specialist, states, "Of course abortion should be legalized, but it won't be while women in this country are considered less valuable than buffalo."[3] (With a population of 22 million, Nepal compares in size to Arkansas—population about 2.4 million.)

In the introductory statements above, Catholic theologians

McCormick and Gudorf place the neuralgic issue of abortion within larger contexts. They remove it from isolation—as a moral category and a widespread human experience—with possible implications for moral evaluation.

McCormick refers to the "consistent ethic of life"—so notably advocated by the late Cardinal Joseph Bernardin—and recommends "taking it seriously." We shall do so in this chapter, inserting population issues within Bernardin's "consistent ethic." We will add to McCormick, asserting that "abortion should be viewed within the larger context of other life-and-death issues…capital punishment, warmaking," *and global population concerns.*

Abortion has enormous dimensions. Statisticians tabulate 1.5 million in the U.S. annually, and perhaps 50 million globally. This phenomenon has held the attention and—it seems factual to add—the ire of Pope John Paul II and the Vatican.

Cairo Population Conference: Vatican Participation

On the global scene the Vatican, through its "permanent observer" status in the United Nations, made its vigorous opposition to abortion a major factor in the 1994 International Conference on Population and Development at Cairo. As *Time* reported in naming the pope "Man of the Year," "The Pope's emissaries defeated a U.S.-backed proposition John Paul feared would encourage abortions worldwide…. In the end…the Cairo conference inserted an explicit statement that 'in no case should abortion be promoted as a method of family planning.'"[4]

For the first several days of the nine-day conference Vatican objections to proposed resolutions concerning abortion and related sexual issues held center stage. One delegate from the Netherlands lamented, "We have just a week and a half to attract the attention of the world, and all we read is abortion, abortion, abortion."[5] Reportedly many shared his feeling.

Finally, the Vatican signed the document as a whole, with some reservations—acknowledging that "the Holy See recognizes the seriousness of the question of maternal death and the dangers to health connected with abortion…[and] the need to provide quality medical care for complications arising from abortion…. For moral reasons, shared by citizens of many nations, it does not endorse legal abortions."[6]

At the two previous population conferences (Bucharest, 1974; Mexico City, 1984) the Vatican withheld participation in the final consensus document. At Cairo, much more positively after much contention, the Vatican ultimately stated that it "wishes in some way to associate itself with the consensus, if in an incomplete or partial manner." Thus, albeit partially, the Holy See participated in a common global effort clearly oriented to population reduction.[7]

Longer range assessments of the Vatican at Cairo (and the entire event) than are possible as this is written will be forthcoming. But it seems likely that at Cairo something religious was gained, while something was lost—good news and bad news.

Good news: the only church with a voice at this top level of global discussion insistently demonstrated a strong awareness of the moral factor, the transcendent factor in human existence, in human conduct, and in policy decisions. While patently wrong to attribute such moral consciousness to it alone, only the Roman Church as a matter of policy and U.N. status can be so forceful and prophetic in the global forum on behalf of moral value. "The Holy See had some important things to say in its own right on matters of development, the education of young girls, human dignity and the need to protect fetal as well as woman's rights."[8]

Bad news: much else in the Church's social teaching seemed submerged in its heavy focus on abortion. (Vatican spokesmen countered that feminists, not the Vatican introduced the topic—but the Vatican was surely prominent in sustaining the discussion.) The Vatican tone often seemed condemnatory, unready to concede good will, less concerned for common ground than for difference. After all, the Vatican has repeatedly acknowledged the reality of global population concerns. But in a singular conference of the global community at Cairo the diplomatic strategy of the Vatican for several days asserted its own concerns and values in contentious fashion.

In today's world the prophet may of necessity be confrontational, as was an Archbishop Romero or Dietrich Bonhoeffer or Martin Luther King, Jr. At other times, interdependent cooperation seems more appropriate. Prior to the conference an entirely sympathetic observer stated that "the Holy See will no doubt have to agree to disagree with certain elements of the Cairo plan. But when it finally does so, it is my hope that a single-issue focus will not obscure just how much (in the overall plan) it positively applauds."[9] Whatever the Vatican's intent, the impression conveyed is that the "single-issue" focus dominated in the official Catholic contribution at Cairo.

Abortion on the Global Scene

At Cairo the Vatican either brought abortion to center stage, or helped greatly to keep it there for several days. However serious the moral questions concerning abortion, it is only one of *many* exceedingly vexing issues and questions in the population arena. Nevertheless, the role of abortion in population issues requires attention here.

The following reports provide some context for discussing this experience on the global scene:

Report: "Although the same number of abortions are performed annually in Brazil and the United States, Brazil records about 400,000 annual hospitalizations for medical complications from abortion. In the U.S. about 10,000 are admitted annually for abortion complications."[10]

Report: "A recent study (by the U.S.-based Guttmacher Institute) carried out in Brazil, Chile, Colombia, The Dominican Republic, Mexico, and Peru found that more than 2.8 million clandestine abortions are performed annually." Of all pregnancies, these percentages end in abortion: Chile 35, Brazil 31, Peru 30, Dominican Republic 28, Colombia 26, Mexico 17. "Abortion is prohibited by every Latin American country except Cuba."[11]

Report: "The annual number of deaths attributable to clandestine abortions in developing countries is believed to be close to 100,000, with World Health Organization estimates as high as 200,000, or between 20 and 40 percent of all maternal deaths."[12]

Report: "Illegal abortion is one of the major direct causes of maternal death. Rough estimates indicate that only half of the 54 million abortions carried out annually around the world are legal. Most illegal abortions are performed under unsanitary conditions by unskilled attendants...."[13]

Report: "Mothers in the developing world die at a rate 50 times higher than those in the world's wealthiest nations."[14]

Report: (In Kenya) "Many girls get pregnant at 12 or 13. Often abandoned by their families, they must leave school to support themselves and their babies. Lacking skills or vocational training, many end up as prostitutes, a life very difficult to escape. Abortion is not legalized in Kenya, so desperate young women end up in the hands of unscrupulous, unqualified abortionists."[15]

Report: "Urbanization, increases in female education and labor force participation, have resulted in more unwanted pregnancies than ever before and have led increased numbers of women to seek to terminate these pregnancies, often at severe risk to their lives and health."[16]

Report: "In the United Kingdom, close to half (of married women) use effective methods of birth control, while in Italy less than a fifth do.... Italy's low fertility rate is maintained only through a high abortion rate. In 1984, nearly twice as many abortions were performed per 100 live births in Italy as in England and Wales combined, 39 as opposed to 21."[17]

Report: "As many as 45.6 percent of married women in surveys in Shanghai in 1987 and 1990 had at least one abortion. More than a third (36.8 percent) of those who had abortions had at least two."[18]

Report: "Women suffering from botched abortions lie two to a bed in many Third World hospitals. These women did not want to be pregnant but were unable to get the contraceptives they needed."[19]

Clearly abortion represents a major health and human issue, globally. The reader will pardon this reminder of the obvious: no man has ever had an abortion; although no woman ever incurred pregnancy without male cooperation, abortion itself remains singularly a female experience. Most if not all the human experiences behind these terse reports involved acute suffering and stress, with a feminine focus. They do not automatically testify, of course, to *population* pressure. But the very emphasis on abortion at the Cairo population conference provides ample evidence of the connection with population concerns, and a general consensus concerning its importance.

The Catholic Issues—A Sorting Out

Within the Catholic standpoint on abortion several elements are packaged together. It is helpful for our discussion to sort them out.

1. The official Catholic moral prohibition, absolute and exceptionless, employs the biblical commandment against killing. Philosophical reflections from "natural law" as well as the concept of "intrinsic evil" also apply. Complicating circumstances in actual life can never justify the taking of innocent unborn life.

2. The Catholic position often *appears* to combine abortion with sterilization and artificial contraception in a single, sweeping prohibition. Whether so intended or not, this is the misleading impression conveyed. Each, however, is a separate and diverse issue.

3. Also frequently combined (in the Catholic position and in the public debate at large) are *two* areas that in fact are distinct (though related): (a) personal, individual, and parental morality, and (b) public governmental policy and legislation at the level of the common good.

4. Whatever benefit may be sought in any particular instance, a factor of tragedy and grave moral challenge inheres in every decision to abort. Hence, serious moral responsibility at some level must always be a consideration—and most assuredly not only by the pregnant female person most directly involved. Realities of individual integrity, personal rights, the new (unborn) life oriented to personal existence, the common good, and social responsibility call out for moral assessment.

A further point must be acknowledged. Inevitably any divergence from the official Catholic position, so vigorously maintained, immediately incurs in some Catholic circles sharp criticism if not outright condemnation. Focus promptly shifts thereby to issues of ecclesial obedience and conformity, to differing concepts of magisterium, to a discrediting of the very processes of gradual self-assessment and correction that have historically served the Church well—extremely well—time after time. That shift to authority, in all good will, nullifies dialogue on the actual issues of prescribing moral absolutes for countless millions of people in matters of great intimacy, diversity, consequence, and suffering.

In this book we cannot and need not explore all these monumental issues. But we indicate their presence and acknowledge their influence. Moreover, within the Catholic community of faith and conscience we examine the official Catholic stance on these reproductive issues—to assess their basic consistence or inconsistence with other major Catholic positions. These other positions notably concern the moral assessment of war (and nuclear weapons), capital punishment, and AIDS. This reaches to the foundations of the Catholic position concerning contemporary population concerns.

A "Consistent Ethic..."

From a remarkable inspiration or intuition Joseph Bernardin, the late cardinal-archbishop of Chicago, provided a fresh impetus to contemporary moral thought, moral evaluation, pastoral action, and decision making—his widely discussed "consistent ethic of life" argument. Bernardin's line of thought can assist us in evaluating official Catholic moral teaching on population issues, although the argument covers a much wider moral ground than abortion alone.

For readers unfamiliar with this approach, consider first the source. In 1983 Bernardin was chairman of two committees of the American bishops: the committee drafting the "letter" on peace and nuclear deterrence; also the Pro-Life Committee, with principal attention to abortion. Moreover, somewhat surprisingly the bishops' pastoral statement on war explicitly linked abortion and the horrendous issue of nuclear deterrence—a linkage stated but left largely undeveloped (five paragraphs out of 339; nos. 285-289). This was several years prior to the unforeseen demise of Communism, the fall of the Berlin Wall, and the dissolution of the Cold War.

On his own, Bernardin undertook to discuss and articulate that linkage—abortion with national security and nuclear deterrence— asserting both issues as application of one "consistent ethic of life." He states, "For the spectrum of life cuts across the issues of genetics, abortion, capital punishment, modern warfare, and the care of the terminally ill. These are all distinct problems...[but] this combination of challenges is what cries out for a consistent ethic of life."[20]

Moreover, Bernardin saw Catholics (and others) who were ardently, even vociferously active against abortion—yet boosters for a military build-up against Communism. In some instances, especially (but not only) concerning U.S. policies toward Central America, their militancy favored and supported lethal intervention there "in a good cause." He considered this a contradiction: they were "pro-life" but supportive of military killing.

The same persons were, often enough to impress the cardinal, lukewarm, indifferent, or even antagonistic toward other programs of support for the life and well-being of society's disadvantaged, impoverished, or disabled members. Again, to him, this was a contradiction, a serious lack of moral consistency.

With no reference to population Bernardin articulated a "moral vision," a "systemic vision of Catholic ethics," a "consistent ethic [that] identifies both (1) the protection of life and (2) its promotion, as moral questions." The Cardinal acknowledged that in the normal limits of time and energy we human beings cannot stress everything at once, but at least can "recognize points of interdependence which should be stressed, not denied."

> Those who defend the right to life of the weakest among us must be equally visible in support of the quality of life of the powerless among us: the old and the young, the hungry and the homeless, the undocumented immigrant and the unemployed worker. Such a quality of life posture translates into specific political and economic positions on tax policy, nutrition and feeding programs, and health care. Consistency means we cannot have it both ways. We cannot urge a compassionate society and vigorous public policy to protect the rights of the unborn, and then argue that compassion and significant public programs on behalf of the needy undermine the moral fibre of society or are beyond the scope of governmental responsibility.

Not everyone welcomed Bernardin's critique. Nevertheless, "These questions along the spectrum of life from womb to tomb create the need for a consistent ethic of life." His call was directed first of all to fellow Catholics.

Perhaps Bernardin does not call for a consistency of strict *logic*. Perhaps he calls for a consistency of values, of human insight and concern, of compassion, sensitivity, and awareness. *The well-being of life* truly requires support and understanding at many points. In terms of conventional categories of Catholic thought Bernardin's call embraces and conjoins moral theology and social theology in a helpful, welcome, and altogether uncommon manner. He has made an important contribution.

Consistency—a Stern Challenge

Some philosopher—an identity blessedly shrouded in the mists of history, or my memory thereof—remarked that a foolish consistency is the "hobgoblin of small minds." Perhaps he meant that we humans face paralysis if held to perfect consistence in everything we espouse, everything in perfect congruence with everything else that we think, feel, and advocate. Indeed, humankind seems in small risk of becoming excessively consistent. So we do the best we can and strive for improvement.

Yet consistency pushes its stern challenge, not so easily dismissed. Bernardin clearly felt so; the sustained response to his observations suggests that others feel similarly. The norm of consistence at least provides a guideline, a radar, a scanner seeking out flaws in our policy or program, our politics or emphases. Like a medical diagnostic instrument, it points to areas needing attention.

Philip Berryman's excellent study of the American bishops' two major documents on war and the economy discusses Bernardin's argument.[21] Berryman turns to Benedictine author Joan Chittister who detects a serious breach of consistency between two major Catholic positions: (1) the absolute prohibition against abortion, *no exceptions,* as contrasted with (2) the *traditional sanctioning of exceptions* under the biblical prohibition "Thou shalt not kill" (applied to Catholic moral tolerance of war and nuclear weaponry, however qualified). She asks, in irony,

> What is a woman to think: that when life is in the hands of a woman, then to destroy it is always morally wrong, never to be condoned, always a grave and universal evil? But when life is in the hands of men, millions of lives at one time, all life at one time, then destruction can be theologized and some people's needs and lives can be made more important than other people's needs and lives.[22]

The reader may or may not find her feminist accents helpful here; her observation, in my view, stands with them or without them. She points to the *significant exceptions* allowed—in practice largely entrusted to and dependent upon decisions of governments to wage war. But *no exceptions* are sanctioned, zero, never, in personal circumstances of pregnancy, no matter how compounded by illness, impoverishment, oppression, exploitation, personal or family risk. We seem to face here on the one hand a moral strictness or rigor that is absolute—contrasted on the other hand with a moral elasticity, however theoretically hedged about.

Sister Joan Chittister only asks what others have asked before her. Archbishop Denis Hurley, "an exceptionally well-trained scholastic theologian" according to Francis X. Murphy, offered a parallel point during the 1980 synod of (world) bishops.

> It is not easy to explain that the act of artificially limiting the exercise of one faculty of life [contraception] is intrinsically evil, while...in certain circumstances a person may kill, as in self-defense or in a so-called just war.[23]

Hurley appeals persuasively to the principle of consistence in juxtaposing two doctrines of morality. He sees the *approbation* of the greater, more destructive and tragic evil (killing in self-defense or in a "just war")—and the complete *non-toleration* of the lesser (e.g., contraception). He raises an important question. And while his statement does not explicitly comment on abortion, his line of reasoning, by extension, would seem to apply.

The "Just War" as Moral Precedent

The Church has for centuries upheld the "just war theory," wisely or unwisely. The American bishops' 1983 analysis of peace issues uses it extensively (while for the first time acknowledging pacifism as a legitimate alternative within the Catholic tradition). By the "just war" concept stringent moral norms are set forth (rarely in fact observed by nations, but surely useful at least as a standard for moral assessment and reflection), with a strong negative bias against the recourse to armed force. But this negative bias or presumption does *not* constitute *absolute prohibition*. In certain circumstances the recourse to war, to attack, to fight, to defend, to enlist the nation's youth (even coercively, the "draft" or conscription) in armed ranks, to kill and be killed, to destroy and be destroyed, to maim and be maimed, to suffer immeasurably (involving family and loved ones accordingly)—is declared morally acceptable, however profoundly regrettable.

Surely, for example, the Polish nation justly defended itself against Nazi invasion in 1939. Few doubted the moral propriety of American armed response to Japan's Pearl Harbor attack in 1941. Addressing the United Nations in 1982 Pope John Paul II stated that "deterrence"—the infamous nuclear standoff between the Soviets and the Free World—"not as an end in itself but as a step on the way toward progressive disarmament, may be judged morally acceptable." That posture of nuclear defense involved trigger-readiness to kill millions by nuclear missile attack (a readiness sustained and constantly refined throughout some forty years). The American bishops adopted and quoted the Holy Father's stance.[24]

I personally agree with this position, and have advocated it in adult education classes many times. The tragedy of world circumstances seemed to make it the best (or least evil) of overwhelmingly repugnant, regrettable choices. My point here, however, is to argue neither the merits nor the defects of the much controverted just war theory, but simply to note its presence and significance in Catholic moral teaching.

I further note here that the Catholic moral tradition sanctions the use of force in personal self-defense, even to the extent of taking life *if necessary*. The use of force by police, even to the extent of taking life if necessary in law enforcement, is similarly sanctioned. The prohibition against the taking of life is clearly not absolute. There is, of course, the serious and deeply respectable stance of absolute pacifism. But this is clearly *not* the official stance of the Church, which is our focal point here.[25]

We thus arrive at a conclusion: it is a questionably "consistent ethic of life" concerning abortion (along with contraception and sterilization, all deeply affecting the stance of the Church on population issues) when the official Church rigorously maintains an *exceptionless* ethic. Why do not the "just war," self-defense, and law enforcement exceptions constitute a model and precedent, in all consistency?

Consistence—Idol or Guide?

Consistency, of course, is not itself an idol, to be enshrined as a measure of all else. Consistency—or inconsistency—as a quality of a line of thought or judgment simply functions as a clue, an indicator. As in a murder mystery or spy story, this or that clue points to avenues of further exploration, so that disjointed facts might at last fit together in a coherent whole, disclosing the truth of the case. As a famous Sherlock Holmes character asks, "why did the family dog not bark?" That fact probably fits with other facts—is consistent with them. Reality itself, the human mind assumes, has a necessary consistency. An internal combustion engine will not operate with water; water, good in itself, is inconsistent with other structures and processes built into this engine.

Our logical concept of consistency is less rigid than an engine, to be sure, less tangible and measurable; nevertheless, the concept points in certain directions. Thus if exceptions are conceivable and legitimate in so grievous, so ultimate a matter as the taking of another person's life— for example, in self-defense and in decisions to wage war—why then is it not similarly thinkable and plausible (consistency suggests) that morally acceptable exceptions occur equally in circumstances of pregnancy?

Concerning abortion, obviously the fetus, however one interprets it biologically and in human terms (person, ensouled, mere tissue, etc.), morally can only be without guilt, wholly innocent. But at the same time from the moment of its conception even the fetus exists within a social context, within a network and community of social realities. Within those realities a balancing of rights, of existential entitlements, is a fact of life from day one, from moment one. If that fetus grows, let us say, *at the detriment* of the mother, father, other children all of whom are already engaged in responsible social living—then we indeed seem to face tragic, regrettable facts, a balancing and assessment of rights *within a community of life, of lives.* The innocence of the fetus in a given instance is quite plausibly no greater an innocence than that of others of the existing family. The moral claims for the sustenance of a fetal life are quite plausibly no greater, no more acute, than the moral claims of others of the existing family in a particular instance.

Theologian Christine Gudorf has addressed abortion issues in the context of Cardinal Bernardin's "consistent ethic" approach. Revealing that she and her husband decided against a recommended abortion in a difficult pregnancy, she nonetheless states, "That the right of a fetal life to continue living must be defended should not, and ultimately cannot, mean that we exclude from the discussion the rights with which that right conflicts." In her closely argued article she adds:

> No matter what helpful criteria we can arrive at by examining hypothetical situations, we cannot merely insert real persons into prejudged situations and do justice to their personhood. There will always be rare cases where even in these extreme situations there are not only serious impediments to moral responsibility, but perhaps the absence of truly moral alternatives.... When the Church recognizes that abortion is as complex, as social, and as conflictive of rights as the issues of war or hunger, then perhaps we, the Church, can address abortion with more evenhanded compassion, and war and hunger with even more rigor.[26]

Gudorf refers to "rare cases." One suspects intuitively, that some decisions to abort are very likely superficial, selfish, hasty, or heedless.

No category of human decision making, consequential or inconsequential, escapes such factors. But equally surely some "rare cases" are characterized by deeply responsible judgment.

In today's abortion conflict one unique husband and wife team has co-authored a respectful, scholarly study seeking a middle ground. Elizabeth Mensch and Alan Freeman, colleagues on the Law Faculty at the State University of New York, "not affiliated with any particular religious tradition," are parents, and both admit candidly to "firsthand experience of abortion." They lament the hostility and rigidity characterizing this issue, and also the proliferation of abortion on demand to a level of 1.5 million annually in the U.S. Both sides, say these authors, hold to an absolute stance, neither acknowledging the values of the opposition; each could and should learn from the other. Their final paragraph appropriately resembles a lawyer's strong summation to a jury.

> The starting point for a discussion about abortion ought to be the frank recognition that the issue is life or death. To abort a fetus is to kill, to prevent the realization of a human life. But to say that much is not to answer the moral question involved. In the "successful" Gulf War (1990-91), we [Americans] killed many thousands of people, some of them civilians, others exposed to danger against their will. That we choose to kill does not make it wrong on that score alone; but we surely need a vocabulary for talking about life-and-death issues in moral terms that underscore the seriousness of any choice for death. Our religious traditions have served for many hundreds of years to offer hope in the face of despair, to offer life in the face of inevitable suffering and death. We discard those traditions at our peril.[27]

An Abortion: One Catholic Woman's Story

We turn to a remarkable account of one Catholic woman's experience of abortion—for insights not available from theory or statistics. Her focus is not on the surgical procedure, but on the life circumstances that produced the agonizing choice itself.

Using the pseudonym of "Madeline Gray" the author (in an established Catholic journal of opinion[28]) tells of her well-ordered life as wife, loving mother of three (ages six, three, one), participating in her local parish—and an unexpected fourth pregnancy.

This unplanned pregnancy finds the author in a state of delicately balanced, chronic ill health: Crohn's disease, an inflammation and ulceration of the digestive tract. She is further subject to depression. Her very supportive husband fears for his wife's life, fears a life alone with four children. An abortion is chosen, by mutual decision, in acute reluctance, and successfully undertaken. (This sketch does scarce credit to her rich account).

For Madeline Gray, considering her entire family to be at risk, black and white moral absolutes provided neither comfort nor guidance. Perhaps she chose that particular pseudonym because for her a compromised gray area—so often the human lot—was the unavoidable realm of reconciling contradictory values and realities.

For the purpose of our discussion within a larger focus on population issues, particular aspects of Madeline Gray's situation deserve emphasis. Her circumstances included: (a) adequate financial resources; (b) available medical attention for ongoing health needs and in pregnancy; (c) a sound marital and family situation. Even with these crucial supports her challenge was severe. It takes little imagination to grasp the added severity present in so many lives, globally, by the absence of one or more of those critical factors.

Natural law rationales, the principle of the double effect, or an ecclesiological interpretation of the magisterium's moral authority (in relationship to individual conscience) seem questionable foundations on which to prescribe for a responsible moral agent in such incomparably intimate, conscience-burdening, permanently consequential circumstances.

Comments of a Catholic Physician: 1

The foregoing account of one episode of abortion finds sympathetic echoes in the reflections of a retired (British) Catholic physician, Dr. Joyce Poole. She comments on conflicts she experienced in her medical practice, facing patients, while seeking at the same time to respect rigid, highly specific Church pronouncements.[29]

> In the whole field of abortion the well-known saying that every case and every situation is different is platitudinous, but still true. We are required each time to make the notoriously difficult decision about who has the greater claim to be our neighbor.... Once again it would seem that

attempts to apply absolute rules to particular cases lead not only to impossible medical dilemmas but to philosophic and theological muddles.

Two further points from Dr. Poole deserve noting here—authority, and intervention in nature as a characteristic of medical practice. While Church authority has its important role, she states, "there is an authority also residing in those of us who have a lifetime of listening in close and frank contact to the problems of ordinary people."[30] Noting the theological objection that contraception, sterilization, and abortion interfere with nature she observes that "the whole business of medicine is concerned with doing this"—that is, *for some proportionate reason* (general health) invasion of the body is allowed (surgery, medication, tests, treatment, etc.).[31]

Comments of a Catholic Physician: 2

In this chapter with a double focus—abortion (as a population factor) and Catholic moral consistence—a reflection on the Catholic role in the AIDS epidemic speaks to the latter.

Jon Fuller, a Jesuit priest-physician and director in the AIDS program at Boston Medical Center, closely parallels the message of this chapter and book in his call for a Catholic moral reassessment.[32] An estimated 28 million persons now carry the H.I.V. (human immunodeficiency virus) infection, with 6 million dead (late 1996) from the resultant AIDS (acquired immune deficiency syndrome). Although condom use is now an important medically established part of prevention measures (in this sexually transmitted disease), Fuller states, the Church opposes it adamantly. Are the moral values in contraceptive activity to be accorded more importance than lethal illness for millions?

Fuller points to historic instances of "reshaping of moral thinking when novel and difficult cases strain the applicability of previously established principles"—seeing such "reshaping" as vigor and vitality in moral thought. The reshaping he recommends will confront a moral stance in which theory not only precedes and pre-judges—but also disregards circumstances, any circumstance, all circumstances. The powerful category of "intrinsic evil" pre-settles the issue. Fuller hopes that the story of AIDS in our time will find the Church as part of the solution, not part of the problem. For that to occur, change is essential.

Capital Punishment: How Consistent?

A further challenge to a "consistent ethic of life" occurs in the moral issue of capital punishment. Two points promptly emerge: (1) convicted criminals, one assumes, are (legally) guilty, unlike fetal life; (2) the foundation of the religious objection to all killing, including capital punishment, is neither sociological nor pragmatic—but the ultimate sovereignty of God over all human existence. For the Christian: how does one square deliberate, *always avoidable*, state-sponsored killing with the example of Jesus? Capital punishment is in every instance *absolutely* avoidable: the condemned person is already imprisoned, often for many years, and has only to be life-sentenced to so remain. The remedy or alternative is not only humanly available—but in fact ready-at-hand and far more commonly chosen. Therefore, such needless killing should be avoided in respect of the Creator's ultimate prerogative. In actual public controversy, of course, rights of the community, of victims and survivors are also advanced, and properly so.

However, in discussing capital punishment the *New Dictionary of Catholic Social Thought* immediately notes that, to the contrary, the authority of the state in this matter "has traditionally enjoyed support from biblical and theological resources in the Christian community."[33] The *Catechism of the Catholic Church* (1994) agrees, approving the death penalty "in cases of extreme gravity" while in the following section urging public authority to "limit itself...[to] bloodless means" of punishment.[34]

In her powerful book against capital punishment—based on sustained, intimate death row experience—Sister Helen Prejean notes that the American Catholic bishops have condemned the practice as "unfair and discriminatory" and a continuance of "the cycle of violence," but nevertheless uphold the "right" of the state to kill.[35]

My point here is a comparison: the *absolute* stance in the fertility-control aspects of population issues compared and contrasted with a *conditional* stance on the death penalty. For the informed Christian with the incomparable example and teaching of Jesus, earlier biblical injunctions of "an eye for an eye" are scarcely credible as a standard or guide. Yet, official Catholicism has been less than resolute on this issue (although the present pope in the later years of his pontificate has adopted a nearly exceptionless stance—to be reflected in a subsequent edition of the *Catechism*).

Our point here underscores in the Catholic moral tradition that the taking of life has been considered morally tolerable for grave, proportionate reason (e.g., the "just war," capital punishment). That is an established fact. How, when, and where that principle properly applies is surely open to differing opinion, conflicting interpretation. But the Catholic moral tradition has not found itself insulated from concession to life's moral complexity and ambiguity, from the dreaded balancing of rights, responsibilities, circumstances, and decisions. It is time to reassess the complexity and ambiguity of global population realities within that official Catholic social teaching.

Conclusion

In this chapter I have taken Bernardin's argument a step further—(without implying his agreement or support)—giving it a new thrust, a new application. I suggest that Catholicism's rich moral tradition of acknowledged, realistic, long-tolerated exceptions is at odds with itself in declaring other areas exceptionless (meanwhile sharply discouraging reevaluation of such declared official positions).

Thus when the Vatican at the 1994 Cairo conference testifies before the world that its stance on explicitly sexual, reproductive facets of population problems consists of absolutes, verities so clear as to be exceptionless—in this critique from the inside one asks for, one wonders about, one recommends reassessment. Exceptionless, and beyond reassessment? In fact, the Catholic moral tradition has often properly and legitimately accommodated exceptions.

Cardinal Bernardin's "consistent ethic of life" captured the imagination of many—a concept new in emphasis rather than moral content. The "signs of the times" now call us more insistently to that particular challenge. One can admire the forthrightness with which the official Church has in fact responded to population issues, and urged its positions. It has not hesitated to face considerable opposition and deserves some praise in so doing.

But there is also a rich wisdom in learning from those who speak a different word to us. Back when I first studied theology, those who saw differently were always categorically "adversaries." We know now in a more ecumenical era that some of them, many, were colleagues. In population issues doubtless the Catholic Church has some genuine adversaries—but also far more colleagues than thus far recognized or acknowledged.

Questions for Reflection and Discussion

1. Does Cardinal Bernardin's "consistent ethic of life" have implications for Catholic moral evaluations? If so, how? What is the value or power of consistence in ethics and morality?

2. Sr. Joan Chittister alleges an inconsistence between the official Catholic stance concerning a "just war"—and sexual morality (in this particular instance, abortion). Do you agree, or disagree? Why so?

3. Is killing ever justified? If your answer is affirmative, how do you square your answer with the Fifth Commandment?

4. What is your assessment of Madeline Gray's account? Does it assist in evaluating the official Catholic position on abortion?

5. The reflections of Dr. Jon Fuller and Sr. Helen Prejean are presented as arguments from AIDS and capital punishment, which are parallel (i.e., basically similar) to the theme and message of this chapter. Are these valid parallels?

6. What is your assessment of the argument that in some instances the circumstances may morally justify abortion? Might the circumstances of impoverished persons in already heavily populated areas render abortion morally justified? (The purpose of the question is not to elicit emotional opinions on this painful issue, but to explore the *moral significance* of humanly encountered, inescapable *circumstances*— economic, health, even political and cultural—on the options that real people sometimes face.)

CHAPTER SEVEN

*According to the mainstream press, there is some
doubt as to the position of the scientific community
on the issue of population policy. This year, however,
representatives from 58 of the world's leading
scientific academies signed a report demanding
immediate action to slow population growth.*

—*NATHAN KEYFITZ*[1]

*The Church and the scientific community will
inevitably interact; their options do not include
isolation.... Each can draw the other into a wider
world in which both can flourish.*

—*POPE JOHN PAUL II*[2]

Church and Science Look at Population: Partners in Dialogue and Challenge

CAN YOU TOUCH A YEAR? IN A SENSE, YES. ON A CHILD'S FIRST
birthday, you can hold that precious youngster in your arms—and
reflect. You hold and touch all the amazing development of that one
year celebrated with cake, candle, and song. You touch a year,
figuratively perhaps, but really.

One recent afternoon on a sunny Montana hillside I touched forty
million years. With a geologist from Western Montana College at Dillon
I grasped a layered handful of loose, stratified rock, the outcropping of
ancient seabeds deposited there, roughly dated at forty million years.

Other formations studied in this week of amateur geology were older by far.[3] But forty million years lightly in my hand was awesome enough. One stands dumbstruck at the dimensions of our world—in age, vastness, grandeur, power, and complexity.

Was I gullible, naive, to accept this assertion from geological science, this partial chronology of our planet's development, which so stuns and outstrips the imagination? Do you, the reader, accept it—as I did? On what basis? Can something that so exceeds experience really be ascertained, known with any degree of certitude? Somewhat similarly we depend on scientific sources for knowledge of global population trends and dynamics.

How Do We "Moderns" Know What We Know?

Hot and cold, pain and pleasure I experience directly. But *forty million years*? For such sophisticated knowledge the intensely organized, sustained network of study and observation, communication and cooperation that we call "science," or some particular branch of science, is necessary.

In our part of the world where science and the sciences flourish, most of us accept those understandings of the world that science, collectively considered, gives us. We probably advert consciously to such acceptance only now and then—the force we know as gravity, the roundness of our Earth (now confirmed by photos from space); coastal tides; explanations of conception, cell division, and gestation; radio waves; our own bodily functions (blood circulation, immune system, brain and neurological processes, etc.)—on and on. Few of us can directly or personally validate this accepted knowledge. Nonetheless we are "sure" of it, on the authority of science and scientists, on the convergence and plausibility of multiple testimonies, on (frequently) the partial congruence of our own experience with those explanations published in popular media or more academic texts.

The pragmatic articulation of science in technology—the wonder of electricity in the light bulb, of airline travel, of medical treatment by surgery or pharmacology—makes believers of us all, or most of us at least. A few may still insist the earth is flat. But now even at the elementary school level some early personal contact with the evidence, the procedures, the logic, the history, and the wonder of various physical sciences is experienced. For many that instructive, world-opening experience continues into university and even professional levels.

And Population?

How do these comments on science connect with population? No one has ever seen a "population problem" as such, in itself, per se. Signs and symptoms of overpopulation, so interpreted: yes, surely. Observers in many countries see famine, migrations, severe poverty and congestion, homelessness, natural resources locally abused or exhausted, economic deprivation or exploitation. But as such they do not see a direct (clearly isolated) causal relationship of population numbers to these lamentable phenomena. That causal relationship is detected, perceived, and formulated as an *interpretation of diverse, scattered data.* Consider this report of environmental problems in Chesapeake Bay:

> A mounting environmental bill is coming due that is a direct consequence of population growth. Consider Presly Creek, a small Virginia inlet off the Chesapeake Bay. At first glance, it looks pristine. But, in fact, it is buckling under the strain of 15 million people (up from 8 million in 1950) who now live in the 64,000-square-mile Chesapeake Bay watershed: polluted runoff from roads, lawns and farms has turned the water murky green and decimated underwater sea-grass meadows. Oyster reefs are gone, as are the sturgeon, American wigeon and redhead ducks…. Silt from plowed fields and construction sites has filled in coves.[4]

The proclaimed connection between "population growth" and the indicated Bay damage is attributed to "polluted runoff(s)" and a near doubling of the resident population. This is a highly sophisticated interpretation of diverse data, a judgment achieved slowly along several lines of observation. Later the same report tells of runoffs from sewage treatment plants and city streets, waste oil, even automobile emissions washed from the skies in rainfall. Again, a connection with population is implied: "Today, for every cubic mile of water in this rich country, there are 800,000 people living in the watershed; the Baltic Sea, by contrast, has 16,000 persons per cubic mile of water, and the Mediterranean Sea just 350."[5]

A decision or conclusion that population levels have become excessive, problematic, and damaging is an abstracted interpretation by science and scientists. Such interpreters of data are a skilled array of demographers, anthropologists, biologists, sociologists, environmentalists, governmental and medical personnel (plus numerous others: professionals, business people, and general citizenry). From them we know what we know of population, isolated and highlighted as a causal factor, its prospects and perils. And their interpretations inevitably confront contrary interpretations. Asking "what kind of planet do we want… can we get?" Harvard environmentalist William C. Clark states that "science can illuminate these issues [e.g., species diversity, climatic change, population size and growth, etc.] but cannot resolve them. The choice is ours to make and our grandchildren's to live with."[6] The official Church as well as informed theologians ought to be among the prominent sources of guidance in formulating such momentous choices.

The Church and Science: History and Theology

Throughout this book we have been surveying the evolving relationship between the official (and unofficial) Roman Catholic Church and population issues specifically. That relationship inevitably reflects, for better or worse, the general stance of the Church toward science, both the natural sciences as well as the social sciences (which deeply interact in population study). At root the Church is as dependent as others on scientific sources for demographic data. These data are hardly self-interpreting; otherwise, we would not face the drastic variations and conflicts in population perspectives.[7]

In this chapter we consider Church responses to population issues within the larger picture of the relationship of Church and science. Here as always, history and background deeply influence present reality and foreground. The relationship of Church to science obviously did not begin with population; but a long history of Church-and-science is one important factor affecting Church response to population issues today.

At the 1994 Cairo population conference (and various encounters preceding, partly discussed in earlier chapters), once again tension and conflict were the predominant impressions conveyed. But scientists and churchmen (and these *are* usually *men*) did not first meet in population conferences, Cairo, Bucharest, Mexico City, or otherwise. The two most notable, or notorious, antecedents in the religion-and-science relationship spring quickly to mind—Galileo in the sixteenth century, Charles Darwin in the nineteenth—both producing rich, reciprocal animosities that need no retelling here.

Yet despite Darwin and Galileo, indeed partly because of them, lessons were learned that eventually produced more positive relationships, albeit still tenuous and developing. Addressing an international gathering of scientists, describing "science and faith [as] both gifts of God," Pope John Paul referred to "regrettable past events of history, such as the 'Galileo case'…[wherein] a tragic mutual incomprehension has been interpreted as the reflection of a fundamental opposition between science and faith. Clarifications furnished by recent historical studies enable us to state that this sad misunderstanding now belongs to the past."[8] Daily news media rarely report these positive steps—quiet, often academic, peaceable, and unspectacular, hardly amenable to TV's soundbite propensity.

A further factor complicates official Church positions on population. The official positions concerning contraception, sterilization, and abortion embody conclusions arrived at by deductive, abstract reasonings, largely based on traditional interpretations of natural law. The resulting prohibitions are presented as universal and absolute, as intrinsic evil. In dialogue concerning population issues these deductive, abstract positions confront and conflict with inductive, concrete data from demographic and related observation.

In the contemporary field of Catholic moral theology, substantial reassessments and reformulations are emerging, wholly apart from population concerns.[9] The role of human experience, of new exploration in numerous fields of study, of Scripture—these and more are accorded new importance. The traditional, official stance is regarded by many as no longer adequate or satisfactory.

Science is respected as a source, generally speaking, of valuable and significant information about God's world that simply was not available in earlier times. This does not mean that science eliminates the need for theology, or can take over its function. Hardly. As early as 1972 Karl Rahner described the new role of science.

> The natural and social sciences, too, by creating modern technological man, by their world-picture and the many questions resulting from it, have changed theology's situation to a profound degree. If we observe very little of this in our textbooks as yet, it indicates a failure, not a legitimate detachment of theology from science.… The sciences are fellow-contributors to the human's self-understanding.… In the concrete situation determined by

the cultural, intellectual, social, and natural sciences, it is science, no longer mediated by philosophy, which constitute theology's partner-in-dialogue.[10]

In many ways the official Church has initiated admirable relationships with science. Population remains an exception. While we need not make an idol of science, scientists, or their data, God's world comes to us also along these relatively new paths. We need to listen.

The Church and Science: Three Areas of Contact

One perceives at least three categories or areas where Church and science relate to and encounter each other (viewed here from the theological or ecclesial side of such contacts):

(1) The Church speaking directly *to and with scientists,* commenting on the enterprise(s) of science, discussing the relationship of the two realms of knowledge: faith and reason. This occurs, for example, concretely in the Vatican's Pontifical Academy of Sciences,[11] and in other settings where the pope or other spokespersons for religious perspectives speak to scientists—or vice versa, equally, in dialogue (academic conferences, regional bishops' committees, etc.). Pope John Paul II has been frequently and admirably active in this milieu along with an increasing number of highly qualified individuals on both sides of the religion-and-science dialogue.[12]

"Dialogue" is mentioned in the first category, occurring in numerous ways. For example, The Center for Theology and the Natural Sciences— "a membership organization affiliated with the Graduate Theological Union" (Berkeley, California)—currently co-sponsors a decade of international research conferences with the Vatican Observatory.[13] The Center's numerous conferences, courses, and publications explore religion and science relationships at a highly sophisticated level.

(2) The Church speaking officially to the public or world at large on issues that *incorporate scientific data*—population, issues of family planning and conception control, environmental concerns, medical and bio-engineering issues, and others. This area often includes, inevitably, a political factor, with implications for national policies or legislation. Vatican participation in the United Nations often exemplifies this area.

(3) Least noticed: the Church *within its own household* promoting a proper assessment, assimilation, and consciousness of those modern scientific understandings, meanings, and insights that touch realities and issues concerning religion. Notably this has applied deeply to issues of cosmology, creation, evolution, environment, applications to biblical understandings, and similar areas. However belatedly, this has nonetheless substantially begun, with a long road ahead.[14] This occurs within schools under church aegis (at all levels), in official church statements, in occasional parish pulpits, and in educational programs (discussed further in a later section).

Scientists and Religious Leaders: Major Statements

Another mode of dialogue was initiated by thirty-two "internationally eminent scientists" with their "Open Letter to the Religious Community."[15] In nine paragraphs the authors state that when "humankind's numbers were small and our technology feeble" the impact on the environment was negligible.

> But today, suddenly, almost without anyone noticing, our numbers have become immense and our technology...awesome.... We are now able to make devastating changes in the global environment.... Problems of such magnitude, and solutions demanding so broad a perspective, must be recognized from the outset as having a religious as well as a scientific dimension.... We scientists...urgently appeal to the world religious community to commit, in word and deed, and as boldly as is required, to preserve the environment of the Earth.

Among the most difficult issues, the scientists include "a voluntary halt to world population growth—without which many other approaches to preserve the environment will be nullified."

This urgent, respectful declaration readily acknowledges that "efforts to safeguard and cherish the environment need to be infused with a vision of the sacred."

In an article concerning that "Open Letter," one of the signatories, astronomer Carl Sagan, points to the role that the scientists themselves have played in environmental devastation.[16] "Many of us didn't even bother to think about the long-range consequences of our inventions....

In too many cases we have lacked a moral compass." Praising a new level of rapport between religion and science, Sagan quotes words of Pope John Paul II (see head of this chapter). Sagan describes the religious response to the scientists' appeal as "overwhelming... signed by hundreds of spiritual leaders from 83 countries including 37 heads of national and international religious bodies."

These religious leaders acknowledge the role of science in partnership with the religious role.

> The scientific community has done humankind a great service by bringing forth evidence of these perils. We encourage continued scrupulous investigation and must take account of its results in all our deliberations and declarations regarding the human condition.[17]

At the same time the religious spokespersons affirm that the environmental crisis "is intrinsically religious...sacred creation is being violated." The appeal from the scientists "calls us to new levels of joint commitment."

In June 1991, in New York City, a further declaration was issued by 24 religious leaders. This rich statement carries these pointed references to population concerns:[18]

> No effort, however heroic, to deal with these global conditions and the interrelated issues of social justice can succeed unless we address the increasing population of the Earth—especially the billion poorest people who have every right to expect a decent standard of living. So too we must find ways to reduce the disproportionate consumption of natural resources by affluent societies like ours.... Steps must be taken...to slow the dramatic and dangerous growth in world population through empowering both women and men, encouraging economic self-sufficiency, and making family education programs available to all who may consider them on a voluntary basis.

As if this New York proclamation were insufficient, another was published by 150 religious and scientific authorities jointly in Washington, an impressive group including such Catholic notables as the president of Catholic University, three bishops, representatives of the U.S. Catholic Conference, and Father Thomas Berry (Catholicism's true environmental pioneer).[19] Other distinguished religious and scientific leaders participated. Their wide-ranging but compact statement notes the centrality of population issues and acknowledges that an increase of religious sensitivity to "environmental integrity" comes "significantly as a result of fruitful conversations with the scientific community."

> The human community grows by a quarter of a million people every day, mostly in poorest nations and communities.... We believe there is a need for concerted efforts to stabilize world population by humane, responsible and voluntary means consistent with our differing values.... Special attention must be paid to education and enhancing the roles and status of women.

These statements surely apply to Roman Catholic relationships with the environment, with science, and with population.

All three of these foregoing statements (the 1990 "Open Letter" from scientists, the 1991 New York declaration from religious leaders, and the 1992 Washington declaration by religious leaders) pledge effective implementation. The 1991 statement concludes by recognizing that "in this challenge may lie the opportunity for people of faith to affirm and enact, at a scale such as never before, what it truly means to be religious.... There can be no turning back."

Incidentally, how revealing it might be to conduct a poll of the various religious bodies and congregations represented, locally and nationally, to learn if the average attendee at their respective religious services, conferences, and programs has ever heard these topic(s) mentioned— not to say emphasized.

Church and Science—An Assessment

As mirrored in finance, human experience is a compound of debits and credits, assets and liabilities, income and expenditures. Properly accounted, we achieve a balance, preferably with a surplus on the credit side. Relating to science, does the Catholic Church today enjoy a positive balance? In my estimate, yes, soundly so—naturally enough retaining some debits and deficits. Today's more positive relationship of science and religion is still young, still emerging from more troubled times. But the appeals and responses between scientists and religion discussed above clearly imply more trustful, more cooperative mutual attitudes. Nevertheless in his rich survey of the still-emerging dialogue, theologian Christopher Mooney states that "only with extreme reluctance can scientists and theologians get themselves to speak with each other today."[20]

David Byers, executive director of the American Catholic Bishops' Committee on Science and Human Values, states that "Granted good will on both sides, the future of the science/religion dialogue depends critically on how seriously the partners take one another."[21] That comment may seem obvious, but is in fact crucial—for the tendency, one suspects, is naturally toward a posture slightly dismissive of the other, slightly diminishing the other, assuming a role of superiority. But Protestant theologian Wolfhart Pannenberg warns his colleagues that "if theologians want to conceive of God as the creator of the real world, they cannot possibly bypass the scientific description of that world."[22]

The late medical scientist-author Lewis Thomas noted that "the greatest of all the accomplishments of twentieth-century science has been the discovery of human ignorance," presumably as applicable to theologians as to scientists. "We live, as never before, in puzzlement about nature, the universe, and ourselves most of all." Thomas emphasizes that an awareness of what we *don't* know has itself become significant, a factor in our decisions and evaluations. The realized complexity of our world now compels "living in a condition of intellectual instability for the long time."[23]

Two cautionary comments are appropriate. First, we have no basis and no need to idolize or idealize science or scientists as all-knowing, all-wise, or automatically correct. Nor, second, do we accept assumptions that science provides fact and objectivity, free of bias, while religion provides only opinion, preference, subjectivity, and sentiment. Theoretical physicist and Anglican priest, John Polkinghorne testifies that

> I need the insights of both science and religion. Each is concerned with the search for truth, but they survey different aspects of our experience. It is not the case—as many suppose—that science deals with real knowledge of a world of reliable facts, whilst religion trades in individual opinion which might be "true for me" but which cannot be just plain "true." In fact, such ideas are literally mistaken.[24]

By establishing the Vatican Observatory in 1891 (now with new facilities at Mt. Graham, Arizona) and the Pontifical Academy of Sciences in 1936 (currently with eighty members from widely diverse international backgrounds) the Catholic Church acknowledged natural science. Innumerable Catholic universities as well as secondary and elementary schools fully embrace modern science. The present pope's address to the Pontifical Academy in 1989 was a masterful summary of "the dynamic relationship of theology and science" today.

At the same time one notes the ambiguous (if not flatly contentious) manner—alternately acknowledging and minimizing—when the Holy See turns to population issues. Granted, no one would expect or respect supine acceptance of every demographic assertion or hypothesis. But it is discomfiting to hear that the Holy Father "was reportedly infuriated" when "eight lay experts" of the Vatican's own Pontifical Academy of Sciences, a consultative body, issued a set of opinions and recommendations different from his own in population matters.[25] The Academy report stated:

> There is an unavoidable need to contain births globally in order to avoid creating the insoluble problems that could arise if we were to renounce our responsibilities to future generations…. It is unthinkable that one can indefinitely sustain a birthrate that goes much above the level of two children per couple, which is enough to guarantee the replacement of generations.

Because it was issued five months before the 1994 Cairo conference in which the Vatican took a highly public, specific, and unyielding stance, one can appreciate a certain awkward quality in the Pontifical Academy's independent diplomacies, timing, and public utterance. Yet members of the Academy of Sciences are not Vatican employees or staff, not scholars or apologists for hire, not even necessarily Catholic. They have their own integrity, personal and professional. The pope's wrath was unwarranted.

The "population community"—demographers and advocates alike—is as capable of ideological advocacy, exaggeration, and competitive antagonisms as any other group or movement, including various religious bodies and groups. It too needs challenge and dissent. But the Vatican's *Ethical and Pastoral Dimensions of Population Trends* (see Chapter Five) is characterized by the following dismissive comment on so momentous an issue: "Christians and all people of good will are urged to become aware of the fact that the tactics employed always make use of simplistic economic and demographic information and approximate, that is, inexact, projections."[26] "Always" and "simplistic" are antagonistic and inappropriate for serious dialogue. (The quote speaks, of course, not only to scientific sources but other population advocacy groups as well.)

Church and Science: "Within Its Own Household"

Of the three categories where church and science meet (see pages 146-147, above) the first two have been discussed. Now, the third: "the church within its own household, promoting a proper assessment and understanding of the science-religion relationship."

The Church is a church, not a school. So why care what constituents think of science? At the most, is not the religion-science relationship an extramural, high level matter for officials, clergy, and professors—of little pertinence in the average congregation?

The noted Jesuit humanist Walter Ong has written pointedly on this.[27] An astute observer of culture, Ong sees the changes wrought by science pervading modern life, sometimes at a less than conscious level. We absorb the values and impact of science in schools, popular magazines, television, our modes of travel, the immediacy of communication, our technological devices, and services of all sorts.

But what if all this is *absent* in perspectives presented from pulpits, liturgies, and religious educational settings? Ong asserts that a sense of unreality, of discontinuity will surely occur to some, perhaps many. The great Christian themes, if true and timeless, must apply to and connect with modern reality, surely including the world of science.

> We cannot manage to keep the questions indefinitely unarticulated. To do so is suicidal intellectually, and will do no good to Christian faith.... These questions are ultimately not just speculatively theological although they involve speculative theology. They are deeply pastoral and devotional.

Twice in his incisive essay Ong refers to "the overwhelming questions of population and ecology" as being among those "which clearly have massive theological repercussions."

Ong further suggests that this challenge of the science-religion relationship may well be "the major problem framing, at least subconsciously, most of the major problems confronting Christian faith in the decades just ahead." Integration of faith values and perspectives with contemporary understanding of our world and the human role in it is imperative. Perhaps the profoundly unfinished—indeed barely begun—character of such pastoral and pedagogical integration *helps to explain the lagging, inadequate Catholic response* thus far to global issues of population and environment.

An observation by Ong's Jesuit colleague Karl Rahner sheds further light. Early in his classic *Foundations of Christian Faith*, Rahner notes the substantially changed circumstances within which a theologian works today (any theologian, that is, who would be more than catechetical). In former days theology faced a much smaller, more clearly defined, more tidy intellectual heritage.[28] But today the knowledge of human nature, and all nature, rushes in from multiple sources: art, drama, literature, the physical sciences and social sciences, history, psychology, economics—and more. No one can master it; yet, theology would isolate itself from such knowledge only at great peril. As Lewis Thomas stated, we become aware of our ignorance.

Final Words—a Look Back

We have reflected on the growing and increasingly fruitful relationship of religion and science. This relationship inevitably provides a context within which Catholic perspectives on population are situated. That relationship thus becomes one standard or criterion according to which church population pronouncements and positions are evaluated.

Moreover, despite our focus on Roman Catholic involvement, this is another area where ecumenism is richly experienced, indispensable, and utterly beneficial. Often yesterday's denominational barriers provide today's bridges.

Some basic premises and conclusions:

1. The Church today has a far more positive record vis-à-vis science than seems commonly recognized. This offers a foundation for continued progress and for hope.

2. However, the troubled history of this relationship still influences the present; to ignore that history is to distort the present. Antagonisms and attitudes of suspicion remain a factor.

3. Church policies concerning population strongly reflect and echo decisions, experiences, and perspectives initially developed in *other* categories, *other* circumstances, in relation to *other* problems. The possibility for inappropriate or inadequate application to population thus deserves serious consideration.

4. The Church has a divine mandate as teacher. But the dedicated teacher can never cease to be a learner as well. That always has been true—but is today ever more complex and more urgent.

5. If an alarmist interpretation of global population is unwarranted, nevertheless a direct, activist interpretation is *warranted*.

In short, the world needs the Church. And vice versa. In the words of Pope John Paul II about science, "Each can draw the other into a wider world in which both can flourish."

Questions for Reflection and Discussion

1. How would you summarize the basic point of this chapter—the line of reasoning?

2. What importance, if any, does data from science have for theology? Or should theology simply function "on its own," without outside influence or contribution?

3. How do you understand the comment of William C. Clark (p. 144) that science can "illuminate" but not "resolve"—and "the choice is ours to make"? What choice?

4. Do you see any importance in the contrasting approaches of the Church and science—that is, deductive and abstract, and inductive and concrete? How does this apply to population issues? What impact might it have on moral theology?

5. Please summarize and evaluate the "Open Letter (of 32 scientists) to the Religious Community."

6. Please summarize and evaluate the comments of Walter Ong (p. 152).

The long-run threat of population to the environment is a real one.... It is the isolationist view of population growth that should be rejected.

—AMARTYA SEN[1]

Today, the dramatic threat of ecological breakdown is teaching us the extent to which greed and selfishness—individual and collective—are contrary to the order of creation, characterized by mutual interdependence.

—POPE JOHN PAUL II[2]

Theology, Ecology, Population: New Complex Relationships

IN 1988 YALE HISTORIAN PAUL KENNEDY PUBLISHED A WIDELY acclaimed book, *The Rise and Fall of the Great Powers.* But in a subsequent open forum concerning that book he found himself challenged (as he later reported).

> [I was asked] why hadn't I used my time better, to write about much more important and interesting issues, those forces for global change like population growth, the impact of technology, environmental damage, and migration,

which were transnational in nature, and threatened to affect the lives of us all, peasants as well as premiers?

So in a subsequent book (in which the words above appear in the Foreword), Kennedy addressed those "transnational" issues. Not surprisingly, his first two chapters focus on today's population challenges.[3]

In this chapter we address a triangle of just such "transnational" issues and realities:

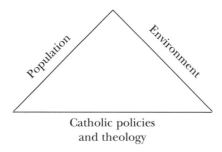

Catholic policies
and theology

Our overall purpose is to explore the interaction of population pressures and the environment, and to evaluate the Catholic response to those realities.

In Section One we consider population's impact upon environment; we report and evaluate Vatican comments on the population-environment relationship. Further discussion covers a major University of Michigan research project in population-environment relationships, and the enormous nation of Brazil as a "case study."

Section Two surveys and evaluates the Church's response to population issues as *part of* its still emerging response to the environmental challenge generally.

Section One:
Our Damaged Environment—
Should We Blame "Population"?

Chapter Seven discussed the role of science in population issues, intersecting with religion generally and the Catholic Church in particular—often cooperatively, but sometimes in conflict. William C. Clark, a Harvard researcher in the relationships of population and environment, was quoted, stating that science can illuminate but cannot resolve these questions.

To speak now of ecology is to speak once more of science, which can, must, and does indeed illuminate. Participants in these issues constitute society itself, nothing less. *Everyone* is affected, however inattentive many may be, or seem to be.

If the issue of "science and religion" seems "up in the air" to some, "religion and ecology" is surely "down to earth"—as real as exhausted fisheries, beaches declared unfit for swimming, and skin cancer from a depleted ozone layer. Religion sees these as God-given natural resources—fish, water, and shoreline, ozone and sunlight—now damaged, abused, degraded. But is this environmental deterioration somehow connected with *excess of population?* If so, how so?

To explore this issue we turn first to the unlikely partnership of a Protestant progressive theologian with a (former) World Bank economist. John Cobb and Herman Daly co-authored a remarkable book, *For the Common Good: Redirecting the Economy Toward Community, the Environment, and a Sustainable Future.* Their Introduction begins with a terse summation of three global environmental concerns: a deteriorating ozone layer, our greenhouse/global warming phenomenon, and an increase of habitat and species extinction. They connect these to population growth.

> All of these facts appear to us to be related in one way or another to one central underlying fact: the scale of human activity relative to the biosphere has grown too large. In the past thirty-six years (1950-86), population has doubled (from 2.5 billion to 5.0 billion). Over the same period gross world product and fossil fuel consumption have each roughly quadrupled.[4]

Some observers attribute global (and regional) environmental deterioration directly and primarily to factors of excessive population. Is this the more likely, the more plausible explanation? Does it really matter how we envision or formulate the relationship of population growth to environmental damage?

With a focus on local or regional environmentalism, resource and population economics, Partha S. Dasgupta considers these relationships significant. He describes how a spiral occurs—truly a vicious circle or cycle: poverty stimulates fertility, which stimulates environmental destruction, which in turn promotes poverty. He offers the following example.

> Fetching water in Rajasthan, in the west of India, takes up to several hours a day for each household. As resources become increasingly sparse and distant, additional hands become more valuable for such daily tasks, creating a demand for families to have more children. The burgeoning population puts more pressure on the environment, spurring a need for even more offspring in a cycle of increasing poverty, population, and environmental damage.

In such a cycle Dasgupta interprets research data as revealing *reciprocal influences* at work—not *exact causal* relationships.

> Recent findings by the World Bank on sub-Saharan Africa have revealed positive correlations among poverty, fertility, and deterioration of the local environment. Such data cannot reveal causal connections, but they do support the idea of a positive-feedback process such as I have described.[5]

Environment and Population: Vatican Statements

An official Vatican statement prior to (and in anticipation of) the 1994 Cairo population conference discussed the alleged connection between population issues and environmental concerns. "According to a frequently repeated affirmation the number of the earth's inhabitants will cause growing pollution or *the degradation of the environment....* However, no one has ever shown any direct cause and effect relationship between population growth and the degradation of the environment." The statement then notes that in fact some densely populated "developed countries" have "less signs of pollution" while others display "very elevated" levels. The Vatican authors later acknowledge that

> The environmental problem also exists in the developing countries...from badly controlled exploitation of natural

resources, recourse to antiquated agricultural methods which exhaust the soil, or the disorderly introduction of industries, often foreign, which are highly polluting.... In any case it would be simplistic to accuse populations of these regions of being responsible for the acid rain or the fears raised at times about the ecological balance of the planet.[6]

In his address to Dr. Nafis Sadik of the United Nations (see Chapter Four), Pope John Paul commented similarly, devoting one brief paragraph to the subject. These Vatican observations both partly concur and partly conflict with other professional sources.

The issue is inherently elusive, frustrating to anyone who expects statistical exactitude. Yet it appeals to common sense to say that if people affect the environment (including its undeniable degradation; recall the words of John Paul II at the head of this chapter), then numerical increases of people probably affect it more, and more severely. Is it really "simplistic" (as the Vatican asserts) to regard regional populations as at least contributory to local degradation of the environment, as at least one significant factor in the situation, sometimes? Can this all be so easily dismissed? Is it really advisable to deny all connection between growing populations and growing environmental degradation until we can demonstrate a direct cause and effect relationship?

For example, consider ten nations of Southeast Asia with a 1993 population at 460 million, projected to 593 million in 2010, and 696 million in 2025.[7] It is certainly reasonable to wonder and inquire concerning the impact of such growth (projected, admittedly uncertain) upon finite resources. It seems neither alarmist nor catering to fear to note with William Clark that "every form of life continually faces the challenge of reconciling its innate capacity for growth with the constraints and opportunities that arise through its interactions with the natural environment."

Clark's essay, "Managing Planet Earth" (a title some doubtless find questionable), introduces a special issue of *Scientific American* magazine (September, 1989, subsequently published in book form) devoted to environmental change in several dimensions, population included. He says that, yes, much of the change and many interrelationships cannot yet be rendered in exact terms—as the Vatican document properly asserts. But he also emphasizes that action cannot always await such exactitude.

Our understanding of the science behind global change is incomplete and will remain so into the foreseeable future. [But] surprises like the stratospheric ozone hole will continue to appear and will demand action well in advance of scientific certainty.... Conventional forecasts of population and energy growth could turn out to be conventional foolishness.... [However] there can be no question that...the explorations [reported in the articles accompanying his] all reflect an emerging commitment to get on with the task of managing planet earth in a responsible manner.[8]

Environment and Population: a University Project

Similarly, both in harmony and discord with the Vatican stance, a remarkable interdisciplinary and international seminar at the University of Michigan (over several years) is entitled the "Population-Environment Dynamics Project." The 450-page volume reporting the project states, "The real world is one in which population and environment are closely related...[yet are] neglected in teaching and research."[9]

An example of one focus in the University of Michigan symposium: a study of the tight relationship between a confined environment and population in nine villages in northwest Benin (west Africa). A team of four researchers describes the tribal residents, farming systems and resources, wood resources, and available protein and fish resources. Villagers are driven to poaching in the nearby national park because of their poverty. "All of this combines to create severe population strains on a narrow strip of land." With water supplies vulnerable, famine and malnutrition a regular threat, "one foresees a formula for looming disaster in the tightly linked population-environment dynamics of this constrained ecosystem."[10] Members of the team continue to work with the villages beyond the requirements of their project.

Oversimplifying enormously, but for the sake of conveying some sense of the research undertaken, I include the report's conceptual or theoretical framework chart (figure 2), with four explanatory comments (in my words) following:[11]

1. Box (left), *Population:* six basic variables that demographically define a population.

2. Box (right), *Environment:* in reference to a total global ecosphere, which divides into ecosystems.

Figure 2: Population-Environment Dynamics Conceptual Framework

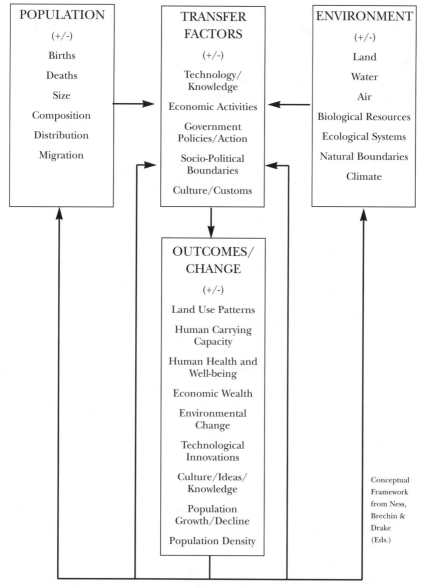

From: Gayle Ness, Wm. Drake, Steven Brechin, eds., *Population-Environment Dynamics*, University of Michigan Press, 1993.

3. Box (middle), *Transfer Factors:* stands *between Population and Environment,* as "mediating conditions." It is important to note that population and environment thus interact mediately, not directly. Hence, "The absence of arrows directly connecting population and environment is quite deliberate."

4. Box (below), *Outcomes/Changes:* the interaction of the foregoing three factors leads to "outcomes/change." "The mix and character of these conditions will define how many people will be supported by the land, at what level of well-being, and at what costs to both current and future resources of a specific set of ecosystems."

The editors conclude their impressive report with these words.

> The research agenda is long and complex. Much work remains to be done in developing useful concepts, in operationalizing those concepts, and in making the detailed field observations implied by any research agenda. This exercise in attempting to think about the population-environment dynamic has, we believe, helped to lay out some of the details of that agenda. If the work ahead is difficult, the stakes are very high. They may well include more than mere symptoms of ecosystem ailments. They may well include the very existence of the planet's ecosystem as we know it. Let the work go forward.[12]

Our Goal: a Learning Process

The editors of the University of Michigan report admit that "population and environment relationships still defy clear and comprehensive understanding"[13]—providing some support for the cautionary tone of the Vatican statement above. Nevertheless a striking contrast is unmistakable when in three Vatican paragraphs this major relationship (environment/population) is discussed and dismissed with such seeming certitude and finality. In the University of Michigan study, on the contrary, the same relationship merits some forty-one "interdisciplinary pilot projects" ranging over rural Zimbabwe, southeast Asia, Brazil, Indonesia, and elsewhere. This surely testifies to intense interest and concern, an effort to learn, to illuminate, to protect and inform about our unimaginably complex, distressed Earth-home.

But our principal purpose here goes much beyond a critique of

Vatican positions. The goal rather is a learning process in which one places hope. The goal is also to show that values honored in Catholic social thought (human welfare, social justice, ecological integrity and stability, et al.) are often affirmed, reflected, and studiously developed in such academic explorations as the University of Michigan project.

We concluded an earlier chapter (Six) by asserting that although the Church surely has adversaries it has "far more colleagues than thus far recognized." Some of those colleagues are at work in the indicated university attempts to illuminate the difficult, dynamic interactions between environment and population—subtle, nuanced, shifting, significant relationships. These are attempts to become more precise, more exact in understanding how human beings interact with their surroundings—affecting it, affected by it—with a view to progress, to improvement and assistance.

We concluded another chapter (Seven) by asserting that the world needs the Church, and vice versa. Pope John Paul in his contributions to the dialogue between science and religion has claimed that each can "draw the other into a wider world." An intriguing claim! What might it concretely mean? Scientific studies in environment-population relationships can have just that effect on the Church-side of the relationship—drawing the Church into wider perspectives and deeper insights. The institutional Church as yet has only a slender, incipient record of comment and guidance in the multiple areas of ecology and religious understandings of our relationships with nature. The Church must be a learner here, while at the same time it seeks to teach and preach—a delicate, responsible role. Any teacher who is no longer a learner becomes quickly obsolescent in today's world.

A Case Study: Brazil

Vatican emphasis is decidedly cautionary and skeptical when looking at connections—whether alleged, intuited, sensed, or perceived—between population growth and environmental damage, regionally or globally. The University of Michigan project in its own way also expresses reserve, since these complex relationships "defy clear and comprehensive understanding." At the same time these scholars seek to spell out those relationships in more specific, more properly documented terms.

In their "Conceptual Framework" (fig. 2) several "Transfer Factors" serve as media that color, filter, and influence the interactions of population with environment. Thus population itself is not bluntly and solely perceived as "the cause" but rather as a prominent element (more or less, represented as +/-). To some extent this concurs with the Vatican position, which protests what it sees as all-out campaigns of population control—ignoring other major factors that contribute to poverty, inequity, and environmental degradation. Brazil provides, briefly, a case study exemplifying this.

Reported by George Martine (president, Institute for the Study of Society, Population and Nature; Brasilia, Brazil), Brazil is included in the Michigan project.[14] Martine's report on agricultural modernization there illustrates the role of powerful political and socioeconomic factors in that nation's farming, land-owning, migration, and urbanization patterns.

Brazil has been notable in recent decades for (among other factors) vastly increased urbanization as well as deforestation in the Amazon area. To some, the peasantry would appear as principal cause—too numerous, too fertile, and consequently unstable. Closer analysis reveals the pressures on the peasantry produced by government decisions, policies of credit preferential to large landholders, speculators, and agribusinesses. "As of 1980, only 21 percent of all farmers had access to credit; moreover 10 percent of all establishments received 60 percent of the total value of all loans conceded.... Sharecroppers, tenants, small owners, and their families were ousted by the demand for land.... Close to thirty million people left rural areas for the cities between 1960 and 1980."[15]

It is revealing to look at Brazilian populations in their two largest cities, suggesting a strong shift to urbanization:[16]

	RIO	(millions)	SÃO PAULO
1950	2.9		2.4
1970	7.0		8.1
1990	10.7		17.4
2000	12.5		22.1

Urban statistics come alive in a lengthy (2½ page) journalistic report on Brazil's poverty and population.

> Rio is an earthy city of sunny beaches, carnivals, lusty music and lost weekends. There is another side to this capital of gaiety, though, where life is not so pretty.

> Some 550 slums or *favelas* ring Rio. They are racked with poverty, violence, joblessness, and disease. Few...who occupy the *favelas* set out to have children who end up begging in the streets. But hungry kids with hollow eyes are part of Rio's grim landscape.

> Ignorance is the main reason these children are born to lives of destitution. Contraception remains a mystery in much of Brazil, even to poor parents eager for some education. One of the most popular forms of birth control is female sterilization, a crude practice administered even more crudely by callous physicians.... Politicians routinely offer women free sterilization in exchange for votes.[17]

Socioeconomic alignments in Brazil have been characterized by "profound inequity," states George Martine. The U.N. *Human Development Report 1993* speaks similarly of Brazil. "Poverty is widespread, with enormous income disparities."[18]

Visiting Brazil in 1991 Pope John Paul addressed the issue of migration and the environment. At Mato Grosso, "Gateway to the Amazon," he spoke of "families uprooted...[who] cannot find even a poor dwelling in which to take shelter." While making no reference to population he spoke of "coming into contact with the environmental problems of both the Amazon and the Mato Grosso highland."[19]

Other observers comment on Brazil. Frances Moore Lappé and Rachel Schurman emphasize the Brazilian paradox of low population density, relatively high acreage of arable land per capita, along with "significant hunger."

> The slash-and-burn agriculture of Brazilian peasants often gets the blame. But if land in Brazil were not the monopoly of the few—with two percent of the landowners controlling sixty percent of the arable land—poor Brazilians would not be forced to settle in the Amazon, destroying the irreplaceable rain forest. And surely the logging and cattle ranching, also destroying rain forests, reflect *not population pressures* but market demand for meat and wood by better-off consumers, largely in the industrial countries.[20]

With an estimated population of 157 million (1994) Brazil—fifth largest land area in the world—is hardly overcrowded. Indeed, birth rates are projected in *decline*, from 2.3 (1960-94) to 1.3 (1994-2000).[21] Consider some comparative figures on population density, i.e., persons per thousand hectares of land:[22]

Argentina	120
Brazil	179
Canada	29
Colombia	316
Cuba	975
Japan	3294
Netherlands	4437
United Kingdom	2382
United States	275
Developing nations, average	541
Industrial nations, average	225

Brazil's social imbalances and inequities remain at high levels. Other authors spotlight the severe problems of Brazilian children[23] and women.[24] The annual Brazilian rate of inflation (1991) was a staggering 428.5 percent (Colombia 29.7 percent; Argentina 127.8 percent; Japan 1.9 percent; USA 3.6 percent; average inflation rate for developing countries: 39.9 percent).[25] These are the cold statistics of suffering and injustice.

One example is only one example, granted. But one suspects firmly that many national parallels exist, that the social injustice component of human suffering is widespread. Demographics and human fertility indeed matter, and require direct attention—*but in conjunction with the total social, economic, and political situations* within which people actually live and to which they are deeply vulnerable. Insofar as cautionary Vatican emphases call for deeper scrutiny of these complex, interactive factors, they appear to be supported by current sophisticated studies, such as reported here.

Section Two:
Church, Theology, and Environment—
New Perspectives,
New Assessments

Population issues and environmental issues mix and mingle, tangle and interact. The exact formula may be elusive, but people do deeply affect their environment and vice versa.

But only in recent decades have we witnessed the emergence of life and environmental sciences achieving new degrees of headline prominence. We see environmental volunteer action and school curricula at every level. We see policy disputes and legislation—even, alas, ecotourism. Some theologians, Protestant and Catholic, have responded with remarkable acumen. Local congregations and pulpits, however, remain largely uninvolved. The *Catechism of the Catholic Church*, all 2857 paragraphs thereof, makes very little mention of the environment or ecology (though some elements under "creation" and elsewhere are doubtless applicable).[26] Fortunately, as noted earlier, Pope John Paul II and the American bishops have shown a keener awareness.

What Has the "Official" Church Said?

The Church can hardly claim leadership in this field. Fortunately, however, neither is it guilty of wholly ignoring the issues. Arriving late is better than missing an event altogether.

One might first ask, "Does it matter? Why so?" For our discussion, what the official Church says does matter; it fills an important place in the argument, in the case at hand. If the Church has taken a stand, we then ask: (1) what is that stand, (2) what are the merits of that stand, and, for this discussion, (3) does it apply adequately or inadequately to population issues? We shall return to these questions.

An assumption underlies this inquiry: population issues and dynamics interact deeply with environmental issues and dynamics. Ultimately inseparable, each entails the other. The University of Michigan project abundantly demonstrates the relationship as elusive, variable, but real— "closely intertwined in real life, [but] separate in much of our thought and action."[27]

For the World Day of Peace (January 1) 1990, Pope John Paul presented his statement on *The Ecological Crisis: A Common Responsibility,* which (to this date of writing) remains his major utterance on this issue. He has returned to the theme briefly several times. His statement testifies unequivocally to a global ecological crisis. The pope avoids the minimizing reservations, suspicions, and even antagonisms that characterize Vatican approaches to population—a topic unmentioned in the ecological statement. One reason is obvious: in the broad ecological area the official Church does not encounter the challenge to its established positions on reproductive issues that it encounters in population concerns.

The pope states that "proper ecological balance will not be found *without directly addressing the structural forms of poverty.*" How does the pope perceive such "structures"?

> Rural poverty and unjust land distribution in many countries for example, have led to subsistence farming and to the exhaustion of the soil. Once their land yields no more, many farmers move on to clear new land, thus accelerating uncontrolled deforestation, or they settle in urban centers which lack the infrastructure to receive them. Likewise, some heavily indebted countries are destroying their natural heritage, at the price of irreparable ecological imbalances, in order to develop new products for export. In the face of such situations it would be wrong to assign responsibility to the poor alone for the negative environmental consequences of their actions. Rather, the poor, to whom the earth is entrusted no less than to others, must be enabled to find a way out of their poverty. This will require a courageous reform of structures, as well as new ways of relating among peoples and states.[28]

The pope clearly sketches here the interaction of distressed populations with their environment. Not surprisingly but eloquently the pope emphasizes that "the ecological crisis is a moral issue"—part of a larger "profound moral crisis of which the destruction of the environment is only one troubling aspect." Merely "better management or a more rational use of earth's resources," albeit crucial, is not enough, not reaching the source. A "moral problem" is thus more than pragmatic, more than efficiency or inefficiency; rather, it penetrates to the level of human choices, human values, decisions, exploitations, and patterns of deliberate domination, of privilege rigidly (often brutally) maintained. As someone stated when the American bishops issued their 1986 statement on economic justice, "Many see the economy like an engine; the bishops see it resembling a family"—subject to choices as well as to deep, chronic, humanly deliberate dysfunction.

In 1991 the American bishops issued a well-crafted statement, *Renewing the Earth: An Invitation to Reflection and Action on Environment in Light of Catholic Social Teaching,* a more detailed analysis than the pope's.[29] After an interval in which this document seemed simply unknown to the general public the U.S. Catholic Conference issued and widely disseminated an excellent resource workbook for parishes. This contains the bishops' statement plus numerous materials well adapted to pastoral use, moving the Church toward action beyond words.[30] A long road stretches ahead.

The bishops cover some of the same ground as the pope, but offer a more directly didactic analysis. Despite a very brief scriptural section, they expand richly on "Catholic Social Teaching and Environment" under nine categories. One of these, "Consumption and Population," asserts bluntly that "Consumption in developed nations remains the single greatest source of environmental destruction."

After discussing "sustainable development" as an instrument toward population balance, they recall the acknowledgments of Popes Paul VI and John Paul II of "a demographic problem." Unsurprisingly they reiterate the established position on contraception, twice objecting to "coercive population control programs"—overlooking the non-coerced desires for fertility assistance of unnumbered couples worldwide. The bishops close with appeals to nine groups (which covers everyone) to recognize responsibility in these issues.

While advocating that the Church can and should move beyond the familiar "established position" I nonetheless applaud the general ecological sensitivity and pastoral initiative of these statements, papal and episcopal. They deserve a genuine pastoral welcome and wide utilization.

Ecology and "The Common Good"

Another factor in Catholic social teaching applies powerfully to environmental and population issues alike—"the common good."[31] Catholic theology is deeply communal; we human beings are created by God for more than our own individual well-being. We are social, societal, and community beings. Consider the following three sources.

1. Vatican II (*Constitution on the Church in the Modern World,* no. 26) emphasizes that human beings are created social—indispensably needful of each other in countless ways, needful therefore of society itself. Today "because of the closer bonds of human interdependence and their spread over the whole world we are witnessing a widening of the role of the common good—the sum total of social conditions which allow people, either as groups or individuals, to reach their fulfillment more fully and easily."

2. Pope John Paul II (*On Social Concerns,* encyclical 1987, no. 38): "It is above all a question of interdependence, sensed as a system determining relationships in the contemporary world in its economic, cultural, political and religious elements, and recognized in this way, the correlative response as a moral and social attitude, as a 'virtue' is solidarity. This then is not a feeling of vague compassion or shallow distress at the misfortunes of so many people, both near and far. On the contrary, it is a firm and persevering determination to commit oneself to the common good; that is to say, to the good of all and of each individual because we are all really responsible for all "(note: the pope's favored term in this regard is "solidarity").

3. The American Catholic Bishops (*Economic Justice for All,* pastoral letter, 1986): over two dozen references to the "common good."

Today's community is global. Today's common good is global. Population problems are, in Paul Kennedy's phrase (above) truly "transnational." Although net population increases concentrate in the developing world, the resultant problems cannot really be confined or constrained. Destabilizing migrations, aggravated regional antagonisms (e.g., competition for water resources in the volatile Middle East) are only some of the problems that can, as Jennifer Mitchell states, "ripple out...to encompass the world as a whole."[32]

Surely, reading these "signs of the times," we meet considerable pressure for change on behalf of the global common good. If that reality is little recognized by the average citizen and government, a similar limited vision ought not characterize the Church. "Horrendous gaps in minimal decency of life for millions" *must* have their impact on theological and ecclesial vision.

Without reference to population, Jesuit theologian Philip Land sees our conventional and accepted notion of the common good as now in need of reassessment.

A number of observers have found the Catholic concept of the common good inadequate to meet the reality of the eco-challenge. For it must now embrace the entirety of creation, inanimate as well as human society.... My formulation of an extension of the principle is two-fold: (1) the common good should include the ecological in the conditions of social living of humanity; (2) equally important, the object of the common good, the community served by it, should embrace the entire creation.[33]

In Land's persuasive comment I particularly underscore his reference to the "social living of humanity"—emphatically, our compassionate focus here. In the encyclical quoted above (*On Social Concerns*), the pope also ties the common good to ecological concerns, and to "the moral character of development." Preeminently and inexorably, environmental concerns involve the common good, transcending borders of every sort.

A 1997 report from the Johns Hopkins University, *Population Information Program,* documents the *absence* of the common good on the transnational horizon.

In many developing countries rapid population growth makes it difficult for food production to keep up with demand. Helping couples prevent unintended pregnancies by providing family planning would slow the growth in demand for food. This would buy time to increase food supplies and improve food production technologies while conserving natural resources.

While the global economy produces enough food to feed the world's 6 billion people—if food were better distributed—many people lack access to enough food for a healthy life. In particular, the UN Food and Agriculture Organization (FAO) has identified 82 poor countries that are at particular risk, do not produce enough food domestically, confront serious constraints to producing more food, and cannot import enough to make up the deficit....

Each year about 18 million people, mostly children, die from starvation, malnutrition, and related causes. An estimated two billion suffer from malnutrition....[34]

What are the implications for a Church (and nations) sensitive to the common good?

What the "Unofficial" Church Says About Ecology

Across a broad Christian spectrum, religious appreciations of the natural world are growing steadily. I wish here more to record and evaluate that plain fact than to itemize it at any length. Many theologians, religious thinkers, authors, and educators—the "unofficial" church—now participate in the dialogue.

So substantial now is this body of thought and action—while still undeniably in early stages of development—that Max Oelschlager can construct a well-reflected case that the very future of society's environmental wisdom and practice depends on the church. He states that "environmentalism is more than anything else a debate over the common good"—a debate to which only religion can bring the indispensable ethical and spiritual values.[35] You may agree or disagree with his thesis, but its very presence testifies to and interprets a growing body of thought, writing, and action. Popes and Catholic hierarchy, although acknowledged, are only some voices in this large choir.

From Catholic sources the following few titles demonstrate and typify the increasing theological attention to the environment.

• Barbara Ward, *Progress for a Small Planet* (Norton, 1982).

• Albert LaChance, John Carroll, eds., *Embracing Earth: Catholic Approaches to Ecology* (Orbis Books, 1994).

• Drew Christiansen, Walter Glazer, eds., *And God Saw That It Was Good: Catholic Theology and the Environment* (U.S. Catholic Conference, 1997)

• John Haught, *The Promise of Nature: Ecology and Cosmic Purpose* (Paulist Press, 1993).

Thomas Berry, Passionist priest and "geologian," stands as Catholicism's singular pioneer in ecological reflection. The following spell out his perspectives.

• Berry, *Dream of the Earth* (Sierra, 1988).

• Berry with Thomas Clarke, *Befriending the Earth: A Theology of Reconciliation Between Humans and the Earth* (Twenty-Third Publications, 1991).

• Anne Lonergan, Caroline Richards, eds., *Thomas Berry and the New Cosmology* (Twenty-Third Publications, 1988).

Clearly, an environmental consciousness is growing, religiously. And concern for population issues must fit coherently and with consistence into our overall theology of the environment. Excessive population as well as excessive consumption and abuse of resources damages the environment. A deteriorated environment reacts on human well-being, regionally, and, even, in the long run, globally. Neither consequence is compatible with the eco-justice—the common good—to which, under God, we are committed.

Conclusions About Population, The Global Context

Earlier, as we began a brief survey of official Catholic comment on environment, ecology, and nature, we asked three questions: (1) What is the "official" stance? (2) What are the merits of that stance? (3) Does that stance *deal adequately or inadequately with issues of population?* We return to those questions now.

The first question is answered in our survey itself. The Church has belatedly but substantively responded at both the Vatican and the U.S. levels. Second, the merits of that stand, collectively considered: genuinely favorable—appreciations were stated along with acknowledged limitations. The crucial final question remains: application to the issues of population. These official Catholic statements remain partial and inadequate, measured against the stern nature of population issues.

"Inadequate" is not synonymous with "wholly unsatisfactory," but at least in this instance we see a road as yet only partially traveled. We spoke earlier (Chapter Four) of the Catholic theological tradition of doctrinal development, which inherently (and humanly) always includes an element of inadequacy preceding a transition to a new level of adequacy. In that sense one may thus ascribe a certain theological "normalcy" to that which is inadequate, assuming openness to further growth and development. There can be no delusion, however, as to the difficulty in this instance, because of the enormous official insistence on the present position.

The official Catholic position affecting population issues, concentrated upon and radiating from the *Humanae Vitae* prohibition of "artificial birth control," conflicts with the Vatican's own acknowledgment of demographic challenges of truly broad dimensions. A moral position rooted in private, individual ethics is inadequate. This exceptionless ethic neither accepts nor accommodates to the stark realities commonly involved for numberless individuals, couples, and families in straitened circumstances.[36] Nor does it accommodate to the stark realities facing many individual nations, and at last the global community itself.

At the same time, paradoxically, there is a strong, appreciated element of *adequacy*, of strength, in the Vatican position—insistently demanding attention to the socioeconomic imbalances so significant in sustaining impoverished structural situations. This adequacy pertains as well to underscoring Western patterns of excessive consumption, and the role of this consumption in sustaining global inequities and even high fertility in Third World areas.

Thomas Berry and others have helped us see how profoundly we humans are social beings, community members. Individuality is by no means lost or smothered thereby; someone has well said that "orchestras do not mean the end of violins." This wider, widest orchestral context is each person's ultimate human reality and responsibility, under God.

Questions for Reflection and Discussion

1. The opening quotation from Amartya Sen summarizes a major emphasis of this book. What is meant by an "isolationist view of population"? Isolated from what?

2. How would you summarize the point or purpose of this chapter? How do population and environment relate to each other?

3. Not unlike evidence presented in a court trial, what does the "evidence" from Brazil prove—or at least suggest?

4. What valuable points do you see in the statements by the pope (1990) and the bishops (1991)? Is it appropriate for the official Church to speak about such issues?

5. How does the concept of the common good apply to these issues? Does the common good imply an obligation of some sort? If so, why and for whom? Do you see a connection between the common good and the opening quotation from Pope John Paul II?

The accelerated pace of history is such that one can scarcely keep abreast of it. The destiny of the human race is viewed as a complete whole, no longer, as it were, in the particular histories of various peoples: now it merges into a complete whole.

—SECOND VATICAN COUNCIL [1]

The achievement of this unity of humankind is a task for Christians: not a mere side-interest but a task for all, and especially for authorities in the churches....

—KARL RAHNER[2]

A Global Religious Vision—and Population

The dictionary defines "catholic" as first of all universal, all-inclusive. A catholic interest in art might range from prehistoric cave drawings to Salvador Dali. Religiously it implies that the Roman Catholic Church reaches out to all, is concerned for all; globe-traveling popes symbolize that essential aspect of the faith. In his splendid history of the papacy Cambridge University's Eamon Duffy states that "For Roman Catholics the story of the popes is a crucial dimension of the story of the providential care of God for humankind in history." Note, "humankind," all, despite many sins and failings.[3]

This wide embrace of the faith is the focus of this chapter (involving population phenomena inescapably). Thus when we speak of the human family we refer not only to the role of family itself in personal and societal life—but to humankind totally, viewed as a family under God.

Humankind: One Family of God

In Pope John Paul II's "apostolic exhortation" on the family (*Familiaris Consortio*), after extensive discussion of the family within God's plan—including an impressive fourteen-point "charter of family rights"—we encounter this poignant statement.

> There exist in the world countless people who unfortunately cannot in any sense claim membership in what could be called, in the proper sense, a family. Large sections of humanity live in conditions of extreme poverty in which promiscuity, lack of housing, the irregular nature and instability of relationships and the extreme lack of education make it impossible in practice to speak of a true family.[4]

Discussing poverty, population, and development, sociologist Ivy George provides evidence documenting the pope's words. She tells of "poor Indian parents driven to sell their children into bonded labor to nearby carpet factories, which export their product to the United States."[5] In neighboring Pakistan Jonathan Silvers reports that

> child labor has assumed epidemic proportions...estimated realistically in the region of eleven to twelve million...at least half under the age of ten...[including] yoked teams of three-, four-, and five-year-olds who plough, seed, and glean fields from dawn to dusk.... The child labor pool is inexhaustible, owing in part to a birth rate among the world's highest and to an education system that can accommodate only about a third of the country's school-age children.

He further states that "the worldwide population of children under fourteen who work full-time is thought to exceed 200 million."[6]

These children scarcely live a human life, much less a family life. Such bitter realities for parents and children alike deserve sensitive appraisal in formulating moral judgment and criteria—a challenge to any "one size fits all" morality, any concept of moral demand that discounts brutal facts of life—or non-life. The international and interfaith conference on population (Genval, Belgium, 1994, reported later in this chapter) said pointedly, "Issues concerning these needs are as urgent to faith communities as are debates over reproductive rights and policies."

We celebrate the *individual* family where it can flourish, and lament it when afflicted or absent. But a religious sense of the human family *in toto*, in the largest meaning, is also incumbent on all who attempt to see humankind itself with "the mind of Christ," his values and perceptions.[7] Paul encouraged us to take on that Christ-mentality—the antithesis of a merely private morality, any exclusive "save my soul" emphasis in religion, too common, too rarely challenged.

The Catholic and general Christian theological tradition carries strong sensitivity to themes of humankind as a family. Whatever, therefore, threatens the well-being of that family-totality requires a response from the Church. Whatever might contribute positively to an increase of that well-being also calls to the Church. One can admire the global travels of Pope John Paul II as one acknowledgment of that call, with human dignity and the welfare of families among his constant emphases.

In a richly provocative phrase Karl Rahner speaks of "the growing unity of mankind as a positive task for mankind" (which, he adds, forces "faith into a situation that has never hitherto existed"—a "situation" and "task" that in this book we have closely connected to population concerns, issues, and phenomena).[8] One has only to reflect on the torrent of international crises—wars, natural disasters, migrations, environmental threats, ethnic antagonisms, political and economic instabilities—to grasp the reality of all this. Even if these are usually remote from the average individual's daily concerns for making a living, sustaining relationships, and coping with the pressures at hand, their reality remains.

Jesus himself insistently spoke of God with a family metaphor, "Father"—emphasizing not gender, but a parental-type, familial-type relationship of love, intimacy, guidance, and nurture. "And when *you* pray, say Our Father...."

This underscores a faith perception of humanity itself as a family, *in toto*. While not employing the term "family," Wilfred Cantwell Smith, a noted scholar of world religions, states that "one of the most determinative characteristics of any human being is whom he or she means in saying 'we.'" Who, ultimately and totally, are included in "we"? The growth of religion and civilization itself calls on us now to mean nothing less than

> "we human beings," across the globe, across the centuries: we persons on earth, in all our vast diversity of historical development, cultural particularism, and in our case religious commitment. It requires erudition, critical acumen, imaginative sympathy, and penetrating understanding; it takes time, effort, and dedication; but it is now possible, and therefore requisite, to learn to say, and to mean, that we human beings on earth are diverse but not incongruous. Our solidarity precedes our particularity, and is part of our self-transcendence. The truth of all of us is part of the truth of each of us. [9]

This unity of humankind, increasingly realized, stands as a norm and measure of all that is right and all that is wrong in humanity's often agonized, occasionally exhilarating struggles within itself. However largely ignored or grossly violated, the Christian religious or theological or doctrinal foundations for such a global perception of humankind's foundational unity, of human familyhood before God, are easily highlighted. Consider these Christian doctrines—with room for more.

1. A common Creator and common destiny for all humankind, individually and collectively.

2. Common sinfulness, alienation from God, needful of redemption and reconciliation.

3. A common Savior and Redeemer, expressing God's love for all by living, dying, and rising for all.

4. The biblical injunction to love one's neighbor, generically, whomever and wherever that "neighbor" be—without reference to ethnic or national boundary. Indeed, even to love one's enemies!

5. A common home, Earth, on which every human being is equally dependent in every moment of existence for air, food, water, shelter, and mutual human support. The goods of the earth (considered as basic necessities), as Pope John Paul repeatedly emphasizes, were "originally destined for all"—but to which millions have utterly inadequate access.

6. The common obligation of reverence toward the Creator, and toward the creation of which we are a part and on which we mutually depend.

7. A common need for those fundamental benefits that sustain growth and support of the body, the mind, and the spirit (e.g., education, peace, basic political and economic stability).[10]

The Genval Conference (reported below in eleven themes) provides one very practical expression, urgent and analytical, of a unitary perception of humankind as a family, a network of living relationships, of responsibility and caring.

Another Vatican Voice

One does not customarily consult *The Wall Street Journal* (from the world of business and finance) for the latest religious news or theological insight. But in that unlikely forum, shortly before the 1994 Cairo population conference, the Vatican's chief press spokesman, Dr. Joaquin Navarro-Valls, wrote an essay for the editorial pages.[11]

Dr. Navarro-Valls wrote—primarily in reference to volatile abortion disputes—that at Cairo, "Civilization is at stake. We would be foolish to see... anything else." But the existence or reality of a "world population crisis, however much disputed on empirical grounds [is]... a doubtful view," he states, minimizing the very purpose for which the massive conference was convened. He does, however, grant that "the issue of human life and population undergirds all others." In our "dishonest age," Navarro-Valls praises Pope John Paul, "courageous enough to stand firm when everyone else compromises with the essential dignity of man"—a gratuitous disparagement of any who disagree with the pope.

Yet as this chapter is begun, National Public Radio reports that China's population now stands at 1.2 billion, five years earlier than predicted, with 1.5 billion forecast by the year 2040.[12] This latest level is reached despite "a growth rate already slashed by more than half after almost two decades of a strictly enforced policy of one child per couple." China's mixture of (a) double-digit economic growth in one of the world's largest markets, (b) a limited resource base, and (c) an expanding population, provokes considerable anxiety. However one evaluates China's Draconian government, or its abysmal human rights record, population prospects in that vast land are undeniably problematic. And if China has a problem, *we all do*—in an ever more tightly interdependent world.

Another current report turns to global water constraints. In 1980 1.8 billion global citizens lacked safe drinking water; 1.7 billion lacked adequate sanitation. The United Nations organized a decade of remedial effort that newly supplied 1.3 billion persons with safe water, 750 million with sanitation. Within *the same time frame*, however, population growth continued at about 90 million annually—so that at the end of the decade the number lacking minimal water resources remained approximately unchanged.[13] Sandra Postel, specialist in water resources, states, "It's an *Alice in Wonderland* situation; you have to run as fast as you can to stay in one place."

Dr. Navarro-Valls is surely entitled to his view, and the Vatican's, that such phenomena are of dubious import. Many others see it differently. Some of them convened in the conference detailed below.

An Interfaith Conference: Population and Development

Preceding the historic 1994 Cairo conference on population issues, Chicago's Park Ridge Center for the Study of Health, Faith and Ethics convened an "International and Interfaith Consultation: World Religions and the 1994 United Nations International Conference on Population and Development," at Genval, Belgium, May 4-7, 1994. The Genval conference comprised thirty participants from Protestant, Jewish, Catholic, Muslim, Hindu, Buddhist, Japanese, Chinese, and African religions. (The invited participants at Genval were not necessarily "official" representatives of their respective faith traditions and communities.)

Conferences on global issues are often discounted as largely rhetorical exercises, harmless adventures in socialization and blandness. But in the relative newness of global population challenges, at a time when ecumenical consciousness struggles for authentic engagement and expression, this conference deserves attention. Vigor, courage, and initiative characterize the conference report—a unique pooling of religious energies with the U.N.'s "secular" efforts. Genval exemplifies the maxim that much can be accomplished in this world if we disregard who receives the credit. Here the "common good" was respected as a reality, a motive, a compelling force—which it should be for those for whom the God of creation is all in all—"in whom we live, and move, and have our being."

The "Preface" of the 20-page Genval Report[14] sets forth the purposes of the event.

The religious communities of the world have a large investment in issues connected with the words *population* and *development.* All would explain that the root of that concern lies in a witness to what is sacred.... The intent was practical: to articulate the interests and witnesses of religious communities on the themes of the [then forthcoming; Cairo, 9/94] U.N. International Conference on Population and Development and to seek points of convergence on these urgent issues.... The faiths share a regard for human persons both as individuals and in communities.... What impressed conferees at Genval was the surprising number of themes on which there was convergence.

With admirable brevity and readability the Genval conference (or "consultation") developed eleven themes to articulate common religious affirmations, their "points of convergence on these urgent issues." Listing these eleven themes (with excerpts from the Report's comments on each) suggests the positive direction and potential of interfaith collaboration in population concerns.

1. On freedom of religion and conscience, and in the role of religious communities in international debate on public policy. "Religious groups themselves must respect the beliefs and values of others, because no single faith may claim final moral authority in international discourse."

2. On the population and development crisis. "People of faith across the boundaries of particular traditions, because of their religiously inspired concern for the health and well-being of persons and the environment, agree that a population and development crisis exists.... Most recognize complex linkages among the issues and an urgent need for the international community to address these factors simultaneously."

3. On the development, consumption, and the maldistribution of resources. "Overconsumption by individuals and within whole societies is seen as problematic in virtually all faith communities and their classic texts. This concern is intensified when overconsumption results in pollution of the environment and depletion of irreplaceable resources. No consensus exists on how overconsumption by the affluent may confound development in poorer countries. But virtually every religion instructs adherents to attend to the needs of the poor...."

4. On humans and the natural environment. "God-centered religions speak of the natural environment as the work of a creator or creators.... A sense of the intrinsic value of nature, long prevalent in some traditions, now grows in other faiths as well. The human may be sacred but is not alone sacred."

5. On the role of women in issues of population and environment. "The witness of religions to the equal dignity, rights and freedom of women and men has not been uniform or unambiguous. Many ancient texts and modern interpretations reflect cultures of male dominance.... Basic rights require the participation of women in the formulation and implementation of policy, particularly in those areas where their lives are most directly affected...reproductive health, population growth, development, the environment.... Women need access to education, resources for reproductive health, opportunities for personal development and socio-economic advancement."

6. On religious communities' valuing of families in their various forms. "Religious communities regard the family as the chief place in which the religious and cultural values are transmitted.... Children require material and human resources for their survival and development, and the capacity to provide for these essentials should be a factor in family planning. Issues concerning these needs are as urgent to faith communities as are debates over reproductive rights and policies."

7. On the special circumstances of adolescents. "Neither faith communities nor civil societies can expect responsible sexual behavior on the part of adolescents without providing them information, moral guidance, and education."

8. On contraception as an instrument of reproductive and public health, family planning, and population stabilization. "Almost all the world's religions endorse contraception as a means of improving reproductive and public health, promoting family planning and responsible parenthood, and contributing to population stabilization. Contraception is also seen as an effective way of reducing the incidence of abortion.... Religious communities object to any form of contraception that is coerced...."

9. On abortion. "While abortion is universally treated as a serious moral and religious concern it is treated differently among and within religious communities.... Decriminalization of abortion is a minimal response...protecting the life and health of women at risk.... The view of any particular religious tradition should not be imposed on others."

10. On sex education, particularly in the context of sexually transmitted diseases and the AIDS crisis. "Many faith communities in diverse cultures have been so protective of traditional ways and so defensive about sex education under the auspices of 'others'—secular agencies and other religions—that they have neglected to offer such education on their own and to their own.... Religious communities...should counter those elements of mass media and global popular culture that undermine a full appreciation of human sexuality and responsible sexual conduct."

11. On human migration in a time of unsettlement. "Religious texts address the plight of those left abandoned, homeless, or impoverished from war, exploitation, and natural disaster. Those without homes deserve special attention and compassion.... Religious communities recognize urgent reasons to connect the themes of dislocation and resettlement with those of population and development."

Such minimal recitation risks presenting what might at first glance seem mere platitudes. But the full Genval report clearly exemplifies the value and indeed the necessity of collective religious thinking, exploring, and acting. It constitutes a pioneering, sophisticated, religiously based, ecumenical analysis, a foundation from which others can start and on which they can build. For each religious community to act alone in the face of global challenge seems predictably futile, and assuredly inadequate. Would it not be a remarkable contribution if the major religious bodies undertook an interfaith, international population and development conference? After all, as Hans Küng has well said, "Whether particular tormented, violated, or rejected people are ultimately helped on the basis of a Christian or Buddhist, Jewish, or Hindu attitude may initially be all the same to those concerned."[15]

Genval: Further Implications

The eleven themes of the Genval conference again demonstrate the complexity of the issues we have been discussing. At first glance the logical response to alarms of "overpopulation" would seem simply to be "reduce the number of people." What else? If there are too many, cut back, slow down.

On more careful consideration such response proves eminently inadequate, as the eleven complex themes suggest. Slow down? Cut back? Yes, but how? When profit margins are imperiled, today's large corporations simply discharge hundreds, even thousands of employees, termed "downsizing"—a wretched plight for the "downsized." But it's not so simple to downsize the human race. Any truly humane program of direct fertility control (1) must include the responsible *cooperation* of the participants, (2) must be solicited, not coerced, and (3) lead to a better life-path or life-style.

Again at Genval, working within rich religious motivations, a multifaceted picture emerges: maldistribution of resources, overconsumption by the affluent, attitudes toward the environment, family and child and feminine well-being, sex education, contraception, and migration. Nor would anyone regard the list as complete. As the comment on the second theme states, "we recognize linkages among the issues and an urgent need for the international community to address these factors simultaneously."

The *Chicago Tribune* introduced a major seven-part series on global population by emphasizing this same deeply human, complex character of the challenge.

> Anyone who thinks a nation can pass some law or institute a government program to stop people from having too many children should think again. Government fiats don't work, for the motives behind these births involve emotions and aspirations as complex and enduring as life itself. In fact, many government programs seem to backfire.
>
> The evidence suggests that parents curb their quest for children only when they have hope for a better life and the education to achieve it. The evidence also suggests society ignores this problem at its peril.[16]

A Religious "Solution"?

On today's global horizon of troubled population prospects, however much economists, biologists, demographers, and others may dispute among themselves, the needs of humankind's enormous family persist relentlessly, in seemingly undiminished suffering and deprivation. Religion must do far more than assess, condemn, prohibit, or moralize. We are called to love, to be compassionate, to act, to participate, to take steps, to go beyond and above the barriers that historically divide and restrain us. Indeed, nothing was more characteristic of Jesus Christ than the transcending of boundaries and barriers.

Some may object, "This is no solution." Granted; it is not so intended. Religion, Christian or otherwise, has no "answer," no "solution." But religion has nevertheless a singular, crucial role to play, as the Genval conference exemplifies, a call to develop attitudes and values, to establish and advocate for priorities, to foster readiness to act, to accept involvement, to accept colleagues, to engage in collegial effort.

Questions for Reflection and Discussion

1. Humankind as a family? Can you accept that? Is it at all realistic, considering the wars and antagonisms we see? Are there theological reasons for such a view?

2. If, as Rahner claims, the "unity of humankind is a task for Christians," do issues of population fit into that task? If so, how so?

3. Is there any reason why a Christian in the U.S.A. should care about child labor in Pakistan, or any other distant country?

4. How do you evaluate the Genval conference report? Do any of its themes strike you favorably? Any unfavorably? Since such a conference cannot "solve the problem," of what value is it?

CHAPTER TEN

Even an appeal to God and the gospel does not produce answers to such concrete problems as the population explosion, hunger in the world, or the structure of a future society offering more freedom and justice.

—KARL RAHNER[1]

Every couple has a right to as few or as many children as it wishes. That sounds fair enough, until one meets up with the parallel assertion that every child has the right to adequate nutrition.

—NATHAN KEYFITZ[2]

Population: A Challenge to Moral Theology

IN THIS FINAL CHAPTER WE RETURN TO NINE POINTS RAISED earlier (Introduction, Part II)—part of the current revisioning of Catholic moral theology. We summarize the population perspectives of this book, proposed as part of such revision, with significance for all of us.

Christ and "Social Responsibility"

No parable in Scripture is more poignant than Lazarus depicted by Jesus sitting at the gate of a rich man's estate, begging.[3] His hope even for scraps from well-stocked tables was in vain. But Christ's vivid scene of afterlife shows the roles reversed. The story, of course, reflects a major emphasis in Christ's whole life and teaching.

In his 1987 exhortation at Hart Plaza, Detroit, Pope John Paul II spoke of this parable as "a marvelous lesson in social responsibility which Jesus left us." He recalled that eight years earlier, in Yankee Stadium, he had similarly "proclaimed the gospel charge contained in this parable of the rich man and Lazarus." He then pointedly asked, "What have you done with that parable?"[4]

The pope's message in Detroit was a rich, ringing call for compassion in personal, national, and international life, for sensitivity to the needs of impoverished sisters and brothers of our own time. Explicitly discussing "the international dimension," the pope asserted that "nobody can say any more 'let others be concerned with the rest of the world.' The world is each one of us."

Pope John Paul has repeated that crucial message around the world, forcefully. I acknowledge his emphasis with gratitude. Nevertheless, I have been suggesting throughout this book—in the spirit of Cardinal Joseph Bernardin's "consistent ethic of life" (see Chapter Six)—that a *compassionate reassessment* of official Catholic prohibitions touching population issues is now justified, now sorely needed. Today's destitute are over one billion; unrestrained reproduction increases their numbers and their misery. That parable of "social responsibility" calls to the Church itself as much as to the world at large.

Karl Rahner, Nathan Keyfitz

They never met, esteemed theologian and noted demographer, and surely never before were teamed until quoted together at the head of this chapter. They are admittedly an "odd couple." But I propose them as tenor and baritone, in harmony.

Karl Rahner (1904-1984), a German Jesuit seen by many as the leading Catholic theologian of the twentieth century (perhaps to be ranked among Catholicism's historic scholars), did not specialize in moral theology. Nevertheless elements of his prodigious output carry moral implications, increasingly realized and studied. The quote above comes from his essay "Morality Without Moralizing" in which while speaking to all readers, he speaks especially *to* and *about* the institutional or official Church. The Church, he states, certainly has a highly significant role in moral teaching and proclamation. But this role should be exercised without pretense at knowing all the answers (overly specific, self-righteous), with a realization of the vastly increased complexity of modern life, and a readiness to learn and to change. Ultimately moral decision making before God is the responsibility of those directly involved, directly confronted and encumbered. Rahner thus points to

> autonomous and responsible decisions in the concrete, complex situations of human life which are no longer completely solvable down to the last detail, in fields never considered by the older morality, precisely because they were then unknown, and even now cannot be adequately mastered by a rational casuistry.... Today we see that there are many things which cannot be covered at all by moral theory or casuistry and nevertheless may be matters of conscience of the greatest moment.

Such "matters of conscience" inexorably include decisions by husbands and wives in Bangkok or Rio, in Nepal or Nicaragua about the management and regulation of family size, of fertility in their particular (often sorely straitened) circumstances. Most of these persons, one is aware, give no heed to Catholic teaching. But Catholic teaching ought to be realistic, human, and compassionate in terms of such very real lives.

Nathan Keyfitz has been called the dean of demographers. He is a Harvard and Ohio State scholar emeritus, former head of the Population Program at the International Institute, Austria. His statement above typifies the moral dilemmas that bedevil population studies, policies, and real life situations. He points to a prerogative proper, it would seem, to any married couple (staunchly advocated by the Church). But then Keyfitz asks, "Suppose the world is made in such a way that these two rights [reproductive freedom, right to basic sustenance] cannot both exist once [population] density goes above a certain point? Such incompatibilities of moral principles are not usually acknowledged in official documents."

Moral values, moral challenge, moral dilemmas, and decision making abound in population studies and realities. Who can prescribe, abstractly and from above, the proper or just formula or resolution? Painful decisions in the real world face individuals, regions, governments, social services, churches and missionary units, and the United Nations.

The Church, of course, has never claimed to have the "answer" to population problems. But its absolute prohibitions on key reproductive aspects imply a moral certitude pertaining to the decisions of billions of human beings, in any and all unimaginable circumstances. Those personal decisions are inescapably some part of the problem, or some part of the solution. In that sense, the official Church inserts its own assessment and verdict into a vastly complex arena wherein almost everything human is percolating, interacting, and ineluctably moving toward some future status as yet unknown.

So, we hear both Rahner and Keyfitz, tenor and baritone. Keyfitz warns of massive real world dilemmas. Rahner affirms that Christianity and Catholicism properly and necessarily contribute by helping to create a moral context of compassion and support, of a loving God's care even (especially) for the most burdened, of respect for life (born and unborn), teaching the purpose of a just sharing of earthly necessities, and the obligation of those who have to the have-nots (the Lazarus of today). As in Pope John Paul's discourse in Detroit, the Church already brings singular power to this role. Much moral sensitivity is needed. But, adds Rahner, "God does not relieve us of our secular problems, does not spare us our helplessness. In the Church, therefore, we should not act as if God did so."

Catholic Moral Theology Today—and Population

If God does not "spare us our helplessness," and moral dilemmas such as Keyfitz describes abound, then we have no alternative but to face them and struggle as best we can. And a struggle it is, as so much of life is, with no owner's manual, no blueprint, no clear-cut rule book to consult. In the area called "moral theology" we pull together the best of our religious tradition and our human wisdom to provide some guidance, some modest ground on which to stand in that struggle.

Catholic theology generally, and moral theology in particular (as indicated earlier), experience today considerable ferment, often called *revisioning* (a good word—new vision, taking a fresh look). I hope to contribute to that new vision here.

First, two central points as preamble, as background and foundation. (1) If Christ himself identified love of God and neighbor as the whole of "the Law," that must be central in moral reflection.[5] Clearly, such love does not usually provide answers. Just as clearly, it provides motive and goal, orientation and determination, to be concretized by individual decisions of conscience. (2) The sense of God's holy mystery, and the holy wonder of life given to each of us by God must be vivid. "Oh the depth of the riches, the wisdom and the knowledge of God!.... Who has known the mind of the Lord?" Thus we affirm the unimaginable dignity and drama of our lives—and the inevitable diversity of perceptions both within the Church and worldwide.[6] Our theology in the past has been sometimes charged with having "God in a box," too sure, too certain. God does not so accommodate, any more than the ocean to a cup.

Our Introduction: Part II identified nine points in moral theology that spring repeatedly to mind when moving amidst population data. Let us look at these again, emphasizing how massive social problems— such as population—contribute to a revision, a fresh look at each point.

1. Natural law.[7] This concept, crucial in Catholic moral thought, has received multiple interpretations. Officially an excessive significance has been attributed to physical or organic systems, especially reproductive. Sean Fagan calls this the "blueprint theory" of natural law.

Less emphasis has focused on the indefinable scope of human rationality, which is at least as natural as semen and ovum.[8] Yet rationality is that essential instrument and power with which we confront such daunting complexity as the twentieth-century acceleration of population, nuclear war, moral conundrums within capitalism and macroeconomics, etc.

Natural law can be discerned in the basic human intuition for justice. One of the child's earliest laments is "It's not fair." And, at root, the child is right—fair and unfair, just and unjust, right and wrong, are part of the natural order. The United Nations Declaration of Human Rights as well as our American Declaration of Independence speaking of "unalienable rights" implies the same. A moral structure resides at the heart of human experience, independent of our affirmations or violations.

But the Judeo-Christian mandate of love of God and neighbor stands first. Love of neighbor implements the social nature of the human person, a natural law by which we teach and strive to carry out a loving compassion—for example, to facilitate that "adequate nutrition" of which Nathan Keyfitz speaks.

Natural law interpretations are too readily abstract, theoretical, impersonal. Population issues, on the contrary, involve the well-being of millions of real people who are anything but abstract, and are utterly personal. Let natural law reflection contribute, but not alone dominate. Christ's law of love (John 15:12) requires nothing less.

2. Intrinsic evil. The problem lies less with the concept than with the sweeping use of it by the official Church, an abstract judgment that covers whole categories of acts and thus persons as well. But real actions and real people are not abstract, and not categories.

Like a blinding spotlight, "intrinsic evil" obscures real circumstances, real motives, real pressures in actual circumstances. A landless, unemployed peasant father and husband is said to face the same moral constraints as the Monaco yachtsman, husband and father, cruising the Mediterranean. Do both share a common humanity? Yes. But do both face similar pressures? Does hunger differ from affluence? Did Christ assess Lazarus the same as the rich man?

3. Modes of reasoning: deductive, inductive. Deductive reasoning in moral theology blends well with the formation and application of "intrinsic evil"—first an abstract judgment, then a direct, straight-line application to particular instances, ready-made, evaluated beforehand.

To some extent the deductive process is surely valid and inevitable. In moral study and discussion we *must* make theoretical judgments, in the abstract; we all do it, commonly. But problems arise when there is exclusive or predominant reliance on the deductive; real people don't live their lives in the abstract.

Population data have emerged precisely because our world and humanity have now become known globally, *in toto.* "Globalization" has become a household term. That simply was not possible two hundred years ago. Today we know not only of statistical magnitudes, but a bewildering cultural, economic, ecological, and religious diversity. Inductive reasoning respects all that, and strives to assess its impact and meaning.

4. Basic methods in moral decision making. In the Introduction: Part II, three modes or methods were summarized. All have validity and value. But, as noted above, Catholic moral theology in revisioning gives new respect, new emphasis, to the breadth of human experience, to the changes that occur historically, giving new weight to the relational/responsibility approach.

When Lyndon Johnson, a Texas senator, became president he promoted the civil rights of black citizens in a way then unacceptable to many Southern colleagues, and different from his own earlier position. Asked to explain, Johnson replied, "I know more now."

We all know more now, more about our Earth, our universe, and more about our fellow human beings, globally. Christianity has always proclaimed human solidarity. But now we know much more how necessary and how imperiled such solidarity is. A relational/responsibility approach, while not rejecting other modes, adds a sensitive open-ended response. "We know more now." What do we do about it, as a consequence?

5. Consistence. The official Church, as noted several times, acknowledges "a demographic problem." Yet the prohibitions it maintains in basic reproductive issues, absolute and exceptionless, are simply inconsistent with its own (appropriate) tolerance of exceptions in other areas also of great moral consequence.

The same prohibitions necessarily oppose efforts to provide desired, uncoerced fertility controls—one important part of development (thus poverty relief) efforts. This too is inconsistence, touching the gospel mandate that puts love first. (See "option for the poor" below.)

6. Truth, fixed or evolving? Is not the truth true? What else need be said?

But what we hold to be true at any given time is the expression of human certitude—combining fallible human reasoning with available information. How *true* was certitude of the sun circling the earth, before Copernicus and Galileo observed otherwise?

For traditionalists in moral theology no change can or should occur, because what was true yesterday is necessarily true today. And the seal of the official Church guarantees it so. This attributes a complete and finished quality to our knowledge. Or do we invoke a kind of miraculous quality to Catholic knowledge, insulated from human history?

Demographic knowledge, in historical perspective, is recent. It is new truth, partial, still emerging, moving toward a future as yet unclear. To assume that such a portentous phenomenon (the acceleration of human numbers in the last 150 years), as much as we know it, requires only responses inherited from yesteryear is, to many, an unwarranted assumption.

In a 1992 address to the Pontifical Academy of Sciences, "Lessons from the Galileo Case," Pope John Paul II had this important observation.

> The birth of a new way of approaching the study of natural phenomena demands a clarification on the part of all disciplines of knowledge. It obliges them to define more clearly their own field, their approach, their methods, as well as the precise import of their conclusions.[9]

Those words, it must be noted, were not said theoretically, but in reference to major historic errors by the Church itself. In population issues today we are surely looking at "natural phenomena."

I recommend those wise words to moral theologians, and to the Church itself.

7. *Scripture*. Demographics as such do not involve Scripture. However, in these pages I have noted (1) the Vatican II call for new sensitivity to Scripture in moral theology, and that (2) the abstractly rational quality of natural law would be counterbalanced by such sensitivity. As an example, I cited a scripturally based compassion (Chapter Five), an appropriate response to the suffering of a billion people in absolute poverty.

In a rich discussion of "the moral life," Irish theologian Vincent McNamara states that the biblical text will confront us with "not just a neutrality but an advocacy stance in certain directions—in favor of the poor, of blacks, of women, of the marginalized."[10]

Lazarus at the gates of the rich man, as well as reminders of the mystery of God (eloquently conveyed in Scripture), further illustrate Scripture's rich contribution.

8. *"Preferential option for the poor."* Intense concern for the poor characterizes much population and development literature. The United Nations' *Human Development Report 1997*, an extraordinary publication, is devoted to poverty.

> The world has the material and natural resources, the know-how and the people to make a poverty-free world a reality in less than a generation. This is not woolly idealism but a practical achievable goal.[11]

But what has this to do with moral theology? If morality is a following of rules, perhaps not much. But if morality is the Christian life—inseparable from our total response to God—then the gospel worldview comes alive. "I was hungry, and you gave me food; thirsty... a stranger... naked... sick... in prison...."[12] This surely ranks with the most dramatic passages in the Bible, strongly underscoring why Vatican II called for a renewed emphasis on Scripture in moral theology. The latter then becomes much more attuned to solidarity with the world's victimized, the marginalized, the oppressed.[13]

The U.N. Population Fund's *State of the World Population 1997* has as its theme "The Right to Choose: Reproductive Rights and Reproductive Health." This theme deals entirely with improving the lot of poor populations, stating that "the most practical and effective population and development policy is to create an environment in which people can freely make reproductive choices and decisions."[14] That observation closely coincides with official Catholic emphases.

The Johns Hopkins University's *Population Reports* on "Winning the Food Race"[15] is similarly oriented to what in Catholic terms is the "preferential option for the poor." The Church has colleagues; the "preferential option" (albeit an awkward term) captures an element truly central in Christ's life and teaching.

9. Conscience. I return to a family in Rio de Janeiro (Chapter Eight, notes 17, 36): Somalia and Absolom da Silva and their eight children. Catholics, "all of their children were unplanned, the products of love and ignorance." Living in "one of Rio's more than 550 slums," where only about 2 percent "have even been to high school," both Somalia and Absolom are illiterate, both working. "Hunger is so common that the children learned long ago not to complain," children who "in this most famous of beach cities have never seen the ocean."

The Chicago Tribune's 2½-page account of the da Silva's severely complex, pressurized lives suggests many questions. Who has the right to tell these struggling, well-intentioned people which decisions they must or must not make, before God, in managing their lives? Even the poor have moral obligations and constraints, but ultimate decisions are their own to make. This is conscience.

Choices—Complex and Consequential

Nathan Keyfitz states that Joel Cohen's book, *How Many People Can the*

Earth Support? shows "how biologists and social scientists can resolve their differences…and how we can escape from the population trap…an enormous service to science and scholarship that could help all disciplines."[16] Cohen emphasizes that whatever the future holds for humankind will largely be the result of decisions—choices—made humanly. Or not made.

Such decisions will affect the dimensions of population as well as quality of life for large segments of humankind—and ultimately affect *all humankind,* in all likelihood. Inevitably, choices do get made; as a bit of folk wisdom says, even "not to decide is to decide."

Cohen discerns eleven questions, areas for decision and choice, that face governments, religious bodies, non-governmental organizations of innumerable sorts, scholars, and concerned world citizens.[17] He asks

How many people can the earth support?…

1. at what average level of well-being? (food, water, housing, manufactured goods, health)

2. with what distribution of material well-being? (regional wealth vs. regional destitution)

3. with what technology? (can technological inventiveness keep pace with growth?)

4. with what domestic and international *political* institutions? (standards of liberty and political participation)

5. with what domestic and international *economic* arrangements? (levels of physical and human capital; tools, employment)

6. with what domestic and international *demographic* arrangements? (birth and death rates)

7. in what physical, chemical, biological arrangements? (e.g., global warming, toxic wastes)

8. with what variability or stability? (secured levels vs. extreme variations)

9. with what risk or robustness? (security of citizenry concerning natural or human disaster)

10. for how long? (100 or 1000 years)

11. with what fashion, tastes, values? (cultural values, family and employment values)

Surely such consequential choices are matters of morality as well as the greatest practicality. Such consequential choices involve personal ethics as well as social ethics, private and personal issues as well as vast structural issues. As such the participation of the Church's best and most sensitive minds is critical.[18] At the same time Catholic and general Christian participation can only occur in modest collaboration with numerous other concerned persons. In Chapter Seven we saw scientists urging people of religion to just such participation.

Cohen, in other words, is not a determinist, does not see the future of humankind as fated or wholly subject to automatic, self-propelling processes. It's not all cut and dried. There are always natural momentums that we humans face, as with the great storms or weather phenomena of whatever sort, as with the unstoppable dynamisms of birth and death, growth and aging that we all experience. But choices are made. Responses are decided upon. Decisions matter, determining how we face the challenges, influencing how our world develops.

The wise prayer of Alcoholics Anonymous comes to mind: to accept what we cannot change, change what we can, and seek the wisdom to know the difference. Cohen spells out, as best he sees it, some of the major factors of part two of that AA prayer: change what we can. Choices are to be made, many choices, consequential and determinative choices.

If Pope John Paul could so rightly refer to the global ecological crisis (or plural, crises) as *moral*,[19] the population crisis (closely related, as suggested in Chapter Eight) shares that character. Cohen's delineation of areas in which choices will be crucial speaks to the moral quality of what we have been discussing throughout this book, with implications for the revisioning of Catholic moral theology today.

Granting that predictions of the future and earth's "carrying capacity" can at best be conditional and tentative, Cohen says of such questions, choices, and estimates that "their true worth may lie in their role as goad to conscience and a guide to action in the here and now."

A Final Word

Theologian John Haught (Georgetown University) has for many years taught about the interactions of religion and science. He comments on the preoccupation of traditional moral theology with personal issues—but today new and far broader realities demand attention.

> Our classic moral traditions have been so obsessed with questions of individual rights that they have overlooked the interdependent, relational nature of our existence and that of all beings. It is true, of course, that the ethical emphasis of the god-religions has been powerfully relevant on issues of social justice, but we are just now beginning to recognize that social justice is inseparable from eco-justice.... The pro-life ethic has been associated too narrowly with issues surrounding human sexuality. If it is to be seriously "open to life" it cannot turn away from the global population problem and the additional pressures placed on the earth's systems by the sheer force of human numbers.[20]

Finally, in his history of the popes Eamon Duffy refers to Pope Paul VI having "the greatest but most troubled pontificate of modern times" (1963-1978)—spanning the glory of Vatican II and the contentious encyclical involving birth control. A brilliant and holy man, Cardinal Montini, shortly before becoming Paul VI, spoke these words to the priests of his diocese.

> The Church is looking for itself [in Vatican II, then under way]. It is trying, with great trust and with a great effort, to define itself more precisely and to understand what it is.... The Church is also looking for the world, and trying to come into contact with society....by engaging in dialogue with the world, interpreting the needs of society in which it is working and observing the defects, the necessities, the sufferings, the hopes and aspirations that exist in human hearts.[21]

Those words still ring true, perhaps because they describe a task that is never-ending, never complete. Keenly aware of the limited nature of my own perceptions of these monumental issues of the modern Church and the modern world, I submit these pages as part of that vital process that a future pope so well described.

Questions for Reflection and Discussion

1. Karl Rahner (opening quote) says, "the gospel does not produce answers." If not, of what value is it? Do we not need "answers"?

2. Christ's parable of Lazarus depicts only one poor man and one rich man. How, then, is it a "parable of *social* responsibility"?

3. The opening quotation from Nathan Keyfitz: what is his point or meaning?

4. What is the proper role of the official Church in such large issues as population? Are there similar issues to which the Church does or should pay attention? Can the Church provide answers or solutions? Can it contribute? If so, how?

5. As in the Introduction: Part II, again nine factors from moral theology are highlighted. Do any impress you favorably? Or unfavorably? Why so?

6. Quotation from John Haught: do you agree that "the global population problem" is a "pro-life" issue? If so, how so?

Appendix One: Population Issues in Context

Only when an economy distributes resources so as to allow the poor an equitable stake in society and some hope for the future do couples see responsible parenthood as good for their families.

—AMERICAN CATHOLIC BISHOPS,
RENEWING THE EARTH, 1991 (III-H)

In a concise editorial, Aaron Sachs, Staff Researcher of the Worldwatch Institute(*World Watch*, September/October 1994), encapsulated many of the same perspectives and emphases on population issues advocated in this book (and by the American bishops, above). He underscores that broad human context to which I have attempted to contribute theological reflection. In the final analysis these—the human and the theological—should converge and integrate. The full editorial follows.

Misconstruing the "Population Problem"

The creation of a growing public awareness that the earth's limited resources cannot support unlimited population growth represents a major achievement for the global environment movement. But that movement may also have created a monster. Because the population debate touches on such inflammatory issues, from abortion to the fear of losing scarce resources and jobs, it tends to rile people up before they have a chance to think about what's really happening. Faced with worsening social tensions and uncertain economic prospects, people yearn for a quick and easy solution. They want to blame everything on "overpopulation"—on a horde of irresponsible parents somewhere far away, who are simply having too many children.

In Western Europe, for example, the hottest political issue by far is immigration. Many voters have registered their opinion that "overpopulated" North African countries have no business sending their human surplus to Europe to take away jobs that should belong to native Europeans. In the United States, natives of California have been known to blame not only unemployment but also crime, environmental degradation, and even traffic congestion on Mexican immigrants and their fertile parents.

Just in the past couple of years, however, people with wide-ranging expertise—in women's issues, reproductive medicine, social development, and demography—have come to a remarkable consensus that resoundingly rejects this scapegoating tendency. Overpopulation, the experts have agreed, is not the *cause* of the world's problems, but the *effect* of an underlying socioeconomic inequity— between rich and poor, and between the industrialized and developing worlds. It is not the disease, but only a symptom.

Of course, higher population densities do exacerbate the core problem of social and environmental decay. But population stabilization alone would not make jobs and resources less scarce, or stop political violence, or stem the flow of migrants. There is still enough food in today's world, for instance, but millions are starving because they have no money to buy their fair share of it. In any case, we will never be able to achieve real population stability unless we first create a more equitable social order—unless we actually treat the disease. Many impoverished women will not have smaller families until they can depend on more of their children surviving past infancy; and until they have other means of attaining financial and social security besides rearing large numbers of children.

The legacy of this September's [1994] gathering of United Nations delegates, then—too often referred to as "the Cairo population conference," but actually titled the International Conference on Population *and Development*— should not be a frenzied race to reduce fertility by whatever means. It should be a comprehensive population policy designed to promote universal human justice and well-being. The UN delegates won't have succeeded unless they manage to impress on all of us—but especially on those of us who have enough wealth to look beyond our immediate needs—an awareness that those problems we associate with overpopulation are not just someone else's responsibility, but very much our own.

(For responses to Sachs, see *World Watch*, January/February and May/June 1995.—Reprinted with permission of Worldwatch Institute, 1776 Massachusetts Avenue, NW, Washington, D.C. 20036.)

Appendix Two: Whole Nations in Poverty

Any strategy that reduces poverty sets the stage for a shift to small families.

—LESTER BROWN[1]

If Lester Brown is correct, then any strategy that attacks poverty, whether at a local or international level, will set "the stage for a shift to small families."

Global poverty—especially the poverty of whole nations within an increasingly globalized world economy—is a massive and bewilderingly complex phenomenon. Its major dimensions are dimly suggested by the data below. Bleak statistics of the 1960-70 period are by 1990 diminished further, in each of the five categories.

These "signs of the times" (which undergird population pressures) bespeak the suffering of millions, and call to Christian conscience. In a wired world of instantaneous global investment, jet travel, and satellite communication, our impoverished "foreign" sisters and brothers in God's one family are truly near at hand, irreversibly, as never before.

Share of Poorest 20 Percent of World's Population in Global Opportunities
(percent of global economic activity)

	1960–70	1990
(Global)		
G.N.P. (gross national product)	2.3%	1.3%
Trade	1.3	0.9
Domestic Investment	3.5	1.1
Domestic Savings	3.5	0.9
Commercial Credit	0.3	0.2

Comment:

Poor nations cannot participate on an equal footing in international market opportunities or extend market opportunities to their own people. Poverty is a formidable barrier to participation, whether within or between nations. The very poverty of poor nations denies them international credit, and barriers on the movement of both goods and people cut their potential earnings. The *1992 Human Development Report* estimated that poor nations are being denied $500 billion of market opportunities annually— about ten times the annual flow of foreign assistance they receive. The poorest twenty percent of the world's population now receives only 0.2% of global commercial credit, 0.9% of global trade and only 1.3% of (GNP) global income (table above)....

Participation (the central theme of the *1993 Human Development Report*) is a plant that does not grow easily in the human environment. Powerful vested interests, driven by personal greed, erect numerous obstacles to block off the routes to people's political and economic power.[2]

The 1997 *Report* recalled the much-quoted metaphor of a "rising tide." "The greatest benefits of globalization have been garnered by a fortunate few. A rising tide of wealth is supposed to lift all boats, but some are more seaworthy than others. The yachts and ocean liners are rising in response to new opportunities, but many rafts and rowboats are taking on water—and some are sinking."[3]

Appendix Three: Poor Nation Debt: "A Noose Round the Necks"

Once progress is made here, other concerns start to fall into place—environment, population control, health, education, for example.

—NATIONAL CATHOLIC REPORTER, EDITORIAL (BELOW)

Many poor countries, particularly in sub-Saharan Africa, have accumulated massive debts which are totally unpayable and which hang like a noose round the necks of their economies choking off any likely prospect of future prosperity.

—CARDINAL GEORGE BASIL HUME,
NATIONAL CATHOLIC REPORTER, 3/1/96

In each nation as well as in the global community at large, population pressures exist within a larger context—or perhaps more accurately, within *several contexts*. Surely *that* is the message rendered earlier in Figure 1 (Chapter Five) and Figure 2 (Chapter Eight). Hence, if direct efforts at reproductive control and restraint (contraception, etc.) are to be effective in the long run—*simultaneous efforts* directed to the larger realities affecting people's lives also seem utterly essential.

Some of those "larger realities" appear in a recent report from the United Nations Research Institute for Social Development[1]: a staggering 83 percent of global income goes "to the richest fifth of the population"—at the top. A microscopic one percent goes "to the poorest fifth"—at the bottom. With no explicit reference to population pressures, such a wildly skewed profile of the global economy hints powerfully at the destitution that encourages high fertility in the poorest regions.

The National Catholic Reporter (*NCR*) in an editorial (3/15/96, reprinted below) sketches some of those vital connections, interactions, and relationships in the global economy. *NCR* underscores the international debt picture—largely ignored in the daily media and political discourse—as a major context perpetuating stagnation, paralysis, and misery in many impoverished nations.

The editorial was sparked by comments of England's ranking prelate, Cardinal George Basil Hume, O.S.B., Westminster—addressing "a February 12 (1996) seminar he organized with senior executives of The World Bank and The International Monetary Fund to discuss the multilateral debt burden" (*NCR* 3/1/96). In introductory remarks to the seminar (whose summary report carries no reference to population issues) Cardinal Hume emphasized the concern of his Church for global poverty.

> The servicing of these unpayable debts imposes intolerable and impossible burdens on the most vulnerable members of the poorest societies in our world. The Church is concerned not only out of compassion for, and in solidarity with, the many people who are suffering as a result. There is above all a moral obligation, particularly on those who can influence decisions, to do what they can to ensure that urgent and effective action is taken by the appropriate governments and financial institutions, and that the solutions they adopt are just. Because it is a question of justice, the Church has not only the right but the duty to be involved.

In his message following the Synod of African Bishops in September 1995, the Holy Father made an explicit appeal to the episcopal conferences of the industrialized countries to present this issue to their governments and the multilateral institutions. I see Cardinal Hume's seminar as one small, but I hope helpful, response to that appeal.[2]

The message in this book: population pressures do not exist in a vacuum.

The *NCR* editorial follows.

Poor Nation Debt Calls for Jubilee Year Relief

It was uplifting to hear Cardinal George Basil Hume of Westminster propose recently (*NCR*, March 1) that the celebration of the third millennium begin with rich nations forgiving poor nations' debts. He called those debts a "noose around their necks." He added: "We are on the threshold of a new millennium, which for Christians is a jubilee[3]—a time traditionally when debts are forgiven."

We have not heard much talk of debt forgiveness during the 1996 [U.S. presidential] primary debates. Third World debt is not exactly a household phrase. Yet the debt crisis can—and must—be solved, above all to give new hope and opportunity to the world's poorest countries but also to prevent new threats to global peace and security.

Thirty-two countries are now classified by the World Bank as severely indebted, low-income countries—SILICs—25 of which are in sub-Saharan Africa. The overall debt stock of these countries stood at just under $210 billion in 1994. This was four times higher than in 1980.

Viewed globally, these debtor nations represent small change compared with wealthier nations' debts: around 10 percent of the total debt. However, measured in terms of ability to pay, the debtor-nation burden is insupportable. The precarious position of these debtors is reflected in their relentless accumulation of arrears on their debt payments.

Last year, repayments of $16 billion fell due to these nations, according to Oxfam International. This is equivalent to almost half of their export earnings. SILICs were able to repay less than half of this amount. The rest was simply added to principal and interest arrears. And the nations fall backward yet again.

Today, interest payments account for about one-half of total debt servicing. Arrears, meanwhile, have quadrupled since 1989 to $56 billion.

The case for debt forgiveness stems from a convergence of moral imperatives, economic logic and self-interest. The moral imperative for multilateral debt relief derives from a simple proposition: It is wrong to accept such large-scale suffering and the poverty caused by the debt. No nation should tolerate a situation in which an unpayable debt burden perpetuates the evils of mass malnutrition, disease and illiteracy.

The economic case for debt reduction is similarly overwhelming since it would release the productive potential of marginalized communities and help create a framework for more self-reliant growth. Investment in human capital is being undermined by repayments on debts that are self-evidently unpayable.

Meanwhile, the costs of these repayments are being borne mostly by poor women and children for whom debt is destroying opportunities for health, education and employment.

Additionally, in an increasingly interdependent world, the dangers to stability posed by the deepening poverty associated with debt—such as the prospect of increased conflict, refugee flows and environmental degradation— cannot be discounted.

Debt profiles are usually expressed in financial terms. But the ultimate expression is to be found in the enormous human costs associated with it. Oxfam International offers these human examples:

• In *Uganda*, $3 per person is spent on health compared with $17 on debt repayments. This is despite the fact that one in five children in Uganda does not reach her or his fifth birthday because of diseases that could be prevented through investment in primary health.

• In *Zambia*, between 1990 and 1993, the government spent $37 million on primary school education. Over the same period, it spent $1.3 billion on debt repayments. Repayments to the International Monetary Fund alone were equivalent to 10 times government spending on primary education.

• In *Tanzania*, spending on external debt is double the level of spending on water provision. Yet more than 14 million people lack access to safe water, exposing them to the threat of waterborne diseases, which are the main cause of premature death and disability.

• In *Honduras,* total public spending on debt represented more than spending on health and education. This is a country where more than half of the population lives in abject poverty.

• Finally, in *Nicaragua* one of the most prominent factors contributing to the economic crisis is the burden of the national debt, which stands at $11 billion. Interest payments alone to international lenders sap $260 million from the country's budget each year—more than Nicaragua earns from the products it exports, like coffee and meat.

International efforts to resolve the multilateral debt crisis are at a watershed. Last year, a World Bank task force acknowledged for the first time both the extent of the multilateral debt difficulties facing many countries and the need for debt reduction. Nevertheless, there is substantial resistance to debt reduction at the International Monetary Fund and the World Bank as well as among some recalcitrant governments.

Their message is that multilateral debt relief is unnecessary, or that it would have a potentially destabilizing effect on the international financial institutions, or that it would be "morally hazardous," that is, rewarding the indigent.

The truth is that in many cases the culprits who borrowed the money to begin with have long left the scene of the crime, and those who are paying it back through economic belt-tightening never saw its benefits in the first place. International lenders are not without responsibility either.

Digging to the roots of Third World poverty is never easy. Debt is one serious, but not the only, factor. Others include rapid population growth, instability and unrest caused by civil wars, widespread government corruption and business mismanagement.

Some have likened Third World corruption to the

disease of alcoholism. Nothing much changes before the drinker first acknowledges the problem and takes steps to end long-established patterns. Some international development experts say they see little point in further investment until corruption and mismanagement end.

To get serious dialogue rekindled between debtor nations and international lenders, debt forgiveness, like today's international refinancing arrangements, will have to be tied to measurable development targets, like building hospitals and schools and ending gender disparities.

There is no reason, in principle, why a multilateral debt-initiative should not be linked to specific targets, with the savings from debt reduction used for investment in social priority areas.

Thank you, Cardinal Hume, for reminding us that millions are trapped in desperate financial schemes from which there is no escape. The debt-forgiveness discussion will develop in the years ahead as linkages are made between forgiveness and reform. The essential need is to end the suffering and the poverty. Once progress is made here, other concerns start to fall into place—environment, population control, health, education, for example. If there is will, the paths can be found. Justice, mercy and self-interest all require us to act— and the beginning of a new millennium is the perfect time to get serious about the task.

(Reprinted with permission of *The National Catholic Reporter*, 115 E. Armour Boulevard, Kansas City, Missouri 64111.)

Note:

Population Data for Nations Mentioned[4]

	1960	1994	Doubling Date (projected at current rate)
Uganda	6.6 (million)	19.1	Year: 2019
Zambia	3.1	7.9	2022
Tanzania	10.2	29.2	2022
Honduras	1.9	5.5	2019
Nicaragua	1.5	4.0	2020

Appendix Four: Reflections on Official Catholic Moral Teaching —From a "Third World" Perspective

I am dealing with persons at the concrete lived level of experience.

—ANON. (BELOW)

When beginning work on this book I wrote to a missionary priest, a longtime friend, asking about his contemporary experience with Catholic moral doctrines in a Third World situation. Obviously, I did not know what response I might receive, if any. But the response was prompt and abundant, very much "from the heart." With the author's permission (and requested anonymity) I am pleased and privileged to share it here. The reasons for his anonymity become evident in his text.

His combined pastoral, philosophical (ranging from Aristotle to Descartes), and theological sensitivity will be evident. He was aware of my work concerning population, and wrote with that as the background to his remarks.

I have edited his remarks slightly, but retained the informal style of personal correspondence. I leave untouched his abbreviations: "JPII" = Pope John Paul II; "CDF" = the Vatican's Congregation for the Doctrine of the Faith, under Cardinal Joseph Ratzinger; RC = Roman Catholic; NT = New Testament; AA = Alcoholics Anonymous. The Roman Curia refers to the pope's inner circle of advisors and administrators.

His letter follows.

Dear John,

I was thrilled to get your letter which I just received, so without, perhaps, organizing my thoughts too logically I will talk to you of some very deep convictions which come from my heart.

I no more than you go in for Church "bashing." After all, the Church is you and me—and we all, I presume, are searching for the truth. What I set forth here has a certain tentativeness about it, because I respect the complexity of the real order, and also the limitations of human thought towards plumbing the depths of reality.

First of all: some positive considerations. If I were pope, I presume I too would be sensitive to the world of our times that seems to have lost some of its moral foundations. So perhaps my emphasis would go toward a catechesis at a fundamental level, to address some basic needs of the present.

But as pope I would *propose* what I said, and not *impose* my message. I believe TRUTH ultimately has its own intrinsic appeal, and I do not have to authoritatively use clout to *force* submission to what I say. Least of all do I want to bypass the complexity of issues about which I myself lack certitude. I can live with uncertainty; I can accept risk, and I want to mature to *personal responsibility* for my own decisions.

Let me address the issue of overpopulation at a practical level. I just came from a parish dinner; there were four hundred children, most with no shoes, very dirty clothes (some probably will die of cholera). But the parish priest feeds them every day with a contribution of ten cents from each kid (provided they can pay even that). The kids had some fish soup, rice, bread, sufficient to maintain life.

I was talking this week to a man who said he was going to have a vasectomy. I was totally in accord with the decision he had reached. But in order to protect my loyalty to the Church I could not tell him I agreed with his decision. The episcopate here, more or less, puts out the line that vasectomy is mutilation. Now, let me theologize on this with you.

If I am in a world of absolute substances, I might come to this same conclusion (vasectomy, mutilation). But reality crashes with this position head on. I do not know of a single man who, for the delight of experiencing what it would be like to have sexual relations after a vasectomy, *mutilates* his body for the fun of it. I find essential motivation rests on the reality of *relations* in the marriage.

Aristotle in his *predicaments* moved from observing cosmological change to a conclusion of substance (same substance perdures throughout the process of *accidental* change). *Substance* was the basic predicament; then came the various *accidents*—place, time, etc. Last of all came *relation*. Somehow this may fit satisfactorily in cosmology, but it does not fit God's plan of salvation (as far as I comprehend it). *Relation* has a primacy: relation to myself, to my neighbor, relation to God. I don't know that God ever entered Aristotle's *worldview*—an immobile "prime mover," some kind of a primordial force. But certainly nothing of the Christian God, who in the incarnation calls us friend, approaches us in intimacy, and is not only transcendent, but immanent presence within my heart.

When a man wants a vasectomy I find he wants to respect the purpose of his marriage, to form a "community." *Life* and *love*, which Vatican II had the common sense to say, are purposes of marriage, of equal importance with procreation and education of the children. Hence, vasectomy, it seems to me, has a legitimate purpose in the context of marriage understood as a relationship of life and love. I'm talking here in the realm of relation, light years away from the human being conceived as *substance*, in a non-relational perspective. So I told this man what so often I tell penitents in confession: I cannot give you permission for this operation. *You* have to make the decision! Paul VI and John Paul II will not take your place at the judgment. Your responsibility is to foster the values of life and love in your marriage. The decision is *yours.* This, to me, seems to be the honest pastoral conclusion.

I want to protect my role of serving the people and feel this is the ultimate limit to which I can go without someone reporting me to the bishop, that I'm not in accord with Church teaching. Above all, I am dealing with persons at the concrete lived level of experience. I search for truth with them and they are more experts than I in the lived experience of their marriage. I wish the "magisterium" would be more respectful of lived reality instead of claiming it has arrived at certitudes which can be imposed on suffering persons without listening to their experience.

In the time of Galileo the world of science was saying to the Church, "Look through the telescope." Reply of the Church: "We don't have to; we have concluded through the gift of the Spirit to our absolute conclusion." John Paul II recently apologized on behalf of the Church for its intemperate action of that time. Why continue to impose "certitudes" that are not the result of taking evidence from the involved persons into account? Too often the Church imposes "certitudes" which contradict lived experience of the faithful.

It is my conviction that the pope is a gift to the Church— but that he has nothing to define infallibly unless he does deep homework. Especially when the pope chooses to speak to persons of experience he has a need to *listen* to their *experience.* The Church is the pilgrim people of God, not just the magisterium—and Peter's role (at least according to Jn 21, "Feed my lambs..." in contrast to Mt 16:18, "Thou art Peter...") is a pastoral role. *Splendor Veritatis* purports to be doctrinal; I would rather see an emphasis on the pastoral. After all, "If I *know* all the secrets of the universe, and do not give the primacy to love, I am sounding brass," etc. (1 Cor 13).

Person, relation, and the subject are at the heart of what salvation history is concerned with. I appreciate a principled morality—but ultimately each person must live honestly from the depths of his personal conscience (his heart: we do not live life at the cerebral level, but out of our gut convictions). I believe there is such a thing as *connatural knowing* as against ricochet living by the conclusions others reach and would impose on me by way of law. (Psychology's discovery of the unconscious enters here.)

The Church has not caught up with the psychological advances of the past century. Institutions move slowly, but they should not grind people up in the process by imposing insupportable burdens. I am a little more sanguine here than these last statements indicate. Actually psychology is "sneaking in" through a side door. For example, pre-Vatican II annulments were practically never allowed. The Church's doctrine was all so cut and dried: "Did you pronounce your vows before a priest? The marriage is *ratum*. Did you consummate the marriage after your vows? The marriage is *consummatum*. What God has joined together let no man put asunder." (In the 1950s could a Catholic be a divorce lawyer?)

All this has so much certitude (just like a priestly vocation, and the lamentable "reduction" to the lay state). The whole trouble is that the earlier view did not respect reality, especially the reality of *relation*. The head level and the lived level are somewhat different formalities. Descartes wanted philosophy to be as clear and distinct as mathematics. But Cartesian clarity (for which all too often the Roman Curia opts in its quest for certitude, certitude to avoid the messiness of real life, and maintain, it seems to me, its authoritative power to impose) never quite comes off.

Today it seems to me the Roman Curia reaches its conclusions deductively with Cartesian certitude, but at the cost of credibility. In the era of Galileo we didn't need to look through the telescope. Today: "We don't have to listen to the laity, or to women; we (CDF, pope) have the guidance of the Holy Spirit (you pilgrim people do not). Therefore accept what we say." JPII might as well go on to say, "I will take your place at the final judgment, because this help of the Holy Spirit is what you must accept from me." Somehow there is too much extrinsic authority (juridical authority, not existential authority). Ultimately the Roman Curia will grant, "You must follow personal conscience"—but it certainly throws up all kind of roadblocks that inhibit the laity from accepting its true existential authority. Certitude, certitude is the desire of the Curia. I would as soon take the risk of my personal life. It is my conviction that every person must do this; but I think the Holy See is throwing up real roadblocks.

I adverted to psychology entering by the back door into annulments. There still is the *matrimonium ratum et consummatum*. But today lived *experience* is invoked to clarify a distinction that respects psychology. The couple *clearly* knows what the *words* "til death do we part" mean. But rational certitude and Cartesian clarity must yield to an *experience* at a deeper level: call it compatibility, connatural knowing, or whatever. It is the thing moralists hint at (it seems to me) in the *fundamental option*. This is at a gut, heart level of lived experience. Lived experience has to be invoked, and it's a hard thing to clarify with Cartesian clarity. So psychology, or lived experience, enters into the deepest commitments of life, and they have to be lived out of my own heart and not out of conformity to the expectations of others, including CDF and the Roman Curia.

It seems to me that this ambiguous, "messy" level of my own inner certitudes of the heart has to be respected. "The heart has reasons" that knows not reason (the level of cerebration and the Cartesian dualistic certitudes). The Holy See has yet to probe these depths. ...*Love* is in the order of relationship, in the order of risk and growth; without love, forget the whole enterprise of salvation history. History forever presents us with new moments, with (at times) dis-continuities such as Paul's message for the (unclean) Gentiles. CDF too much lives on past "certitudes," does not admit errors (witch burning, crusades, maltreatment of heretics, etc.). We're always right. Simply, I deny it!

Today the pastoral need *may* be for a reversion to moral certitudes. But as a "creative" theologian I want to respect the work of the Spirit ever leading us *forward* to a new moment of history. Merely to look backward to protect the gold deposit of Fort Knox is to me inadequate. Truman once said, "If you can't stand the heat, get out of the kitchen." JPII has the courage of his convictions and the Lord continually writes straight with crooked lines (as I perceive in my own—and his—life). God bless this strong-headed Pole; he's the instrument of God and God is ever full of surprises.

I would be so much more content if the *monita* of the encyclicals and the Holy Office were to state, "After prayerful conclusion and with a sense of our responsibility to offer to the faithful the best that our current investigation (research) allows, we *propose* to the Church the following *guidelines*." Respect for the human person demands respect for the context of the pressures and the ambiguities with which people live their lives. Our certitude has to be proportioned to the object (subject) we are studying. The human person is forever enshrined in mystery. We cannot hope to have covered every aspect of the sexual and relational complexities in our present proposal.

The Church does not have a good track record on sex, as far as I am concerned. Psychology assures us that repressed emotions grow in strength and we are dominated by them. We are like sentries nodding at the gate, watching for what might emerge from the depths. We need a far more temperate and respectful approach than the CDF's (psychologically naive) insistence on will power—when calling for conformity to its norms. Certainly (to argue analogically) most persons would concur with the Church's judgment years ago that alcoholism ruins families, etc. But the stern words of the confessor, "Take the pledge, don't you see the damage you're doing!" just never worked. Understanding and support by peers (AA) who understand the problem and work compassionately and pastorally with the alcoholic are effective. Condemnation solves nothing; moral righteousness seeking to introject inadequately understood imperatives on personal conscience can exacerbate the problem.

I think the current wave of sex problems in the clergy stem somewhat from angelism and dualism in classical church morality. I think some of these repressed sex emotions and denials wrought by our inadequate psychology and spiritual training reap the whirlwind today.

Questions have to be put: where is the psychological and sexual and spiritual maturity? Grace builds on nature, but I think the stern prohibitions against "lower" nature are reaping their consequences today. I don't want to sound like I've got the answers to maturity in these complex dimensions of the human person, but the inadequate results of classical morals' condemnations are not correct, as far as I'm concerned. On masturbation my own pastoral counsel takes the form: "You are a good Christian, and would like to dominate your impulses, so I congratulate you. But probably you are not going to find yourself free of these persistent urges. But don't focus on them. Masturbation is a weakness, an act totally introverted—but not because you have a perverse heart. Far from it, far from it! But do consider putting into practice a good action in favor of your neighbor, a compassionate word to a depressed person, a glass of water to someone thirsty, a kind deed at home or for your neighbor. I think you could die immediately after indulging the weakness of masturbation and that Jesus will receive you, saying 'Thank you for the glass of water, etc.,—I have not come to condemn but to save.'"

I was talking to a priest from Brazil today, and asked him about the situation there. He told me that many have abortions (my experience here also), and others get vasectomies. I talked to a woman yesterday—six children, three abortions. They want to forget them, but I tell them they will never forget them. But let them place themselves before Christ on the cross. His life was being aborted even as was the innocent life of your three children whom you will be with forever in eternity. Jesus says of you as you kneel before the cross: "Father, forgive her, she knows not what she does." Your children know you are their mother; they accept you, they pardon you, they love you. Carry on a conversation of a loving mother with her child. You cannot forget them, but start to relate to them in a loving way. This is what the miracle of Christ's pardon wants to work in your heart.

I think the Holy See works with "nature," with "substance," "essence," with abstraction. Then you come up with immutable essences that you have concluded to with metaphysical certitude on the third level of abstraction. C'mon: deal with *person*, not with your deductive absolutes. And immerse yourself in anthropology, psychology, the social sciences, and the expertise of the persons involved. Forget your ineluctable certitudes which do not run the risk of human ambiguity and error. This would be far more credible than what you are doing at the present. The worst thing seems to me to be the imperative written into the Curial pieces of moral reasoning. "These are our conclusions; we have the responsibility for your salvation, and *you are to appropriate our conclusions* in the concrete circumstances of your life." I think this reduces Christians to conformists who are supposed to be unquestioning in their loyalty to whatever the magisterium proposes. It seems to me that this is too much a denial of human freedom, of personal conscience. How can the CDF have such certitude on birth control, forbidding for even one moment that you could approve this immoral practice, an (intrinsically) evil act? With practically all the rest of Christendom on the other side of the issue, I find a huge credibility gap in Rome's authoritative decree.

Newman used to say, "The very first 'vicar of Christ' is the sacred inviolable conscience of the individual Christian:

two toasts to personal conscience, one to the pope." It is still RC doctrine, so far as I know, that the ultimate moral norm of concrete behavior must be the individual conscience. Rome too easily bypasses the concrete ambiguity of human life, and would *impose* moral imperatives arrived at deductively without respect for daily life, taking into consideration the concrete circumstances in which Rome's imperatives are to be lived.

Jesus said, "Let the weeds grow with the wheat; be careful about rooting them out ahead of time." Our "head gardener" in Rome at times wants too pure a harvest before Christ comes to proclaim to all the effectiveness of what He has done to save us. There is too much condemnation, a prophecy of gloom, coming from Rome. I just don't see it as the *good news*. Ultimately I am a believer in grace. The 1789 French Revolution, "liberty, fraternity, equality" wound up with too much of the guillotine and very few of the human aspirations achieved. I am a thorough believer in Christ and the Church as well as the sinfulness of man— which includes the pope and Cardinal Ratzinger. But again Church is the pilgrim people of God—all of us weaving our precarious way forward. Why can't we accept the human ambiguities, and propose guidelines instead of imposing timeless inherent absolutes?

Too much Curial "we don't have to search for the truth." We already are in possession of this transcendental (usually a body of thought alleged as beyond the reach of the rest of us). And even *if* the Church (magisterium) did possess *all* the truth, she still should follow the steps of the Master who did not coerce the freedom of the prodigal son, the adulterous woman, etc. Today there is too much *fear* in the Church (on part of priests who must be conformists or get disciplined out of their seminary work, etc.). Helder Camara's seminary is closed. Cardinal Arns, one of the great champions of the poor (São Paulo, Brazil) had his diocese carved into four portions for conservative auxiliaries to mute his liberating voice. The indigenous theologies from Africa and S. America are muted today by calls for conformity to Rome: a far cry from the ecumenism and religious liberty of Vatican II.

This thing about getting into the depths of the human person is something quite serious. I think that when the CDF practically demands an *inner assent*, this is going too far. The inner sanctum, which is something of a "holy of holies" in every person, calls for more delicate treatment: never, never imposition.

There was much talk of Newman's development of doctrine during Vatican II. Excellent, but there also has to be openness to absolutely new discoveries of our time that do not come as organic growth out of NT cosmology. To wit the new factors you are trying to come by in your research on the population explosion, etc., as this should affect the Church's message in our time. Vat II opened windows, talked of a New Pentecost, etc. Let's carry that forward. "When I was a child, I thought as a child, etc.—but now...!" We can't have our hand on the plow and be looking backward to conserve and defend what we did with lesser insights of yesteryear.

To me the RC faith is still the best religion around, and I don't know of another religious leader of the stature and influence of JPII. But Scripture still admonished Peter to (1) put away the sword (as Jesus heals the severed ear)—the Gentiles use clout, such does not become you; you are to serve, not to dominate. (2) Peter protested against the washing of feet, but he needs it as much as any beggar off the street on Maundy Thursday. (3) Don't withdraw from the real world into the clouds of Tabor. (4) Your three-fold denials are to be faced and repented, etc. etc.—So a little less triumphalism, much less certitude, and more openness to the mystery of person and world.—You can add your own notes, John!

My esteemed and eloquent correspondent suggests "you can add your own notes." This entire book is my effort to do just that.

Introduction: Our Perplexing Population

1. Nathan Keyfitz, "The Growing Human Population," in *Managing Planet Earth*, Jonathan Piel, ed. (New York: W. H. Freeman, 1990). Keyfitz is Professor emeritus of Sociology and Demography, Harvard University, past president of the Population Association of America.

2. Jodi L. Jacobson, *Planning the Global Family*, Worldwatch Paper 80 (Washington, DC: Worldwatch Institute, 1987), 11.

3. *International Human Suffering Index* (Washington, DC: Population Crisis Committee, 1992). Poster format. Rates and ranks 141 nations on ten measures of human well-being.

4. Marguerite Holloway, "Population Pressure, the Road from Rio Paved with Factions," *Scientific American*, September 1992: 32. See also Chapter One, note 12 for related reflections.

5. Nathan Keyfitz, "The Scientific Debate: Is Population Growth a Problem?" *Harvard International Review*, Fall, 1994.

6. For readers unfamiliar with Catholic terminology: the "official or institutional Church" refers to three levels. (1) The pope (or papacy) personally; (2) the Vatican, the overall Catholic administrative offices and departments, which often speak and act on behalf of Church policies, programs, and activities; (3) bishops in their respective regions and dioceses around the world. Pope and bishops together are "the hierarchy."

"The Vatican" is situated in Vatican City, the world's smallest sovereign state, in Rome. The Vatican has permanent observer status in the United Nations, unique among religious bodies. "Church" capitalized refers to Roman Catholic specifically; "church" refers to Christians broadly and totally.

7. *Commonweal*, editorial, January 30, 1998. Also, Thomas P. Rausch, "Divisions, Dialogue and the Catholicity of the Church," *America*, January 31, 1998. In controversy, Rausch emphasizes, "the truth is always greater than ourselves...[and] to be Catholic is to be open to truth in all its expressions." He calls for "a certain theological humility."

8. Robert J. Blackwell, *Galileo, Bellarmine & the Bible* (Notre Dame, IN: University of Notre Dame Press, 1991), 179.

9. An impressive volume of scholarly Catholic reflection on global-moral issues came to my attention too late for this book: Maura A. Ryan, Todd D. Whitmore, eds., *The Challenge of Global Stewardship—Roman Catholic Responses* (Notre Dame, IN: University of Notre Dame Press, 1997). It covers many areas discussed in this book, demonstrating a rich diversity of views. Includes useful presentations of official Catholic positions on population by Bishop James McHugh and George Weigel. An early book by a Catholic population scholar, Arthur McCormack, now out of print: *Population Explosion: A Christian Concern* (New York: Harper and Row, 1973). A sophisticated analysis of population issues, including two brief chapters on the Catholic role. See Chapter Two below, note 32, for more on McCormack.

10. For an incisive example of new assessments of "natural law" see Cynthia S. W. Crysdale, "Revisioning Natural Law," *Theological Studies,* September, 1995: 464-484. Also, Jack A. Bonsor, "History, Dogma, and Nature: Further Reflections on Postmodernism and Theology," *Theological Studies,* June 1994: 295-313 (esp. 308-312). Also, Judith Dwyer, Elizabeth Montgomery, eds., *The New Catholic Dictionary of Catholic Social Thought* (Collegeville, MN: Liturgical Press, 1994), article "Natural Law" by Joseph Fuchs, who states, "The traditional teaching on natural law is explicitly defended many times in the texts of Vatican II…yet it is possible to show that a tendency to change this teaching also exists (673)." This article has an excellent bibliography.

While not focused on natural law, two additional articles give strong evidence of revisionist tendencies in Catholic moral theology after Vatican II: Richard A. McCormick, S.J., "Moral Theology 1940-1989: An Overview," and John Langan, S.J., "Catholic Moral Rationalism and the Philosophical Bases of Moral Theology," both in *Theological Studies,* March, 1989. This book attempts to situate and validate global population issues (in their moral and pastoral aspects especially) within that broad revisionist movement.

11. "Decree on Priestly Formation," no. 16. All quotations from the Second Vatican Council (1962-65) are taken from Austin Flannery, ed., *Vatican II, Conciliar and Post-Conciliar Documents* (Northport, NY: Costello Publishing Company, 1987).

12. David Willey, *God's Politician, Pope John Paul II, the Catholic Church and the New World Order* (New York: St. Martin's Press, 1992), 184. The quoted statement concludes an incisive chapter on "The Population Explosion." Willey, foreign correspondent in Rome for BBC since 1972, accompanied the pope on several trips.

13. Mary Robinson, "The Appropriate Response to Humanity," *Presidents and Prime Ministers Journal,* July-August 1993: 15.

14. Shridath Rampal, *Our Country, the Planet* (Washington, DC: Island Press, 1992), 207.

Prologue

1. Lance Morrow, "I Spoke as a Brother," *Time*, January 9, 1984: 28.

Chapter One: The Church and Population, Beyond Statistics

1. *Dogmatic Constitution on the Church*, no. 8.

2. (New York: United Nations Population Fund, 1993), 9.

3. Keith Epstein, "Bureaucracy Stalls, Travelers Die," *Ann Arbor News*, March 21, 1993.

4. Marguerite Holloway, "Population Pressure," *Scientific American*, September 1992: 36.

5. Robert Caplan, "The Coming Anarchy," *Atlantic Monthly*, February 1994: 54.

6. Luke 10:25–37.

7. Quoted in *Ministry for Population Concerns* newsletter, January-March 1994. Spoken to the United Nations, September 28, 1993.

8. Michael Teitelbaum, "The Population Threat" *Foreign Affairs*, Winter, 1992: 64. Excellent, comprehensive article. Authoritative sources for demographic data: United Nations Population Fund, 220 E. 42nd, New York, NY 10017; Population Reference Bureau, 1875 Connecticut Ave. NW, Washington, DC 20009.

9. Alex Marshall, ed., *The State of World Population 1997* (New York: U.N. Population Fund), 4. The theme of the 1997 report is "the right to choose: reproductive rights and reproductive health."

10. Jennifer D. Mitchell, "Before the Next Doubling," *World Watch*, January/February 1998: 23. Her emphasis on momentum draws on John Bongaarts, "Population Policy Options in the Developing World," *Science*, February 11, 1994.

11. Joel E. Cohen, "How Many People Can the Earth Support?" *The Sciences*, November/December 1995: 19. This article draws on Cohen's landmark book, same title (New York: W.W. Norton, 1995), especially chapter 13.

12. Charles Mann, "How Many Is Too Many?" *Atlantic Monthly*, February 1993. On conflicting interpretations of biologists (et al.) and economists: Nathan Keyfitz, "Demographic Discord," *The Sciences*, September-October 1994; Keyfitz, "The Scientific Debate: Is Population a Problem?" *Harvard International Review*, Fall 1994; George Moffett, "The Population Question Revisited," *The Wilson Quarterly*, Summer 1994; Ben J. Wattenberg, "The Population Explosion Is Over," *The New York Times Magazine*, November 11, 1997 (responses, Letters,

December 14, 1997); Amartya Sen, "Population: Delusion and Reality," *New York Review of Books*, September 22, 1994, balanced view by a Harvard economist-philosopher. Also, an excellent survey (with bibliography) of diverse ethical perspectives on population: Sissela Bok, "Population and Ethics: Expanding the Moral Space" in Sen, Germain & Chen, eds., *Population Policies Reconsidered: Health, Empowerment & Rights* (Boston: Harvard University Press, 1994).

13. "Stop Coercing Women," paired in debate with Charles F. Westoff, "Finally, Control Population," responding to, "What's the World's Priority Task?" *New York Times Magazine*, February 6, 1994: 30-33. Also, Sen, *Population: Delusion and Reality* (note 12 above) documents coercive measures, and their relative ineffectiveness. See also Jodi L. Jacobson, *Gender Bias: Roadblock to Sustainable Development*, Worldwatch Paper 110 (Washington, DC: Worldwatch Institute, 1992), esp. "Female Poverty and the Population Trap," 39.

14. William Anderson, Bruce Oakley, "The Prevalence of People," *The University Record*, June 21, 1993. Published by University of Michigan News & Information Services, Ann Arbor, Michigan—"The World Bank forecasts that the number of desperately poor people, those living on less than $1 a day, will rise from 1 billion today to 1.3 billion by the end of the decade. About 750 million of them go hungry every day." *New York Times*, April 28, 1995: C3.

15. Sandra Postel, *Last Oasis, Facing Water & Scarcity* (New York: W. W. Norton, 1992), 58.

16. Ibid., 21.

17. Thomas Lynch, Valerie Dillon, eds., *A Positive Vision for Family Life* (Washington, DC: U.S. Catholic Conference, 1985). Contains the papal exhortation *Familiaris Consortio*, 23-48. Quotation, no. 30.

18. "A Future of Their Choosing: A Sierra Roundtable on Population Growth and Family Planning," *Sierra*, September/October 1994: 54. Ford is also senior vice-president of Pathfinder International, a Boston-based family-planning organization.

19. D. Hinrichsen, "Winning the Food Race," Population Reports, Series M. no. 13. Baltimore: Johns Hopkins University School of Public Health, November 1997.

Chapter Two: The Catholic Record

1. Meinhold Krauss, *Karl Rahner: I Remember—An Autobiographical Interview* (New York: Crossroad, 1985), 90.

2. *The Catholic Crisis* (Boston: Beacon Press, 1968), xiii. The late Thomas O'Dea was a distinguished Catholic sociologist, with special interest in the sociology of religion. This book is a critical study of Vatican II and its significance.

3. Pope Paul VI, "On the Regulation of Birth" *(Humanae Vitae)* (Washington, DC: U.S. Catholic Conference, 1968).

4. Pope John XXIII, "Christianity and Social Progress" *(Mater et Magistra)*, in Joseph Gremillion, *The Gospel of Peace and Justice, Catholic Social Teaching Since Pope John* (Maryknoll, NY: Orbis Books, 1976), 182. This remarkable book presents the author's commentary plus the text of twenty-two major church documents. I draw extensively from this book, gratefully.

5. Pope John XXIII, *Peace on Earth (Pacem in Terris)* (Washington, DC: U.S. Catholic Conference, 1963).

6. This call for population expertise in Catholic universities was repeated by the American bishops in 1973 (note 38 below); both calls have been ignored.

7. John Mahoney, *The Making of Moral Theology, A Study of the Roman Catholic Tradition* (New York: Oxford University Press, Clarendon Press paperback, 1989), 261.

8. Ibid., 264.

9. Pope Paul VI, *On the Development of Peoples (Populorum Progressio)* (Washington, DC: U.S. Catholic Conference, 1967).

10. Barbara Ward, "Looking Back at *Populorum Progressio,*" *The Catholic Mind,* November 1978, 10 and 24 respectively.

11. Second General Conference of Latin American Bishops, *The Church in the Present-Day Transformation of Latin America in the Light of the Council,* vol. II, *Conclusions,* 3rd ed. (Washington, DC: U.S. Catholic Conference, 1979), 15.

12. Ibid., 60-68.

13. Stephen Mumford, "The Vatican and World Population Policy," an interview with Milton Siegel, *The Humanist,* March/April, 1993.

14. Gremillion, *The Gospel of Peace and Justice,* 104.

15. Ibid., 106.

16. Mahoney, *Moral Theology,* 172.

17. *National Catholic Reporter,* March 4, 1994. See also Andrew M. Greeley, "Contraception a Baby Among Church's Sins," *National Catholic Reporter,* October 15, 1993.

18. Philip S. Kaufman, *Why You Can Disagree and Remain a Faithful Catholic* (New York: Crossroad Publishing Company, 1992), ii.

19. National Catholic News Service, "The Cologne Declaration," *Origins,* March 2, 1989 (carries the entire statement). Also Richard McCormick, "*Humanae Vitae* 25 Years Later," *America,* July 17, 1993: 8, summarizes widely varied and continuing dissent; McCormick, "The Church and Dissent," *Commonweal,* February 27, 1998. Also, Margaret O'Brien Steinfels, "Dissent & Communion:

You Can't Have One Without the Other," *Commonweal,* November 18, 1994; Elizabeth A. Johnson, "Responses to Rome," *Commonweal,* January 26, 1996: 11-12. See also Karl Rahner's "Criticism in the Church" in Lehmann and Raffelt, eds., *The Practice of Faith* (New York: Crossroad Publishing Company, 1986), 228-236, reprinted from *Theological Investigations XVII,* a notably balanced discussion. Also, Ladislas Orsy, "Magisterium: Assent and Dissent," *Theological Studies* 48 (1987): 473-497. Nine articles on "The Church Confronts Loyalty and Dissent." *America,* June 27, 1970.

20. *U.S.Catholic,* editorial, October, 1993.

21. September 6, 1994. Catholics Speak Out, Box 5206, Hyattsville, Maryland, 20782.

22. Catholics for a Free Choice, 1436 U St., NW, Suite 301, Washington, DC 20009-3916.

23. Pope John Paul II, *The Splendor of Truth (Veritatis Splendor)* (Washington, DC: U.S. Catholic Conference, 1993). For descriptive and evaluative comments see Richard A. McCormick, "Some Early Reactions to *Veritatis Splendor,*" *Theological Studies,* September 1994: 481-506. Neither the encyclical nor McCormick's critique deals explicitly with population, but both contain much that is implicitly relevant. Also Anne E. Patrick, *Liberating Conscience* (New York: Continuum, 1996), 145-169.

24. Pope John Paul, *On Social Concerns (Sollicitudo Rei Socialis) Origins,* March 3, 1988. At least one (non-Catholic) author has personally and directly addressed Pope John Paul II on population issues. Agricultural scientist Keith C. Barrons, Ph.D., *A Catastrophe in the Making—With Letters to the Pope* (Tampa, FL: Mancorp Publishing Inc., 1991), discusses world population trends and Catholic influence, especially in many Third World areas. He includes five substantial letters (thirty-seven pages) respectfully but urgently sent to John Paul II.

25. "Africa and the Cross," *U.S.News & World Report,* February 12, 1990: 16.

26. David Willey, *God's Politician: Pope John Paul II, the Catholic Church, and the New World Order* (New York: St. Martin's Press, 1992), 164. See his Chapter Eight, "The Population Explosion."

27. Carl Bernstein, "The Holy Alliance," *Time,* February 24, 1992. The Reagan administration at this time was politically sensitive to the "Religious Right," a conservative constituency wider than the Catholic elements within it.

28. *National Catholic Reporter,* May 8, 1992.

29. Patricia Lefevere, "Church, UN at Odds Over Population Policy," *National Catholic Reporter,* April 15, 1994. On this occasion the pope, in the formalities of diplomacy, was meeting with Dr. Sadik in her role as secretary general of the then-forthcoming Cairo conference.

30. "Address of Pope John Paul II to Dr. Nafis Sadik, Vatican City, March 18,

1994," from the Permanent Observer Mission of the Holy See to the United Nations, 20 East 72nd, New York, N.Y. 10021.

31. March, 1974, vol. 35, no. 1. Private correspondence with the current editor reports that the topic has not been featured again.

32. In 1992 David Willey (*God's Politician*, 176) devoted three paragraphs to Father Arthur McCormack, "an experienced missionary priest, for 25 years one of the Roman Catholic Church's leading experts in demographic problems. [His] views are, needless to say, not welcome today at the Vatican." See above, Introduction, note 9.

33. Charles E. Curran, *Issues in Sexual & Medical Ethics* (Notre Dame, IN: Notre Dame University Press, 1978), 168-97.

34. Francis X. Murphy, "Of Sex and the Catholic Church," *Atlantic Monthly*, February, 1981: 50f, an extensive report on the 1980 Synod. Also, Richard McCormick, "*Humanae Vitae* 25 Years Later," *America*, July 17, 1993: 8. Also, Peter Hebblethwaite, "Echoes of Old Showdown," *National Catholic Reporter*, August 27, 1993. He quotes Archbishop Quinn, "The personal and demographic problems of the contemporary world must be acknowledged before they can be solved."

35. Thomas Reese, "The Close of the Synod," *America*, November 8, 1980. Reese reported further on the same Synod in *America*, December 20, 1980.

36. *Renewing the Earth, An Invitation to Reflection and Action on the Environment in Light of Catholic Social Teaching* (Washington, DC: U.S. Catholic Conference, 1991), 9.

37. "Population and the Catholic: A Positive Approach," *Origins*, November 29, 1973.

38. See note 6 above.

39. "Global Population," *Theological Studies:* 68.

40. "Population Control," *Theological Studies:* 157.

41. *Faces of Poverty & Population*, edited by Office of Advocacy Education (Monrovia, CA: World Vision, 1993), 6, "An Exodus Story," Roberta Hestenes. This text carries seven articles from World Vision's Washington Forum of 1993.

Chapter Three: The Catholic Stance: Strengths & Achievements

1. Bishops' Second General Assembly, November 30, 1971, in Gremillion, *The Gospel of Peace and Justice*, 513. A statement of singular importance, affirming Catholic social teaching as *essential*—a "*constitutive dimension*" of Catholic life and faith.

2. Willy Brandt, *Arms and Hunger* (New York: Pantheon Books, 1986), 79. Brandt,

West German chancellor 1969-74, won the Nobel Prize 1971, chairman of the World Bank Commission on International Development.

3. Gene Burns, *The Frontiers of Catholicism* (Los Angeles, CA: University of California Press, 1992), 90.

4. *Popline*, November-December 1993. Cartoon reprinted from *Dayton Daily News*, Editorial, "The Encyclical," Werner Fornos.

5. *Earth in the Balance, Ecology & the Human Spirit* (New York: Houghton Mifflin, 1992), 262.

6. Pope John Paul II, *The Ecological Crisis: A Common Responsibility* (Washington, DC: U.S. Catholic Conference, 1990, publication no. 332-9).

7. Vatican II, *Dogmatic Constitution on the Church*, nos. 9-17.

8. Karl Rahner, *The Foundations of Christian Faith* (New York: Crossroad Publishing Co., 1989), 322. Rahner was a theological consultant to two German cardinals at Vatican II, an author whose volume of output was matched only by his singular insight and wisdom. He will be cited in these pages as a master of the Catholic tradition and a bold pioneer of its future.

9. Karl Lehmann, Albert Raffelt, eds., *The Content of Faith* (New York: Crossroad 1992), 487. Reprinted from Rahner's *Shape of the Church to Come* (New York: Seabury Press, 1972).

10. Avery Dulles, *Models of the Church* (New York: Doubleday, 1974) 205.

11. Fritjof Capra, David Steindl-Rast, *Belonging to the Universe: Explorations on the Frontiers of Science and Spiritual Life* (New York: Harper Collins, 1991), 107. An extended interdisciplinary conversation.

12. Vatican II, *Pastoral Constitution on the Church in the Modern World*, especially nos. 47-52.

13. The literature on this subject is extensive. A solid account of the Church's official doctrine: Janet E. Smith, *Humanae Vitae: A Generation Later* (Washington, DC: Catholic University Press, 1991). See also "The Moral Norms of *Humanae Vitae*," *Origins*, March 2, 1989, reprinted from *L'Osservatore Romano*, the Vatican newspaper. Briefer, supportive accounts: Komonchak, Collins, Lane, eds., *The New Dictionary of Theology* (Collegeville, MN: Liturgical Press, 1987), articles on Birth Control, Marriage, Natural Law, etc. Also: Karl Rahner, ed., *Encyclopedia of Theology, The Concise Sacramentum Mundi* (New York: Crossroad, 1989), similar articles.

14. Vandana Shiva, Mira Shiva, "Population and Environment: An Indian Perspective," 47-48 in *Power, Population and the Environment: Women Speak* (Toronto, Canada: Weed Foundation, 1992), Gillian Phillips, ed. The authors are respectively a physicist-ecologist and a physician.

15. Sissela Bok, "Population and Ethics: Expanding the Moral Space" in *Population Policies Reconsidered*, Gita Sen, Adrienne Germain, Lincoln Chen, eds. (Boston: Harvard University Press, 1994).

16. *Reproductive Rights and Wrongs: The Global Politics of Population Control* (Boston: South End Press, 1995, rev.), 71-2. For further discussion of coercion see Christine E. Gudorf, "The Cairo International Conference on Population and Development and The Need to Monitor Its Implementation," *IN/FIRE Ethics* (Newsletter of the International Network of Feminists Interested in Reproductive Health), issues 3 & 4, 1994. "Reproductive coercion has been and still is widespread." See also Gudorf, "Population, Ecology, and Women," *Second Opinion* (Chicago: Park Ridge Center), January 1995: 59-71.

17. See R. E. Ryder, "Natural family planning: Effective birth control supported by the Catholic Church," *British Medical Journal*, September 18, 1993: 723-726. Also: P.W. Howie, "Natural regulation of fertility," in *British Medical Bulletin*, 1993, vol. 49, no. 1: 182-199; "Natural Family Planning: A Good Option," Rosalie Rodriguez-Garcia, ed. (Washington, D.C.: Institute for International Studies in Natural Family Planning, Georgetown University School of Medicine, 1989), 15-page booklet. Much additional data available from this source. Also: *Natural Family Planning*, publication 395-7, (Washington, DC: U.S. Catholic Conference).

18. Michael Harris, "New Life for Family Planning," *Time*, September 19, 1988: 96.

19. Betsy Hartmann, *Reproductive Rights and Wrongs*, 276, 279.

20. Further on Natural Family Planning: Mitch Finley, "The Dark Side of Natural Family Planning," *America*, February 23, 1991, plus responses, *America*, April 6, 1991; Ruth P. Moynihan, "NFP: What it takes," *Commonweal*, November 20, 1992, in "Correspondence"; Luigi Mastroianni, M.D., "The pill is now safe," *National Catholic Reporter*, July 31, 1992; Janet Claussen, "My Argument With Natural Family Planning," *America*, February 11, 1995; Sean Fagan, *Does Morality Change?* (Collegeville, MN: Liturgical Press, 1997), esp. chapter 8, "Responsible Parenting." (Note: this material does *not* generally discuss the use of NFP in Third World settings.)

21. Nathan Keyfitz, "The Growing Human Population," in *Managing Planet Earth* (New York: W.H. Freeman, 1990), 65f. Originally in *Scientific American*, September 1989. Also: Lester R. Brown, Jodi L. Jacobson, *Our Demographically Divided World* (Washington, DC: Worldwatch Institute, 1986, Worldwatch Paper 74), 5f.

22. Susan Power Bratton, *Six Billion And More: Human Population Regulation and Christian Ethics* (Louisville, KY: Westminster/John Knox Press, 1992), 38. Thoughtful, impressive study by an Evangelical scholar, a biologist. It is worth noting the work of Virginia Abernethy, anthropologist, who rejects the demographic transition model in her carefully argued *Population Politics* (New

York: Plenum Press, Insight Books, 1993). She sees "population growth as the most serious threat that we, as a species, have ever encountered"; she strongly emphasizes realization of the earth's *limited resources,* that "real environmental constraints exist." Such constraints are masked or ignored by the transition model, she contends.

23. Joseph Gremillion, *The Gospel of Peace and Justice,* 604.

24. No. 87.

25. "Population Policy in the Developing World," *Science,* February 11, 1994: 781.

26. "Breaking Population Momentum," *World Watch,* January/February 1998: 26. The author is a researcher with the Worldwatch Institute. Her article is a commentary on Bongaarts' (above) and an update on the impact of the 1994 Cairo population conference.

27. Arthur McCormack, "The Population Explosion: A Theologian's Concern?" *Theological Studies,* March 1974: 11.

28. United Nations Development Programme, *Human Development Report 1993* (New York: Oxford University Press, 1993), 180, Table 23.

29. *Managing Planet Earth,* 66.

30. *Human Development Report, 1993* (and) *1997* (New York: Oxford University Press). *Report 1993:* 10. For "Demographic Profiles," see tables 23, 45. *Report 1997:* see "Changing Demographic Structures," 70; Reproductive Health and Family Planning, 108. Tables 22 and 41 ("Demographic Profile" for developing and industrial countries respectively) are summarized ("aggregates") in Table 47. These include:

World Population:	1960	2,994,300,000
(est., millions)	1994	5,553,800,000
	2000	6,025,600,000

Population doubling date	*Least developed nations*	year 2022
(projected, at current growth rates)	*all developing nations:*	year 2036
	industrial nations:	year 2212

Contraceptive availability, 1987-1994 ("prevalence," percent of married women in fertile years or husbands, using any contraception):

Least developed nations	21 percent
All developing nations	56 percent
Industrial nations	71 percent
World at large	58 percent

31. Mahbub ul Haq, interview, *Common Ground* radio program no. 9338, 1993, radio series on world affairs sponsored by The Stanley Foundation (Muscatine, Iowa).

32. "Development: From Exclusion to Inclusion," in *Center Focus,* September 1993. Also see *National Catholic Reporter,* "Measuring Growth," editorial, December 12, 1993.

33. Lester Brown, *State of the World, 1992* (New York: W.W. Norton, 1992), 7. Also: Goodland, Daly, Serafy, eds., *Population, Technology and Lifestyle: The Transition to Sustainability* (Covelo, CA: Island Press, 1992), advocating not unquestioned growth, but global sustainable development. Also: for a deeply skeptical view of sustainable development see Donald Worster, *The Wealth of Nature: Environmental History & the Ecological Imagination* (New York: Oxford University Press, 1993). See his index for multiple references on "sustainable development," but esp. chapter 12. Worster questions the underlying assumptions, the human capacity to *manage* the natural order. "I fear...'development' will make most of the decisions, and 'sustainable' will come trotting along..." (153). Also: Herman E. Daly, John B. Cobb, Jr., *For the Common Good: Redirecting the Economy Toward Community, the Environment and a Sustainable Future* (Boston: Beacon Press, 1994), esp. Chapter Twelve, "'Population,' and 'demographic transition,'" 242-246.

34. Emily T. Smith, "Growth vs. Environment," *Business Week,* May 11, 1992: 69, quoting John D. Sterman, M.I.T. Sloan School of Management. See also Shridath Rampal, *Our Country, The Planet* (Washington, DC: Island Press, 1992), 141, on "sustainable development."

35. Pope John Paul II, *Ecological Crisis,* no. 5. See my Chapter Eight for further discussion.

36. *Renewing the Earth* (Washington, DC: U.S. Catholic Conference, 1991). Italics in original.

37. Max Oelschlaeger, *Caring for Creation, An Ecumenical Approach to the Environmental Crisis* (New Haven: Yale University Press, 1994), 20.

38. "How Many People Can the Earth Support?" *The Sciences,* November-December 1995: 22.

39. Lehmann, Raffelt, eds., *Content of Faith,* 588-9.

40. *Human Development Report 1993,* 1. See also my Appendix Two, "Whole Nations in Poverty."

41. Frances Moore Lappé, Joseph Collins, *World Hunger: Twelve Myths* (New York: Grove Press, 1986), 32. See their Chapter Three, "Too Many Mouths to Feed."

42. David Willey, *God's Politician,* 115, 130. See also: Edward L. Cleary, *Crisis and Change* (Maryknoll, NY: Orbis Books, 1985), esp. chapter 4, "Grassroots Christian Communities"; also, Phillip Berryman, *Liberation Theology* (New York: Pantheon Books, 1987), esp. chapter 4, "Christian Base Communities."

43. Tina Rosenberg, *Children of Cain* (New York: William Morrow & Co., 1991). Chapter 4, "The Laboratory," describes the murderous social environment in El Salvador where the indicated crimes occurred, esp. 253.

44. Ibid., 206.

45. Alfred W. McCoy, *Priests on Trial* (Victoria, Australia: Penguin Books, 1984), 152. This book also contains much material on basic Christian communities in the Philippines. See also my Chapter Five, notes 27, 28.

46. Leslie Wirpsa, "In Colombia, hope walks hand in hand with martyrdom," *National Catholic Reporter,* January 10, 1992.

Chapter Four: The Catholic Stance: Evaluating the Present, Looking Ahead

1. "Open to Life—and to Death: The Church on Population Issues," in Albert LaChance, John Carroll, eds., *Embracing Earth: Catholic Approaches to Ecology* (Maryknoll, NY: Orbis Books, 1994), 44. Toolan is an associate editor of *America.* "Openness to life" is the crucial phrase in *Humanae Vitae,* Pope Paul VI's encyclical prohibiting artificial means of birth control: "Each and every marriage act must remain open to the transmission of life" (no. 11).

2. Toolan, in *Embracing Earth,* 45.

3. Paul Imhof, Hubert Biallowons, eds., *Faith in a Wintry Season: Conversations & Interviews with Karl Rahner in the Last Years of His Life* (New York: Crossroad, 1990), 38.

4. Ibid., 19.

5. (Some) critiques in earlier pages: Introduction—"one-size" morality; Chapter 2—The Cologne Declaration, 1989; *Theological Studies,* comments of seven theologians, 1974; Archbishop Quinn, 1980 Synod; Archbishop Hurley, 1980 Synod.

6. Pope John Paul II, "Address to Dr. Nafis Sadik, Vatican City, March 18, 1994." See also Chapter Two above, notes 29, 30. For a further account of the meeting of Dr. Sadik with the pope see Carl Bernstein and Marco Politi, *His Holiness, John Paul II and the Hidden History of Our Time* (New York: Doubleday, 1996), 519-524. The meeting is reported, apparently based on Sadik's recollections, as tense and one-to-one. No mention is made of the address, discussed here, published by the Vatican. Reconciling or integrating the two sources is not within the scope of this book.

7. *The Challenge of Peace* (Washington, DC: U.S. Catholic Conference, 1983).

8. *Economic Justice for All* (Washington, DC: U.S. Catholic Conference, 1986).

9. Pope John Paul II, *The Ecological Crisis* (Washington, DC: U.S. Catholic Conference, 1989).

10. *Renewing the Earth* (Washington, DC: U.S. Catholic Conference, 1992).

11. Paul VI, *On the Development of Peoples*, no. 37.

12. Quoted in Mark Hertsgaard, "Still Ticking," *Mother Jones* March/April 1994: 71. For a congruent observation from a Catholic source see David Toolan, "Open to Life—and To Death," 44.

13. See Robert P. Heaney, "Sex, Natural Law and Bread Crumbs," *America*, February 26, 1994, excellent analysis by a biomedical scientist recommending the broader *contextual* or *relational* approach to sexual morality. Responses to his article: Janet E. Smith, "Barnyard Morality," August 13, 1994; several letters, September 10, 1994; letter, Janet Smith, November 5, 1994 (all *America*). Exemplary dialogue on this vital moral issue. See also Lisa Sowle Cahill, "Catholic Sexual Ethics and the Dignity of the Person," *Theological Studies*, March 1989: 120-150, esp. 146. Also, Christine E. Gudorf, *Body, Sex and Pleasure: Reconstructing Christian Sexual Ethics* (Cleveland: Pilgrim Press, 1994), esp. first three chapters on a holistic view of "the qualitative nature of the relationship in which the [sexual] act occurs."

14. Play (1964) by Joseph Stein, music by Jerry Bock, lyrics by Sheldon Harnick. Setting: Jewish village life in pre-Revolutionary Russia.

15. Frank M. Esmonde (Merion Station, PA), in "Letters," *America*, November 11, 1993. For the authors to whom Esmonde responds, see note 18 below.

16. Patricia Lefevere, "Church, U.N. at odds over population policy," *National Catholic Reporter*, April 15, 1994. Also in *The Earth Times*, April 4, 1994, which Ms. Lefevere informs me in private correspondence is "an independent paper circulated at the U.N. and daily during the recent PrepCom 3" (sessions preparatory to the 1994 Cairo population conference). She checked the report concerning the German bishops with two German delegates who declared it to be "a substantially correct rendering of the bishops' statement." I am grateful to her for this data.

17. Richard McCormick, "*Humanae Vitae* 25 years later," *America* July 17, 1993, 12.

18. Kevin Flannery, Joseph Koterski, "Paul VI was right," *America* September 25, 1993.

19. "Letters," *America*, November 20, 1993.

20. "*Humanae Vitae*: what has it done to us?" *Commonweal*, June 18, 1993: 14. Undoubtedly for most Catholics this contentious issue is now passé, settled and decided one way or the other. However, literature on the subject continues to appear, and the emphasis of the present pontiff (as in his address to Dr. Sadik) sustains its prominence. It remains central in the official teaching vis-à-vis global population issues, and thus becomes unavoidable in this book. Abortion will be discussed later.

21. Francis X. Murphy, "Sex and the Catholic Church," *Atlantic Monthly*, February 1981: 52.

22. John Mahoney, *The Making of Moral Theology* (New York: Oxford University Press, 1989), 303.

23. Ibid., 218.

24. Charles F. Harrold, *A Newman Treasury* (New York: Longmans, Green & Co., 1943) 92, 83. Has a twenty-three page excerpt from Newman's *Essay on the Development of Christian Doctrine.* See also Vatican II, *Dogmatic Constitution on Divine Revelation,* no. 8.

25. Mahoney, *Moral Theology,* 325. Also: Komonchak et al., eds., *New Dictionary of Theology* (Wilmington: Michael Glazier, 1987), Thomas Rausch on "Development of Doctrine," excellent bibliography (publisher now merged with Liturgical Press). Also *Encyclopedia of Theology: The Concise Sacramentum Mundi,* Karl Rahner, ed. (New York: Crossroad, 1989), "Development of Dogma"; also *Dictionary of Theology,* Rahner, Herbert Vorgrimler, eds. (New York: Crossroad, 1981, second edition), "Development of Dogma."

26. Vatican II: *On Ecumenism,* 4; *On the Church,* 15-16; *On the Relation of the Church to Non-Christian Religions,* 2-4. Also, Mahoney, *Moral Theology,* 194-202.

27. Imhof, Biallowons, *Wintry Season,* 197.

28. John L. McKenzie, *Light on the Gospels* (Chicago: Thomas More Press, 1976), 14.

29. Quoted, *U.S.Catholic,* October, 1993, editorial by Robert E. Burns. Statement attributed to an interview in *The London Times,* undated. Same statement quoted, *Time,* December 26, 1994—January 2, 1995: 72. See also *National Catholic Reporter,* "Time for Ecclesial Bravery," March 31, 1995: 36.

30. Vatican II: *On Ministry and Life of Priests,* 9; *On Religious Liberty,* 15; *On the Apostolate of Lay People,* 14; *On the Sacred Liturgy,* 43; *Decree on Ecumenism,* 4; *On the Church in the Modern World,* 4.

31. Gerald O'Collins, *Fundamental Theology* (Ramsey, NJ: Paulist Press, 1981), 102f, excellent discussion of "signs of the times."

32. Judith A. Dwyer, ed., *New Dictionary of Catholic Social Thought,* 881.

33. Vatican II, *On the Church in the Modern World.* nos. 4, 5.

34. Karl Lehmann, Albert Raffelt, eds., *The Content of Faith* (New York: Crossroad, 1992), "Truth and the Development of Dogma," 406-408, italics added. This remarkable essay excerpted from Rahner's *Theological Investigations,* I, 1961. See also Gerald A. McCool, ed., *A Rahner Reader* (New York: Crossroad, 1989), "The Historicity of Theology," 89, and Chapter 5, "Scripture, Tradition and the Development of Doctrine," 91-107; bibliography of Rahner on these topics, 365.

35. Lehmann, ed., *Content of Faith*, 407-8.

36. *Summa Theologiae*, I, 7-1. Also, Bernard Wuellner, *Summary of Scholastic Principles* (Chicago: Loyola University Press, 1956), no. 378.

37. See Norbert Rigali, "Artificial Birth Control: An Impasse Revisited," *Theological Studies*, December 1986. Excellent analysis of contrasting approaches to birth control controversy. He emphasizes the differences between a "historical consciousness" and a "classicist consciousness." Also, Christine Gudorf, *Body, Sex and Pleasure*, evaluates the impact of historical consciousness on Catholic interpretations of natural law, esp. 62-74. Also on historical consciousness in theology: Jack A. Bonsor, "History, Dogma, and Nature: Further Reflections on Postmodernism and Theology," *Theological Studies,* June, 1994: 295-313.

38. "What Ever Happened to *Octogesima Adveniens*?" *Theological Studies*, March 1995, 39-60. (Document 18 in Joseph Gremillion, *The Gospel of Peace and Justice*, 485-512.) The cited no. 4, says Elsbernd, "highlighted the historically constituted nature of the social teaching of the Church, the role of the local community, and the difficulty as well as the undesirability of a single universal papal message or solution to problems"(39). Elsbernd teaches at Loyola University, Chicago.

39. Komonchak et al, eds., *New Dictionary of Theology*, article "Liberation Theology," Roger Haight, 576; this article carries an excellent bibliography. The literature on liberation theology is substantial. Authoritative as a brief introduction: Gustavo Gutiérrez, "father" of the movement, in Dwyer, *New Dictionary of Catholic Social Thought*, 548-553. Also useful in relating this theology to a larger understanding of *church*: "Church of the Poor: The Ecclesiology of Gustavo Gutiérrez," James B. Nickoloff, *Theological Studies*, September, 1993: 512-535.

40. Phillip Berryman, *Liberation Theology*, 4.

41. James Childress, John Macquarrie, eds., *Westminster Dictionary of Christian Ethics* (Philadelphia: Westminster Press, 1986), article "Population Policy," 487.

42. *Theological Studies*, December 1993: 662-677.

43. Rahner, *Encyclopedia of Theology*, "Church & World," 237-250.

44. "*Humanae Vitae*: 25th Anniversary," *Origins*, April 22, 1993. Reference to Noonan occurs within a substantial presentation of the Church's official doctrine. For additional comment on Noonan's position see Elizabeth Mensch and Alan Freeman, *The Politics of Virtue: Is Abortion Debatable?* (Durham: Duke University Press, 1993), 101. (These authors report Noonan as a member of the special papal commission convened to advise on the contraception issue, prior to the issuance of *Humanae Vitae*.)

45. All three episodes are discussed in Chapter Two.

Part Two
Introduction: Population—and New Vistas

1. "Morality Without Moralizing" in *The Shape of the Church to Come* (New York: Seabury Press, 1974), 64.

2. *Principles for a Catholic Morality* (San Francisco: Harper and Row, 1990, rev.), 221. Concerning natural law see my "Introduction: Perplexing Population," note 8.

3. Ibid., 21-22.

4. See O'Connell, above; Anne E. Patrick, *Liberating Conscience* (New York: Continuum, 1996); Edmond J. Dunn, *What Is Theology?* (Mystic, CT: Twenty-Third Publications, 1998), his Part Two: "Moral Theology"; Sean Fagan, *Does Morality Change?* (Collegeville, MN: Liturgical Press, 1997); "Moral Life, Christian," Joseph McNamara, in Joseph A. Komonchak, ed., *The New Dictionary of Theology*, 676; "Modern Roman Catholic Moral Theology," Charles E. Curran, in James Childress, John Macquarrie, eds., *Westminster Dictionary of Christian Ethics* (Philadelphia: Westminster Press, 1986), 388.

5. *What is Theology?*, 162, 165.

6. O'Connell, *Principles*, 196.

7. Quoted by O'Connell, 278, note 11.

8. Judith A. Dwyer, ed., *The New Dictionary of Catholic Social Thought,* 603. See also my Chapter Four, section 2, discussion of the impact of history in theology.

9. Ibid., 862.

Chapter Five: Scripture and Compassion

1. Monika K. Hellwig, *Jesus The Compassion of God: New Perspectives on the Tradition of Christianity* (Collegeville, MN: Liturgical Press, 1983), 94, 95. Hellwig is professor of theology, Georgetown University.

2. Michael Downey, "Compassion," in *The New Dictionary of Catholic Spirituality* Michael Downey, ed. (Collegeville, MN: Liturgical Press, 1993), 192. In this excellent article Downey adds, "Rather individualistic virtue has been emphasized... [we see] human suffering and pain of enormous proportions, caused in part by social systems and structures born of sin and evil."

3. Judith Dwyer, ed., *New Dictionary of Catholic Social Thought*, 861.

4. William C. Spohn, *What Are They Saying About Scripture and Ethics?* (Mahwah, NJ: Paulist Press, 1984), 1.

5. Anne E. Patrick, *Liberating Conscience* (New York: Continuum, 1996), 10.

6. Hellwig, 121.

7. Ibid., 15.

8. Ibid., 121.

9. *Sojourners,* August 1994, several articles. See also *Transaction, Social Science & Modern Society,* May-June, 1995: 27-29. In an article largely discrediting analyses of "overpopulation" ("What is Population Policy?") Nicholas Eberstadt states that "what most people are talking about when they refer to overpopulation is poverty." He feels that poverty itself is often attributed to "overpopulation"—which is "an elementary lapse in logic." Clearly, poverty is produced and sustained by *many* causes. But whether demographic statistics here and now constitute "overpopulation" or not, it seems evident that "where there is severe poverty...adding more people makes the suffering worse." While resources may decline or remain constant, demand grows greater and more competitive. Eberstadt's is part of a useful symposium of our articles on "Demographic Demons."

10. Brown, Fitzmyer, Murphy, eds. (Englewood Cliffs, NJ: Prentice Hall, 1990), 702, no. 126.

11. *Acts of Compassion: Caring for Ourselves and Helping Others* (Princeton: Princeton University Press, 1991), 160-l. See his Chapter Six.

12. Ibid., 308-9.

13. *On Social Concerns, Origins,* March 3, 1988, no. 40.

14. Libreria Editrice Vaticana, 00120 Citta Del Vaticano, 1994.

15. Ibid., 4.

16. *The Challenge of Peace* (1983), *Economic Justice for All* (1986).

17. Philip Berryman, *Our Unfinished Business: U.S. Bishops' Letters on Peace & Economy* (New York: Pantheon Books, 1989). Excellent study of two major documents. Pages 10-11 tell of extensive prior consultation: for the peace letter from "about thirty-five experts," for the economy letter more than 150 experts. In contrast, the Vatican document refers to "consultation and dialogue with specialists such as theologians, pastoral workers and demographers," and to its own "competence in ethical and pastoral fields involving demography."

18. Pontifical Council for the Family, *Ethical and Pastoral Dimensions of Population Trends,* note 9.

19. *The International Human Suffering Index* (Washington, DC: Population Crisis Committee, 1992).

20. *World Population Data Sheet 1993* (Washington: Population Reference Bureau). "Doubling time" is the number of years until the population will double, assuming constant rate of increase—a projection of possibility, not a forecast.

21. "Impaled Upon the Horns of Faith and Reason," *America,* March 6, 1993.

This issue also contains John C. Schwarz, "Population, The Church and the Pope," and David Toolan, "Second Thoughts on the Population Bomb." To my awareness *America* was thereby the first Catholic "journal of opinion" to spotlight population questions.

22. David Noel Freedman, ed. (New York: Doubleday, 1992).

23. R. Bruce Douglass, ed. *The Deeper Meaning of Economic Life: Critical Essays on the U.S. Bishops' Pastoral Letter on the Economy* (Washington, DC: Georgetown University Press, 1986); see Anthony Tambasco, "Option for the Poor," 37-55. See also Donal Dorr concerning the "option for the poor" in Dwyer, *New Dictionary of Catholic Social Thought,* 755-759. Dorr emphasizes that this option is to be exercised not only by individuals, but by the institutional church at every level.

24. Douglass, *Deeper Meaning of Economic Life,* 42, 51, 53.

25. (Collegeville, MN: Liturgical Press, 1992), 162-63.

26. Alfred W. McCoy, *Priests on Trial* (New York: Penguin Books, 1984), 152, 154. This fascinating book tells of priests learning, growing, and working with the poor in the Philippines, amidst the rich and powerful.

27. Ibid., 154.

28. Within one month two major American journals featured Pope John Paul II. *Time* honored him as "Man of the Year": "In a time of moral confusion, John Paul II is resolute about his ideals and eager to impose them on a world that often differs with him," December 26, 1994-January 2, 1995: 53. The *New York Times Magazine* spoke of "the most traveled, most widely known Pope in history," with a "sternly didactic view of humankind's halting efforts": Paul Wilkes, "The Popemakers," December 11, 1994: 64.

29. Demographic data from *World Population Data Sheet 1993* (Washington, DC: Population Reference Bureau). Church data from *The Catholic Almanac 1994* (Huntington, IN: Our Sunday Visitor Publishing Co.), 356, 102, 105. Opposition by Philippine hierarchy: see "Philippine Health Chief...Stirs Wrath of Church," *New York Times,* August 4, 1993; "Philippino Bishops Decline Dialogue on Birth Control," *National Catholic Reporter,* September 3, 1993.

30. Henriot, "Who Cares About Africa? Development Guidelines from the Church's Social Teaching," in *Catholic Social Thought and the New World Order,* Oliver Williams, John Houck, eds. (Notre Dame, IN: University of Notre Dame Press, 1993), 230. Excellent analytical article.

31. Paul Kennedy, *Preparing for the Twenty-First Century* (New York: Vintage Books, 1994), 24. His first two chapters highlight population issues.

32. (San Francisco: Institute for Food and Development Policy, 1990).

33. Ibid., 13, 32.

34. Ibid., 29.

35. Ibid., 67-8. For a somewhat similar analysis see my Appendix One, "Misconstruing Population...."

36. Ibid.,18.

37. Ibid., 14, 51.

38. Ibid., 29-30, concerning deprivations of freedom. For a confirmatory analysis of global patterns of poverty and disenfranchisement see my Chapter Three above, discussion of *Human Development Report 1993* (New York: Oxford University Press, 1993), especially first and second chapters of the Report.

39. *A Martyr's Message of Hope* (Kansas City, MO: National Catholic Reporter Publishing Company, 1981), 84.

40. Ibid., 81.

Chapter Six: "A Consistent Ethic"

1. "Abortion: The Unexplored Middle Ground," *Second Opinion*, March 1989. Contains his article and four respondents in a symposium. From Park Ridge Center, 676 N. St. Clair, Chicago, Ill. 60611. McCormick presents twenty points concerning moral and policy issues on abortion, seeking a middle ground. The quotation is no. 19.

2. "To Make a Seamless Garment, Use a Single Piece of Cloth," *Cross Currents*, Winter 1984-85, 490. Gives particular attention to problems of seeking to legislate morality in pluralistic societies.

3. Jan Goodwin, "Prisoners of Biology," *Utne Reader*, January-February 1997.

4. December 26, 1994/January 2, 1995: 53, 56.

5. Alan Cowell, "Despite Abortion Issue, Population Pact Nears," *New York Times*, September 9, 1994.

6. Barbara Crossette, "Vatican Gives Up Battle to Block Population Plan," *New York Times*, September 10, 1994.

7. Editorial, "Vatican Played Valuable Role at Cairo," *National Catholic Reporter*, October 7, 1994.

8. Ibid.

9. David S. Toolan, S.J., "Tempest Over Cairo," *America*, August 27, 1994, editorial. (After attending the conference, Toolan commented in *America*, October 1, 1994.) Press coverage during the conference was often critical of the Vatican role. For positive assessments: "Picking a Fight," *Commonweal*, September 9, 1994, editorial; John Leo, "Hardball at Cairo," *U.S.News & World Report*, September 19, 1994; editorial, *National Catholic Reporter*, October 7, 1994.

10. James Brooke, "With Church Preaching in Vain, Brazilians Embrace Birth Control," *New York Times*, September 2, 1994.

11. "Abortion Common Despite Laws," *Latinamerica Press*, September 1, 1994.

12. Barbara B. Crane, "The Transnational Politics of Abortion," in *The New Politics of Population: Conflict and Consensus in Family Planning*, Jason L. Finkle and C. Alison McIntosh, eds. (New York: The Population Council, 1994), 257, note 1. The Introduction to this text is very useful; also "Limits to Papal Power: Vatican Inaction after *Humanae Vitae,*" Charles Keely. See also Susan Bratton, *Six Billion and More* (Louisville, KY: Westminster/John Knox Press, 1992), esp. chapter 19, "Coercion and Abortion in Population Management," ethical considerations.

13. Jodi L. Jacobson, *Planning the Global Family* (Washington: Worldwatch Institute, 1987), 20. Worldwatch Paper no. 80.

14. Janet deMerode, "Part of the Solution: World Bank and Population Issues," *Harvard International Review*, Fall 1994. Issue carries eight articles on population. The quoted statement does not refer to abortion, but (especially) illegal abortion doubtless contributes to this high maternal death rate.

15. Prabha Prabhakar Bhardwaj "Women Nurture the Environment," in *Power, Population and the Environment: Women Speak*, Gillian Philips, ed. (Toronto: Weed Foundation, 1992), 54.

16. Crane, note 12 above, 241.

17. Jacobson, *Planning the Global Family*, 28.

18. Susan V. Lawrence, "Family Planning, at a Price," *U.S.News & World Report*, September 19, 1994.

19. Malcolm Potts, Martha Campbell, "The Philosopher's Stone: Contraception and Family Planning," *Harvard International Review*, Fall 1994: 22.

20. Joseph Bernardin, *The Seamless Garment* (Kansas City, MO: National Catholic Reporter, 1984). Speeches at Fordham University and St. Louis University, and two others. "Introduction" by Jason Petosa gives background data. It should be noted that Bernardin initially used the "seamless garment" imagery of Christ's cloak in a gospel account of the passion (John 19:23–24); subsequently he mostly used the more descriptive "consistent ethic of life" terminology. As early as 1971 Eileen Egan, an Irish pacifist, used "seamless garment" imagery to link concern for the poor with war, abortion, and the death penalty. Also, Cardinal Humberto Medeiros, Boston, advocated a "consistent ethic of life" spanning "the right of the fetus to be born...[with] every person's right to a truly human existence."

21. Phillip Berryman, *Our Unfinished Business: Bishops' Letters on Peace & the Economy*, 151f.

22. Ibid., 154, quoted by Berryman. Originally in *Commonweal*, August 13, 1982.

23. Francis X. Murphy, "Of Sex and the Catholic Church," *Atlantic Monthly*, February 1981: 55. Hurley is quoted extensively in Chapter Two above—the only prelate in the 1974 *Theological Studies* symposium on population.

24. *The Challenge of Peace*, nos. 172-176.

25. *The Challenge of Peace*, nos. 111-126, 143.

26. Gudorf, "Seamless Garment" (note 2, above): 481, 490.

27. Elizabeth Mensch, Alan Freeman, *The Politics of Virtue* (Durham, NC: Duke University Press, 1993). The authors evaluate the Catholic natural law tradition critically but with much appreciation. See esp. their Chapter 2, "Natural Law and the Catholic Tradition."

28. "Giving Up the Gift: One Woman's Abortion Decision," *Commonweal*, February 2, 1994. David Toolan remarks that "The Vatican does not seem to have in mind, except peripherally, the often crushing burdens of unwanted pregnancies, and the desperation that drives women, as a last resort, to have abortions." See his "Open to Life—and to Death," in Albert LaChance, John Carroll, eds., *Embracing Earth*, 43-4.

29. Joyce Poole, *The Harm We Do: A Catholic Doctor Confronts Church, Moral, and Medical Teaching* (Mystic, CT: Twenty-Third Publications, 1993). For further discussion see Patricia Beattie Juna and Thomas A. Shannon, eds., *Abortion and Catholicism: The American Debate* (New York: Crossroad, 1988). Also Lisa Sowle Cahill, "Abortion, Sex and Gender: The Church's Public Voice," *America*, November 11, 1995.

30. Ibid., 7.

31. Ibid., 58.

32. "AIDS Prevention: A Challenge to the Catholic Moral Tradition," *America*, December 12, 1996.

33. Judith Dwyer, ed., *The New Dictionary of Catholic Social Thought*, 109.

34. (Mahwah, NJ: Paulist Press, 1994), 546, nos. 2266-67. See also, "The Death Penalty Is Wrong," editorial, *America*, February 5, 1995.

35. *Dead Man Walking: An Eyewitness Account of the Death Penalty in the United States* (New York: Random House, 1993), 124.

Chapter Seven: Church and Science

1. "The Scientific Debate: Is Population Growth a Problem?" *Harvard International Review*, Fall 1994: 74.

2. "A Dynamic Relationship of Theology and Science," *Origins*, November 11, 1988. Papal statement occasioned by the publication of papers presented at a

study week on the relationship of philosophy, theology, and the natural sciences, at the papal summer residence. Also: Ernan McMullan, "A Common Quest for Understanding," *America*, February 2, 1989, a commentary on the pope's address.

3. David Alt, Donald Hyndman, *Roadside Geology of Montana* (Missoula, MT: Mountain Press Publishing Co., 1986), 6. Describing "the Belt formation of western and west-central Montana": "early sediments continued to accumulate for another 600 million years...."

4. Betsy Carpenter, Traci Watson, "More People, More Pollution," *U.S.News & World Report*, September 12, 1994: 63.

5. Ibid., 64.

6. Jonathan Piel, ed., *Managing Planet Earth: Readings from Scientific American Magazine* (New York: W. H. Freeman, 1990) essay, "Managing Planet Earth," 2.

7. See Chapter One, note 12, diverging interpretations.

8. Speech at Ettore Maiorana Centre (Erice, Sicily), in *L'Osservatore Romano* (English edition), Vatican City, May 18, 1993. Also, Jack A. Bonsor, "History, Dogma, and Nature: Further Reflections on Postmodernism and Theology," *Theological Studies*, June, 1994: 313. Bonsor cites and analyzes Pope John Paul II's acknowledgment (in *Origins*, November 12, 1992, Pope John Paul II and Papal Commission on Galileo, report) that the Galileo case was ultimately a learning experience for the Church, long resisted.

9. See Sean Fagan, *Does Morality Change?* (Collegeville, MN: Liturgical Press, 1997). Excellent overview of ongoing renewal in moral theology. Fagan is a Marist priest, former secretary-general of his order, an Irish scholar of broad experience and insight.

10. From *Theological Investigations XI,* reprinted in Gerald A. McCool, *A Rahner Reader* (New York: Crossroad, 1989), 87-8.

11. *1994 Catholic Almanac* (Huntington, IN: Our Sunday Visitor Press), 543.

12. Excellent overview of this area: Christopher F. Mooney, S.J., "Theology and Science: A New Commitment to Dialogue," *Theological Studies*, June 1991: 289-329. Also: John H. Wright, S.J., "Theology, Philosophy and the Natural Sciences," *Theological Studies*, 1991, vol. 52: 651-668. Also: Capra, Steindl-Rast, *Belonging to the Universe*, a valuable dialogue exploring relationships between contemporary science and theology. Also: John F. Haught, *Science and Religion: From Conflict to Conversation* (New York: Paulist Press, 1995).

13. *CTNS Bulletin*, Winter, 1993, Director's Report: 42. Address: Center for Theology and the Natural Sciences, 2400 Ridge, Berkeley, CA, 94709; particularly rich resource. Article about CTNS: Margaret Wertheim, "Science and Religion: Blurring the Boundaries," *Omni*, October 1994.

14. Walter J. Ong, S.J., "God's Known Universe and Christian Faith: Pastoral,

Homiletic and Devotional Reflections," *Thought,* September 1991: 241-258. Also, David S. Toolan, S.J., "Nature is a Heraclitean Fire: Reflections on Cosmology in an Ecological Age" (St. Louis: Seminar on Jesuit Spirituality, 3700 W. Pine, St. Louis, Mo. 63108; 1991). Both exceptionally fine.

15. *A Directory of Environmental Activities and Resources in the North American Religious Community,* Summer 1992, 158. Published as "A Project of the Joint Appeal by Religion and Science for the Environment," 1047 Amsterdam Avenue, New York, NY 10025. Generously supplied by Robert Russell, Director, CTNS.

16. "To Avert a Common Danger," *Parade* (The Sunday Newspaper Magazine), March 1, 1992. Generously supplied by Carl Sagan, Cornell University.

17. Ibid., 14.

18. *Directory,* note 15 above, 160 (June 3, 1991).

19. *Directory,* note 15 above, p. 162-3 (May 12, 1992).

20. Mooney, "Theology and Science": 311.

21. David M. Byers, "*Pace* Galileo: Present and Future of Religion and Science Dialogue," *America,* April 9, 1994.

22. Cited by Sallie McFague, *The Body of God* (Minneapolis: Fortress Press, 1993), 221, note 5. McFague provides two excellent bibliographies on science and religion: 232, note 5; 234, note 22.

23. "Debating the Unknowable," *Atlantic Monthly,* July 1981. From the opening paragraph of Thomas' article.

24. "Alone is Never Enough: Seeing the World through Both Eyes," *Omni,* October 1994: 4.

25. Alan Cowell, "Scientists Associated with Vatican Call for Population Curbs," *New York Times,* June 16, 1994; also, Peter Hebblethwaite, "Science, Magisterium at Odds," *National Catholic Reporter,* July 15, 1994. My quotation combines the two sources.

26. Pontifical Council for the Family, Libreria Editrice Vaticana, Citta del Vaticano, 1994.

27. "God's Known Universe," *Thought,* September 1991. Additional on Ong: Mark Neilsen, "A Bridge Builder: Ong at 80," *America,* November 21, 1992.

28. (New York: Crossroad, 1978), 7-8.

Chapter Eight: Theology, Ecology, Population

1. "Population: Delusion and Reality," *New York Review of Books,* November 11, 1994: 68. Sen is professor of economics and philosophy, Harvard University.

2. *The Ecological Crisis: A Common Responsibility* (Washington, DC: U.S. Catholic Conference, 1990), no. 8, publication 332-9.

3. *Preparing for the Twenty-First Century* (New York: Vintage Books, 1994), ix.

4. John B. Cobb, Jr., Herman Daly (Boston: Beacon Press, 1994), 2.

5. Partha S. Dasgupta, "Population, Poverty and the Local Environment," *Scientific American*, February, 1995: 41, 44. Dasgupta is professor of economics, Cambridge University. He adds, "Disaster is not something the poorest have to wait for: it is occurring even now." See also *Human Development Report 1997* (New York: Oxford University Press, 1997), 32, 68-9, poverty and environment.

6. *Ethical & Pastoral Dimensions of Population Trends*, nos. 21-23. Italics in original. Also discussed in Chapter Five above.

7. *1993 World Population Data Sheet* (Washington, DC: Population Reference Bureau), concerning: Brunei, Cambodia, Indonesia, Laos, Malaysia, Myanmar (Burma), Philippines, Singapore, Thailand, Viet Nam.

8. Jonathan Piel, ed., *Managing Planet Earth*, 1. Clark is a senior research associate at the Harvard School of Government, and a member of the U.S. Academy of Sciences' Committee on Global Change.

9. Gayle D. Ness, William D. Drake, Steven R. Brechin, eds., *Population-Environment Dynamics: Ideas and Observations* (Ann Arbor: University of Michigan Press, 1993), vii.

10. Ibid., 288, Valentin Agbo, Nestor Sokpon, John Hough, Patrick West, "Population-Environment Dynamics in a Constrained Ecosystem in Northern Benin."

11. Ibid., p. 378 (their fig. 16.1). Explanatory comments based on pp. 379-80. The authors warn, "It is clear that the population-environment dynamic is not as simple and straightforward as [my fig. 2], which shows an unspecified two-way relationship between two equally unspecified elements: population and environment." Each box indicates a variable "more or less" factor, (+/-). Partha Dasgupta (*Scientific American*, February 1995, 41) similarly finds that "none of the three elements [population growth, poverty and degradation of local resources] directly causes the other two; rather each influences, and is in turn influenced by, the others."

12. Ibid., 406.

13. Ibid., 1.

14. Ibid., 167-186, "Phases of Agricultural Modernization in Brazil."

15. Ibid., 170. Martine makes this astonishing observation: "Some farms in Brazil are larger than some European countries and there is no clear demonstration that they are inherently more competitive.... Many of the large properties in

Brazil continue to be unproductive, their main function being to serve as speculative chattel," 180.

16. *The State of the World Population 1993* (New York: United Nations Population Fund), 4. "Urban sprawl is linking giant cities. Experts say that by the year 2010, Rio de Janeiro and São Paulo will be one continuous megalopolis 350 miles long with almost 40 million people" (14). In 1950 São Paulo was unranked among the world's twenty largest "urban agglomerations"; in 1990 it ranked third; in 2000 it is projected in second ranking.

17. Laurie Goering, Kerry Luft, "Unplanned Parenthood—A Mix of Fear and Ignorance in the Slums," *Chicago Tribune*, February 1, 1996: 1, 12-13. Fifth in a striking seven-part series on global population and poverty; series title: "Gambling with Life: Why Parents Defy Odds and Circumstance to Have More Babies."

18. (New York: Oxford University Press, 1993), 55.

19. *Origins*, October 31, 1991.

20. *Taking Population Seriously* (San Francisco: Institute for Food and Development Policy, 1990), 12-13, italics added.

21. *Human Development Report 1997*, 194. Nevertheless, the "doubling time" for Brazil is calculated at 46 years (at the current rate; *1993 World Population Data Sheet*, Population Reference Bureau). See also Cobb, Daly, *For the Common Good*, 237, concerning Brazil's relationship between "an unlimited supply of cheap labor at subsistence wages" and fertility rates.

22. *Human Development Report 1993*, 180, 208. Hectares (metric) 1 = 2.47 acres.

23. Judith Ennew, Brian Milne, *The Next Generation, Lives of Third World Children* (Philadelphia: New Society Publishers, 1990), 147.

24. Gillian Phillips, ed., *Power, Population and the Environment: Women Speak* (Toronto: Weed Foundation, 1992), 36-42.

25. *Human Development Report 1993*, 188, 212; all percentages for 1991.

26. (Mahwah, NJ: Paulist Press, 1994). No. 2415, for example, has a relevant statement under "Respect for the integrity of creation."

27. Ness, *Population-Environment Dynamics*, 1.

28. *The Ecological Crisis: A Common Responsibility*, no. 11. Italics in original.

29. (Washington, DC: U.S. Catholic Conference, 1991), publication no. 468-6.

30. *Renewing the Face of the Earth: A Resource for Parishes* (Washington, DC: U.S. Catholic Conference, 1994), publication 766-9. Contains the Bishops' 1991 statement, and various pastoral materials.

31. *New Dictionary of Catholic Social Thought*, "Common Good," "Solidarity." Also, Vatican II, *Pastoral Constitution on the Church in the Modern World*, nos. 26-32, 74-75; *Catechism of the Catholic Church*, nos. 1905-1912; *The Modern Catholic Encyclopedia*,

Michael Glazier, Monika Hellwig, eds., "Common Good," "Social Teaching of the Church"; Donal Dorr, *The Social Justice Agenda* (Maryknoll, NY: Orbis Books, 1991), 86-9. Also excellent discussion by Dominican theologian M. Shawn Copeland, "Reconsidering the Idea of the Common Good," in *Catholic Social Thought and the New World Order* (Notre Dame, IN: Notre Dame University Press, 1993), Oliver Williams, John Houck, eds., 309-327. Also David Hollenbach, "The Common Good Revisited," *Theological Studies*, March 1989: 70-94.

32. Jennifer D. Mitchell, "Before the Next Doubling," *World Watch*, January/February, 1998, 22.

33. *Eco-Theology* (Washington, DC: Center of Concern, 1991), 18.

34. D. Henrichsen, *Winning the Food Race*, Population Reports, Series M., no. 13 (Baltimore: Johns Hopkins University School of Public Health, Population Information Program, November 1997), 1, 7.

35. Max Oelschlager, *Caring for Creation: An Ecumenical Approach to the Environmental Crisis* (New Haven: Yale University Press, 1994).

36. Laurie Goering, Kerry Luft, *Chicago Tribune* (above, note 17). They extensively describe a Brazilian married couple, Somalia and Absolom da Silva, and their six children, a family in a Rio slum where "only 2 percent have even been to high school," Mrs. Da Silva planned shortly to undergo sterilization. Catholic, uneducated, impoverished, the Da Silvas exemplify "stark realities" and "straitened circumstances."

Chapter Nine: A Global Religious Vision

1. (*Gaudium et Spes*) *Pastoral Constitution on the Church in the Modern World*, no. 5.

2. *Concern for the Church (Theological Investigations XX)* (New York: Crossroad, 1981), 171.

3. *Saints and Sinners: A History of the Popes* (New Haven: Yale University Press, 1997), Preface.

4. Contained in: Thomas Lynch, Valerie Dillon, eds., *A Positive Vision for Family Life* (Washington, DC: U.S. Catholic Conference, 1985), no. 85.

5. "The Propaganda of Prosperity," *Sojourners*, August 1994. Thoughtful article, one of five on population in this issue. On the destitution of children, the *Human Development Report 1993* (New York: Oxford University Press) states, "Each day, 34,000 young children still die from malnutrition and disease" in the developing countries (12); see also "Children of the Streets" (24), "Children Without Childhood (33).

6. "Child Labor in Pakistan," *Atlantic Monthly*, February 1996: 81-2.

7. 1 Cor 2:16.

8. *Concern for the Church*, 165. His strong Chapter 12, "Unity of the Church— Unity of Mankind," includes this: "The achievement of a greater unity of mankind is an urgent task for people today, if mankind is to exist in a human way. This unity itself represents a mysterious and complex task, the precise meaning and content of which become clear only slowly in the historical process itself. This process is repeatedly debased by the sin of human beings and yet remains also their religious and moral task. The achievement of this unity of mankind is consequently a task for Christians: not a mere side-interest for them, but a task for all Christians and especially the authorities in the churches (who) have to answer before God's judgment." (171-2; slightly edited for clarity)

9. *Towards a World Theology: Faith and the Comparative History of Religion* (Philadelphia: Westminster Press, 1981), 102. The title of this remarkable book may mislead, suggesting a blending of all theologies. Rather he analyzes common, shared features of the major religious traditions. His appreciation of human unity demonstrates that as humanity is a shared reality, so our major problems affect *all* of us—not just *some* of us, applicable to population concerns.

10. From my *God's One Family* (Kansas City: Sheed & Ward, 1991). See also David Noel Freedman, ed., *The Anchor Bible Dictionary* (New York: Doubleday, 1992), vol. 6: "Unity/Unity of Humanity," 746-753. Also Rahner, above note 8, esp. 160.

11. September 1, 1994, "The Courage to Speak Bluntly."

12. February 17, 1995, National Public Radio, "Morning Edition" program.

13. Paul Clancy, "Water From Salt and Sand," *Calypso Log*, February 1995. This periodical is published by The Cousteau Society; Clancy is editor.

14. Report available from the primary sponsoring organization: The Park Ridge Center, 211 E. Ontario, Suite 800, Chicago, Illinois 60611. Four Roman Catholics participated at Genval: Christine Gudorf, Dept. of Philosophy & Religious Studies, Florida International University; others from Peru, Colombia, Poland.

15. *Global Responsibility: In Search of a New World Ethic* (New York: Crossroad Publishing Company, 1991), 63. Küng integrates ecumenism with the search for an ethics acceptable across cultures and religions. Ecumenism is thus an inescapable component of global religious cooperation. Küng was a leading spokesman at the Parliament of World Religions, in its statement of a "Global Ethic" (*The National Catholic Reporter*, September 9, 1993).

16. Editors, "Gambling With Life: Why Parents Defy Odds and Circumstance to Have More Babies," January 30, 1996, 1.

Chapter Ten: Population — Challenge to Moral Theology

1. In *The Shape of the Church to Come* (New York: Seabury Press, 1974), 69.

Reprinted in *The Content of Faith* (New York: Crossroad, 1992), 537. Significantly but without comment the editors of *Content of Faith* juxtapose this essay with another, *Existential Ethics*, 543. To complement the prevailing "essential ethics," Rahner calls for ethical recognition of "each particular situation" in which individuals find themselves, and which ultimately only the individual conscience can assess.

2. Cited in Joel E. Cohen, *How Many People Can the Earth Support?*, 292.

3. Luke 16:19–31.

4. From my personal tape recording, September 19, 1987.

5. Mt 22:37. Also Rom 13:9–10; Gal 5:14; Jas 2:8.

6. John Mahoney, S.J., *The Making of Moral Theology* (New York: Oxford University Press, 1987), 337. "Moral theology is concerned at heart with the mystery of God and 'the riches of the glory of this mystery' (Col. 1:27); a renewed moral theology can find its theological identity only by a recovery of mystery." Also, Rom 11:33.

7. See *Introduction: Our Perplexing Population*, note 10, references on natural law. Also, Anne E. Patrick, *Liberating Conscience*, 154-7.

8. Sean Fagan, S.M., *Does Morality Change?*, 69, and entire chapter 5, "Does Nature Change?"

9. *Origins*, November 12, 1992, 372.

10. In Komonchak, Collins, Lane, eds., *The New Dictionary of Theology*, 685.

11. (New York: Oxford University Press, 1997), Foreword, iii. Published for the U.N. Development Programme.

12. Mt 25:31–45.

13. See Patrick, *Liberating Conscience*, chapter 6, concerning "a turn to the oppressed" in moral theology.

14. Alex Marshall, ed. (New York: United Nations Population Fund, 1997), 4.

15. D. Henrichsen, Series M. no. 13 (Baltimore: Johns Hopkins University School of Public Health), November 1997.

16. *The Sciences*, "Peer Review: Letters," January/February 1996.

17. *The Sciences*, November/December 1995. The eleven questions are quoted from Cohen's article, unnumbered there; brief details in parentheses are my own summaries, not quotations. Chapter 13 of Cohen's book (note 2 above) discusses each question in detail. See also my chapter 1, note 11.

18. See chapter 2, note 6, two high level recommendations that Catholic universities undertake population studies, ignored.

19. *The Ecological Crisis: A Common Responsibility*, Section II.

20. *Science and Religion* (Mahwah, NJ: Paulist Press, 1995), 199-200.

21. *Saints and Sinners: A History of the Popes* (New Haven: Yale University Press, 1997), 274.

Appendix Two

1. "Reassessing the Earth's Population," *Transaction, Social Science and Modern Society,* May/June 1995: 10 (part of a symposium on "Demographic Demons"). Brown is president of the Worldwatch Institute, Washington.

2. *Human Development Report 1993* (New York: Oxford University Press, 1993), 27-28 (Table 2.1 and text). Published for the U.N. Development Programme.

3. *Human Development Report* 1997, 9.

Appendix Three

1. *States of Disarray: The Social Effects of Globalization* (London: UNRISD, 1995), cited in *World Watch,* July/August 1996, 39.

2. "Seminar on Multilateral Debt, 12 February 1996, Introduction by Cardinal Hume," and "Summary of (15) Main Points Made in Discussion" obtained from The Catholic Bishops' Conference of England and Wales, General Secretariat.

3. The biblical "Jubilee Year" (Lev 25:8–17, 29–31): every fiftieth year was ideally designated for the righting of inequities in property, enslavement, and poverty. Scripture scholar Roland Fahey states that "Although not realized in the letter, (the Jubilee Year) appreciation for personal rights and human dignity synthesizes much of Old Testament teaching." *The New Jerome Biblical Commentary,* (Englewood Cliffs, NJ: Prentice Hall, 1990), 78.

4. From *Human Development Report 1997,* United Nations Development Programme (New York: Oxford University Press, 1997). Table 22, 194. The Report ranks 175 nations on its "human development index." The indicated nations rank as follows: Uganda, 159; Zambia, 143; Tanzania, 149; Honduras, 116; Nicaragua, 127. (Also on the Human Development Report see my Chapter Three under "Human Development Index.")